Beyond Peyote

Beyond Peyote

*Kieri and the
Huichol Deer Shaman*

Jay Courtney Fikes, Ph.D.
with Jesús González Mercado

REGENT PRESS
Berkeley, California
2021

eBook edition published November 12, 2020

Editing, layout and cover designed by: Entheomedia.net

Manufactured in the U.S.A.

ENTHEOMEDIA
Taos, NM 87571
www.entheomedia.net
entheos70@aol.com

&

REGENT PRESS
Berkeley, California
www.regentpress.net
regentpress@mindspring.com

.

For my parents
J C and Virginia L. Fikes

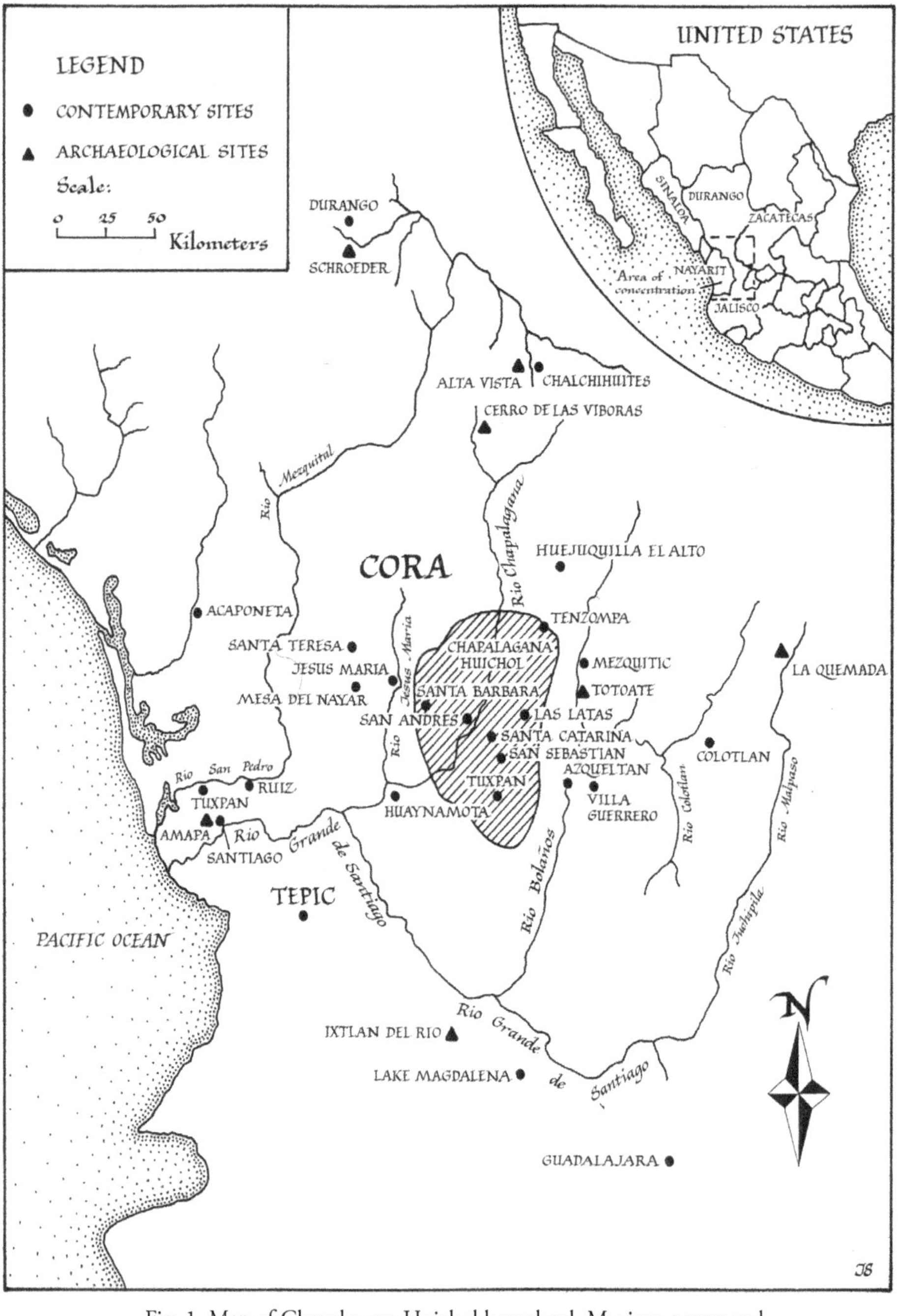

Fig. 1. Map of Chapalagana Huichol homeland, Mexican towns and
archaeological sites. Drawn by Jack Scott.

TABLE OF CONTENTS

TABLE OF ILLUSTRATIONS

ACKNOWLEDGMENTS

I am grateful that Jesús González entrusted me with publishing his autobiography. His willingness to share his deepest personal thoughts and feelings with me, and now with readers of this book, did not come easily. I am also deeply obliged to his son, Vicente González, for his dedicated and competent work in translating his father's narratives, and for having the patience to explain their meaning.

I appreciate all his family did to make me comfortable in their home on several different occasions. I am also grateful to Vicente for permitting me to tape-record information he provided about Kieri in Chapter 6 and the murder of his brother in Chapter 7. Several other members of the González family aided my research in Tuxpan de Bolaños with their hospitality, kindness, and trust. May they all gain some benefit for their efforts.

Professor Phil C. Weigand and Acelia García de Weigand inspired me to adopt their larger spatial and longer temporal view of Huichol society. Their perspective on the Huichol peyote hunt (Weigand 2002) helped me realize that grueling ritual was once central to Huichol participation in a pan-tribal confederacy uniting ceremony, trade and defense. Their support, enthusiasm and constructive criticism of my Huichol research and writing has always been invaluable.

Juan Negrín and I shared something that each of us usually discussed with our Wixarika mentors: our respective numinous experiences during Huichol temple rituals and pilgrimages to sacred sites. Our conversations about Kieri bolstered my confidence enough that I am publishing details about my 1986 pilgrimage to Kieri.

I remain greatly indebted to Mark Hoffman for his meticulous editing and creative design of this book. He wrestled with my words and pushed me to clarify my thoughts. If this book is as readable as I want it to be, Mark deserves much of the credit.

I appreciate the patience and cooperation my wife, Dr. Lebriz

Tosuner-Fikes, demonstrated during the 15 months I just devoted to writing and re-writing this book. During that time I was more irritable and impatient than I should have been. Without her support this book would have been delayed. I am also grateful to her for making five annual pilgrimages with me and Jesús González to the sacred sites near the Pacific Ocean where he and countless other Huichol have prayed for centuries.

Several people read the narrative González dictated about the birth and life of the first Deer Shaman. Dr. Phil C. Weigand read it first, some 15 years ago, and offered several useful suggestions. During the past year Professor Marcelline Krafchick, Karen Kotoske, Dr. Diana Negrín, Phil Cousineau and Karl Poetschke each read Chapter 4 and tacitly acknowledged González' Deer Shaman narrative as a valuable addition to world literature featuring heroic leaders, shamans and prophets. Their remarks and encouragement motivated me to complete this book with a dignified but friendly style, which I believe non-specialist readers will welcome. Wixarika specialists should find my related endnotes of interest.

I am profoundly grateful to Dr. Paul Liffman, Steve Nielsen and Rich Heimlich for their constructive criticisms of early drafts of my chapter about Phil True. I am delighted that Mark Hoffman improved the lucidity and accuracy of this chapter with his insightful comments and diligent editing.

Dr. Paul Liffman has regularly aided me in confronting my deficiencies related to transcribing Wixarika words. I hope he continues to correct whatever mistakes I may have made in this book. Liffman also provided valuable commentary on an early draft of Chapter 7. His personal experiences with the second Huichol leader described in that chapter were published in his doctoral dissertation, as well as a report concerning the murder of Phil True. Together, his coverage of those two topics greatly enhanced my understanding of the unfair treatment typically accorded to "small time" marijuana growers in Mexico's criminal justice system. He also encouraged me to inform readers about the gradual increase in opium poppy production among the Huichol during the past 20 years, as well as the decommissioning of Mexico's federal agency entrusted with serving indigenous tribes during Vicente Fox's administration.

While all of these scholars generously gave of their time and expertise, of course I alone take responsibility for any deficiencies or errors remaining in this book.

Yvonne Negrín graciously allowed me to publish a photo her late husband, Juan, took of a divine Kieri venerated by Huichols as well as the gorgeous yarn painting called "Kieri Awatusa is Feasted and Consecrated." The artist, Tiburcio Carrillo Sandoval (Tutukila), portrays the same Kieri (known as White Antlers) shown in Negrín's photo. Tutukila's yarn painting nicely illustrates the tripartite constitution of Elder Brother (combining Kieri, human and deer) that is presented in González's narrative about the Deer Shaman. I am pleased that Juan Negrín's photo exemplifies a consecrated Kieri, one bearing a name and receiving offerings and prayers. These two images should enable readers to comprehend my most emphatic message to anthropologists who have been misled and who have misled others about the divinity of Kieri and its membership in the genus *Solandra*.

I am honored that Professor Conrad Kottak agreed to endorse this manuscript. In addition to being a first-rate scholar with an impressive command of anthropological information, my wife and I are eternally grateful to him for bringing us together, as young teaching assistants, in his American Culture class.

I would also like to thank my parents, J C and Virginia L. Fikes, to whom this book is dedicated. They were teachers who steadfastly supported my schooling as well as my freedom to explore nature. I remain deeply obliged to them for all they did to enable me to journey beyond the boundaries of American society and return with new knowledge about Kieri and Huichol shamanism.

INTRODUCTION

This is the book I wish I had been able to read when I began studying shamanism in the fall of 1970 with Dr. Robert Levy, a psychiatrist turned anthropologist (Fikes 2011, 21). Following Dr. Levy's guidance, I learned much about Inuit shamanism by reading some of Knud Rasmussen's reports, and about shamanism in general by reading reports of anthropologists, such as S.F. Nadel and Bronislaw Malinowski, as well as the geographer David Sopher. Two of several books Dr. Levy assigned me (Carlos Castaneda's first book, *The Teachings of Don Juan,* and Mircea Eliade's *Shamanism, Archaic Techniques of Ecstasy*) had a profound but short-lived influence on me. This was because neither of them did systematic long-term fieldwork in a specific society. Thus, neither of their works provided an in-depth insider's view of shamanic initiation over multiple generations nor shamanic practices within an historical context of a single society, in the way this book about the Huichol does.

I intend to provide readers with a comprehensive and historical view of the specific brand of shamanism prevailing in Huichol society, using first-person accounts from Huichol shamans, especially Jesús González, as well as ethnohistorical, ecological and political data.

While I must admit that the allegedly first-hand experiences Dr. Castaneda had as a supposed "sorcerer's apprentice" (Fikes 1993) inspired my initial desire to become a Huichol shaman (Fikes 2011), I eventually earned my Ph.D. in social anthropology and became a persistent debunker of Dr. Castaneda's fake ethnography (Fikes 1993, 2008; Austin *et al* 2007). After completing 22 years of ethnographic research with three shamans affiliated with the ceremonial center at Santa Catarina (Fikes 1985, 1993, 2011), I spent another ten years doing research with the shaman, Jesús González, during my brief visits to the Huichol community of Tuxpan de Bolaños.

Soon after meeting González in 1996 (see Chapter 1), I

informed him of experiences I had during my 1986 pilgrimage to solicit aid from a female Kieri (described in Chapter 1). That information prompted him to invite my wife, Dr. Lebriz Tosuner-Fikes and I, to complete religious pilgrimages with him. Knowing I was an anthropologist, he also permitted me to record the core of his remarkable first-hand experiences as a shaman, including those inspired by Kieri, a powerful psychoactive plant in the genus *Solandra* (see Appendix A).

My goal for this book is to convey a coherent and comprehensive interpretation of Huichol shamanism, one that combines personal experiences (mostly González's, and sometimes mine or those of other Huichol shamans) with my historical analysis of significant changes in Huichol shamanic practices, myths and rituals (using mostly González's data). I hope this book offers readers what I wanted fifty years ago, when I began preparing for my journey beyond peyote, by supplementing conventional social anthropology's "participant observation" with enhanced participation or "radical empiricism" (Fikes 2011). Therefore, my observation of Huichol rituals and tape recording of songs and myths they contained was complemented and enhanced by my ingestion of peyote during some rituals and pilgrimages to sacred sites. Taking seriously the hallmark of Huichol shamanism— that shamans communicate with spirits while performing rituals and making pilgrimages to sacred sites—obliged me to fully participate in order to empirically confirm, at least partially, their reports of experiences during rituals and pilgrimages.

Composition of the Book

The biography of Jesús González Mercado is presented in the first three chapters. He was the first Huichol shaman I met, and the last of four Huichol shamans who mentored me. He entrusted me with publishing revelations about his face-to-face childhood encounter with the principal Huichol tutelary spirit, Elder Brother. This shamanic call came to Jesús when he was seven years old, and was produced after he ate potent psychoactive honey made by wasps eating the nectar of the divine plant, Kieri. Elder Brother, incarnate in the Kieri pollen, conveyed extraordinary visions and songs that destined Jesús to become a shaman. Forty-five years later, both he and his wife became ill. To be healed and certified to practice as a shaman, Jesús and his wife completed several pilgrimages together to the Mother Goddess that dwells in the Pacific Ocean. Their sicknesses disappeared once Jesús heeded his long-neglected shamanic call and began performing (singing) at rituals and healing.

His biography discloses details depicting how Jesús diagnoses and heals his patients, as well as decisive childhood experiences such as learning from elders the purposes and methods essential in ritual deer hunting, and coping with the murder of several of his family members during the horrific Cristero Rebellion (1927-1938). Although his comments allude to the poverty and violence he suffered as a child, he did not examine the causes for those chronic problems still troubling the Huichol, or Wixarika as they call themselves.

After publishing an abbreviated version of González's life in 2003 in *The Man Who Ate Honey,* I continued translating interviews and researching the meaning of central themes contained in the copious information Jesús González and his son, Vicente, were confiding in me. Completing my analysis of González's religious narrative about the first Deer Shaman (in Chapter 4) demanded extraordinary effort. After Vicente and I had finished translating into Spanish the ritual text that his father had recited in Huichol, I worked diligently to accurately interpret the significance this sacred narrative held for González. It is clear that his commitment to Elder Brother Tamatsi's integrity and compassion guided all his healing and performing of rituals. Thus, Chapter 4, "The Deer Shaman, Tamatsi, Transforms Society" interprets a narrative that embodies universal themes (such as the hero who overcomes unrelenting adversity) while remaining rooted in the reverence Huichol have for Kieri, deer, and other flora and fauna native to their Chapalagana river valley homeland. This saga of Tamatsi's divine birth, followed by a narrative of the trials and tribulations he overcame in order to defeat the powerful Wolf People, offers us an extraordinary account of compassion, equal to any other world-religious text about divine leadership.

Chapter 5 interprets examples of González's observations of his father and grandfather, during their acquisition of shamanic abilities and clarifies doctrines that guided their use of such skills. González's insider's view of three generations of Huichol shamanism explains how he and his ancestors obtained shamanic power by establishing rapport with the ancestral spirits associated with divine plants (e.g., Kieri), animals (deer, Mexican beaded lizards, rattlesnakes, horned toads, etc) and natural phenomena (Sun, Fire, Pacific Ocean).

González also discussed details central to Huichol peyote hunting and the naming of infants. That information supported my analysis of adaptations connected to the Huichol being incorporated in an annual temple ritual cycle. The Huichol commitment to performing temple (*tuki*) rituals such as the Peyote Dance compelled them to cooperate with more powerful allies, the Cora to their west, and Tepecano to their east (Fikes 1985). Forming inter-ethnic alliances with the Cora and Tepecano significantly altered Huichol shamanism.

González's data in Chapter 5, supplemented by information provided by my two Santa Catarina *kawiteru* mentors, convinced me that the adoption of the temple ritual cycle, especially the peyote hunt, transformed what was a more egalitarian Huichol society in which Kieri was venerated. The most momentous obligation of their temple ritual cycle has been the performance of arduous annual pilgrimages to procure peyote and deposit offerings for the Sun Father at the volcanic mountain where he emerged, near Real de Catorce, in the Mexican state of San Luis Potosi.

This 700 kilometer round trip pilgrimage made on foot became indispensable to insure rain, which is essential for the survival of the Huichol and their maize, and to achieve higher social status, by becoming a *kawiteru*, an authority in ritual oratory. Inviting

Rain Mothers to return to the Huichol homeland at the end of the dry season is accomplished through the performance of the Peyote Dance ritual. This quintessential Huichol ritual requires obtaining peyote and the 'everlasting water,' which embodies the Rain Mothers dwelling in three distinct waterholes. Of course Huichol temple officers must deposit offerings and make prayers to those Rain Mothers before they remove such eternal water, called *Hay+rime* (Fikes 2011). Making such pilgrimages for the benefit of their community significantly increased the prestige of Huichol temple officers and concomitantly diluted Kieri's dominance relative to peyote.

Chapter 6 provides particulars that illustrate the enduring Huichol dedication to the spirit of Kieri, the divine plant whose pollen is the spiritual nucleus of Tamatsi. For the past three centuries, traditional Huichol have been making prayers and offerings to what outsiders see as a saint in the Catholic church at Tenzompa, a town inhabited by Huichol until almost 1910. The Huichol, however, knew that they were still venerating Tamatsi – their powerful, all-purpose, tutelary spirit – inside that church. At that church they solicited various favors from the spirit of Kieri, including success in deer hunting and protection from witchcraft.

González's son, Vicente, witnessed the power of that Kieri spirit after neglecting to deliver offerings he had vowed to make at the church in Tenzompa. His testimony about that transgression, also featured in this chapter, explains why his own "sin of omission" resulted in that Kieri spirit sending punishments. His narrative illustrates why younger Huichol are becoming reluctant to establish pacts with Kieri: because the penalty for failing to abide by one's vows to its divine spirit may bring death, by what appears to be an accident, or bring illness or other misfortune.

Vicente's explanation of the diverse benefits Huichol seek when covertly praying to Kieri at that church exemplify an ingenious practice which became common among Mexican Indians after Spaniards began ruthlessly eradicating their "idols" and punishing ritual practitioners with torture and death: punishments sanctified by the Inquisition. The fact that the worship of Kieri flourishes, despite Franciscan missionary interference, attests to Huichol appreciation of its power.

The final three chapters (7-9) of this book describe chronic economic and political problems facing the Huichol, including the scarcity of arable land, erratic and sometimes inadequate rainfall, poverty, murders linked to marijuana cultivation, and difficulties with tourists who intrude, both in their Chapalagana river valley homeland and in the peyote country, principally around the town of Real de Catorce.

Huichol resistance to a century of land invasions by Mexican cattlemen, interference with their peyote pilgrimages, and the cold-blooded killing of the American journalist Phil True in 1998, are also discussed in these chapters.

Within the transcribed narrative sections by Jesús González and his son Vicente, [Brackets] indicate translator's notes and contextual and explanatory notes; (parentheses) include or translate Huichol words, or contain other notes by Fikes.

Why Write a Fully Contextualized Biography?

Biographies and autobiographies of Native American and Mexican Indians have often neglected to clearly illuminate the domination that European conquerors employed to "Christianize" indigenous people, while at the same time stealing their lands and resources. My first biography of an American Indian leader examined candidly causes of fundamental problems endemic to Native Americans, problems strikingly similar to those troubling the Huichol.

To produce that biography, *Reuben Snake: Your Humble Serpent*, I researched and discussed in detail key issues that Reuben mentioned during our tape-recorded interviews. We intended to make sure readers would comprehend why he and his Ho-Chunk (Winnebago) relatives were still suffering from alcoholism, diabetes and other problems connected to surviving a continuing legacy of racism, religious intolerance and poverty caused by Euro-American immigrants.[1]

To achieve Reuben's goal of putting his autobiography in the "proper context" (Fikes 1996, 18), we provided historical explanations of several examples of Reuben's resistance to injustices, taken from the final 24 years of his life.[2]

In this biography about Jesús González I examine his testimony about Huichol shamanism in an historical, ecological, and sociopolitical context so that readers have in their hands a politically responsible book. Because González and I were focused primarily on documenting his spiritual life, I did not prod him to give me details about his political achievements. Publications relevant to interpreting González's life, especially before 1980, are too scarce to permit me to replicate the kind of "fully contextualized" biography I wrote about Reuben Snake. To compensate for this, his murdered son's political career is the principal focus of Chapter 7. That chapter, and the two that follow it, epitomize my attempt to present a more complete and accurate representation of the historical and social context in which traditional Huichol shamans such as Jesús González lived. My effort to situate González's shamanic practices in the correct context should provide an excellent antidote to the sensational caricature of Huichol peyote use that was widely popularized by Drs. Furst, Myerhoff, and Castaneda (Fikes 1993).

Finally, I ask activists defending Wixarika interests to forgive me for continuing to use the word *Huichol*. By doing so I anticipate that more readers will locate this book and thereby have an opportunity to learn to appreciate the Wixarika as a distinct, inspiring ethnic group. I hope that as readers learn more about the difficult existential issues that the Wixarika confront on a daily basis, at least some will decide to provide assistance.

CHAPTER 1

ELDER BROTHER SUMMONS JESÚS
TO BE A SHAMAN

This book includes the biography of Jesús González Mercado, a Huichol shaman from Tuxpan de Bolaños.[1] Although I first met Jesús González briefly in Tepic in 1976, I did not see him again until I visited Tuxpan de Bolaños in 1996. I went there to "repatriate" film footage archived at the Smithsonian Institution, footage that American anthropologist Robert Zingg shot in Tuxpan in 1934 (Zingg 2004). During my stay in Tuxpan in 1996, González told me that he saw his relatives in the film, and recalled that he was thirteen when Zingg first arrived there. When I reconnected with Jesús in 1996 he had been practicing as a healer and singer for twenty years. He spoke Spanish reasonably well, and had two wives (Maria Jesucita Romero and Maria Micaela de la Rosa). By the time Jesús died, in 2016, he had numerous children, one of whom was murdered by marijuana growers (see Chapter 7), many grandchildren, and a few great-grandchildren

Before my 1996 visit to Tuxpan, I had made some 23 trips (starting in 1976) to learn about Huichol religion from three shamans residing near the ceremonial center of Santa Catarina (some of this research has been published; see references in the bibliography). They explained to me that the orthodox way to be recognized as a healer or singer (shaman) included establishing rapport with an ancestor (what scholars often call a "tutelary spirit") in addition to fulfilling obligations incumbent upon all Huichol temple officers. At least 25 different ancestors, such as Rain Mothers and other essential elements in nature (Fikes 1985, 155; 2011), are served by Huichol temple officers.[2] Each Huichol officer is obliged to serve a specific ancestor such as Great Grandmother Germination, Takutsi Y+rameka, or Kam+kime, the Father of the Wolves, or the Sun Father, for five years. Thus temple officers have the opportunity to ingest peyote and make personal contact with ancestors during pilgrimages to sacred sites, which include the desert where peyote is collected, and while performing temple rituals. Healers acquire their ability during one term of five years of service as a temple officer. Singers must have served as temple officers for two terms, or ten years (Fikes 1985, 1993, 68-69, 2011, 9-10).

Jesús González Mercado did not follow the path to spiritual power that the Santa Catarina shamans I knew regarded as standard. Although Jesús was a custodian of a gourd bowl for the ancestors he served in Tuxpan's edition of the Huichol temple ritual cycle, he did not participate in peyote hunts, as do most temple officers at Santa Catarina. What is crucial is that Jesús was summoned to heal and sing by the spirit of Kieri, a divine plant native to the Huichol homeland.

Jesús' life was irrevocably altered at the age of seven when he was taught songs in a vision induced by eating honey made by wasps which had consumed Kieri nectar. His chronicle describing the origin of the first Huichol shaman (in Chapter 4) credits Buzzard Person with knowing the power of Kieri pollen, and helping incarnate that power in Elder Brother, the first Huichol Deer Shaman. Jesús is convinced that it was Elder Brother who summoned him at seven years old, after he ate psychoactive honey. Jesús then learned songs from Elder Brother, and years later obtained authorization to heal, as symbolized by the sacred paraphernalia inside his *takwatsi* (the shaman's palm-fiber basket). His profound and singular personal visionary experience, as stimulated by psychoactive honey, is amply justified by the myth of the first Deer Shaman and is completely supported by community conviction.

Jesús' delay in practicing as a shaman is noteworthy. His belief that his sickness would disappear once he started shamanizing has yet to be verified as a pattern among the Huichol, but it is recognized as a common component of shamanic initiation in certain central Asian societies (Basilov 1997, Eliade 1964, Hutton

2001, Lewis 1989, Walter and Fridman 2004). Jesús' pilgrimages to the Pacific Ocean, to gain favor with the Mother who dwells there (Tatei Haramara), is a traditional Huichol way to acquire shamanic power. Huichols honor their spiritual Mother (Tatei Werika Wimari) in the First Fruits ceremony, and Jesús praises her for having persuaded Buzzard Person to resuscitate Our Elder Brother, after he was killed while in deer form, by the Animal People (as interpreted in Chapter 4).

The three most significant sources of his shamanic power, Our (spiritual) Mother, Buzzard Person, and Elder Brother (whose spirit is associated with Kieri by Jesús, and with both Kieri and peyote, by shamans of Santa Catarina) are the central characters in Jesús' account of the first Huichol Deer Shaman. I will interpret similarities and differences in narratives that depict the origin of the first Deer Shaman in a future publication.

To enable readers to comprehend what made Jesús a shaman, I supplement his generous description of his momentous childhood spiritual experiences with details explaining how he and his wife were healed, and how he diagnoses and heals patients. To help readers appreciate him as a person, I provide particulars about how the conflict between the Christian militants, called *Cristeros,* and the Mexican government forces allied with Tuxpan Huichol tragically impacted his family during his childhood. His devotion to deer hunting, arranged marriage, and community service as a temple officer and political leader are also discussed.

In these first three chapters below, Jesús declared that at seven years old he learned songs imparted during his extraordinary vision stimulated by psychoactive honey, that he remembered his birth while growing up at the rancho of La Mesa, and that he stayed for one year at a Mexican boarding school established for Huichol children in Tuxpan de Bolaños. Either that was one very incredible year, or his inexact use of "seven years old" really means that each of these distinct experiences happened, "while he was a child." He was probably about 80 years old in 2003, the year we published his abbreviated autobiography, *The Man Who*

Ate Honey: The Revelations of a Huichol Shaman. That booklet gradually evolved into this book, the equivalent to his biography.

Jesús explains how he obtained a blessing from Kieri
(translated from Huichol to Spanish by Vicente, his son):

"I was hunting birds, walking by myself through canyons, armed only with my bow and arrows. My best friend was my cousin. He and I would hunt birds together everyday. My cousin and I were constant companions. We were walking back and forth along a stream. We had no domesticated animals to watch. In the middle of our hunting there was something coming toward us. We were both practically nude, wearing only a wool shirt. As we crossed the stream there were some plants called *Kutamé* (snake's tooth). When we came to these plants there was a honeycomb made by wasps (perhaps *Brachygastra mellifica*, called *Rumáste* in Huichol). My cousin asked me: "Do you see that honeycomb there?" I told him: "Knock it down with a big stick." My cousin decided to knock it down with his bow. It fell on the ground and there were a few wasps, not many. We opened it and tore it apart. I was gathering up the honey. Those honeycombs were beautiful, blue-green in color. Those wasps never stung us.

After we had collected the honey we walked a short distance from that place and began eating honey. After eating the honey we went to the stream. We squeezed the honeycombs to make them like tamales. Then we headed toward home. As we ate the honey we suddenly started vomiting. We lay down under the *Kutamé* to vomit. Our vomit was a very yellow color. We left there and walked until we came to a cave. That is where we threw away our honeycomb "tamales." We continued feeling nauseous as we walked. We arrived at a seep and we wet our heads with water. We drank water and it made us feel worse.

There is a trail that descends to a place called the white rock. The trail passed by it and when I turned to look up I saw a huge rock sliding down. That rock was sliding down toward us (but it was only an hallucination). The rocks were breaking apart at the same time I saw two paths dividing. I fled along the path that was going uphill. My cousin shouted at me, "Where are you going?" I heard him but I did not reply. I continued climbing up the mountain. When I looked up at the summit I saw a boy who spoke to me: "Come on, come on." I climbed up to the top and began walking behind the boy. I followed him until we came to a hill covered with god houses (*xirikite*). The boy declared to the crowd that was present at the god houses: "Here is the boy you ordered me to bring to you." There was a singer's chair (*uweni*) and they sat me down in it. [All this comes from a vision] There were numerous women and many houses forming a circle. Then an old man addressed me: "They have finally brought you here today. I have been searching for you for a long time. I had been looking for you but began thinking that my work would be in vain. Today the child finally found you and now you are here. I have been waiting for you. I have something that I have been waiting to give you. Today I will turn it all over to you and my duty of watching over it will end. Everything you see here, the women that are your sisters, the god houses that form the circle there, you will understand. Listen carefully to everything because you are here to understand it all."

That is what the old man told me. His clothes were torn and had lots of patches. I was listening attentively to the old man, seated where they had seated me. Then he told me: "You know that I have been waiting to give you these things. Pay close attention and focus on what I am going to give you." Then he gave me the *takwatsi*, (an oblong basket containing the shaman's sacred paraphernalia) placing it on the ground in front of my feet. He opened the *takwatsi* and everybody could see the prayer feathers. He began singing the song of *wawe* (amaranth) [This song is used in several ceremonies such as the parching of the corn, and for the bull and when the cornfield is cleared for planting.] "Listen well," he told me and he finished the song. Then he warned me: "Never harm any of your relatives, nor any cattle, horses or corn. If you harm any of them everything will go against you. Nor should you feel envious about anything other people accomplish." Speaking like that he sang five verses and told me: "I am only going to give you these five verses. I am never going to give you a rope, nor a bow, nor an arrow. ["Not having a rope" means that he will not be able to grab a *Kakauyari* (male Ancestor Deity), not having a bow means that he will not be able to shoot an *itauki* (the spirit of a deceased shaman that appears in non-human form), not having an arrow means that he will not be an evil-doer using witchcraft]. Because if I were to give you a rope, or a bow and an arrow it would be to do harm to your relatives, to your corn and your own fortune." That is why he told me I would only receive the five verses. Then he declared: "Memorize these verses and take them with you. Never add anything or subtract anything from these five. Just treasure exactly what I gave you."

After he had told me all this he followed up by taking out a drum. The old man started singing and playing the drum. He sang the song of the daytime and the song of the night-time. He sang five verses of each. He told me: "These are the foundation for each of the songs that I am showing you. You must learn them and use them always during your life on earth." He ended that ceremony by declaring: "This is exactly what you are going to do, directing yourself to the four cardinal directions and ending with their intersection." Next he began the song of the *Hikuli Neixa* (Peyote Dance), using the same format he had in the previous songs. He stated: "This is the way you will begin. This is how you will sing and how you will place the *tepari* [This is not merely the round rock we call *tepari* but also the prayer with all the symbols required to attract the Ancestor Deities. For example, we place the *tepari* in our cornfields to ask our ancestors to protect our corn against the crows, badgers, raccoons etc.] While he was telling me all this suddenly I heard the people shouting and dancing in the same manner that we dance the Peyote Dance today. They were all singing, repeating the words of the old man.

That is the way it happened. I never received anything by my own volition. [This was a gift from the Kieri rather than a response to a person seeking favor from an Ancestor Deity.] I was calm and attentive to what the old man was saying to me. When I woke up the next morning, that is I surely must have awakened, I immediately felt something cold on my head.

I came to my senses and began looking around in every direction. I was expecting to see and hear the same scenes again but I never saw or heard anything more. I was completely alone, sitting with my back against a boulder. Almost all of my body was numb. After I recovered my normal consciousness I spent almost all day laying down there, overcoming my numbness.[3]

I have never been able to understand completely everything that happened to me. Is it that I was born for this purpose, or is it that my ancestors were the ones that selected me? As I live and breathe today I do not worry about anything. Everything I do and everything I know is done without any fear because I never searched for this nor did I solicit it. It was the decision of Tamatsi Kauyumari tukimari (Kieri pollen manifesting Our Elder Brother Kauyumari) and of Hauye Wekame.[4] Nowadays I perform rituals for the welfare of my family, putting into practice all the customs that were revealed to me. I do not envy anybody. I do no harm to anybody. I only heal (carry out the cleansing) my family in accordance with the instructions for healing that were given to me.

Some people criticize me, saying that I am arrogant because of the evil that I do, saying that I am a witch and who knows what other falsehoods. None of this makes me uncomfortable nor do I worry because I am certain that I never do evil things against anybody or any of my family. This is because, for me, permission was never given to do such things. [He was warned that if he were to do evil things it would go against the welfare of his family and his property.]

Anyway, when I returned to my house there was my grandfather.[5] I explained to him everything that happened to me and then he replied: "*Caray* (holy smoke) my little child it appears you are not doing so well. Considering what has become of you and what you were given I am not worthy of taking anything from you. The only thing I can do is rearrange what you have on your body. [The grandfather recognized that Jesús had spiritual pollen, a spiritual trait or mark on his body.] The one thing I can advise you is that you were pitied (given a gift). You must never cheat or dishonor this gift. Such abuses are forbidden and whenever one does not mind the only result will be death. Starting today for the next ten days you must not eat salt. After you fast for those ten days, I will finish your fast for you." That is what happened. According to my grandfather he fasted with me. I completed my vows for five years (this means five years of sexual abstinence). That is what happened up to now in my life. [He did not need to visit the Kieri for five consecutive years. Abstaining from sex for five years was easy, given his young age; his only sacrifice was the salt fast.]

Nowadays, even though it may not be sufficient for other singers, I understand the foundation of my culture (i.e., the gourd bowl and prayer arrow). The rituals that I perform I do in order to obtain abundant life for myself and my family. Will that cause my death? I don't know; only God knows. I fulfill my obligations by performing them. I have numerous descendants that are alive today. I am their tree. I am alive today because of all that happened to me. Whether or not I have fulfilled all requirements, I have survived until today.

If the sun, the earth and the oceans exist, and I listen to their messages, I am the only one who knows, nobody else. These events happened just the way I said they did. It is said that if someone does not fulfill one's obligations, that person will die.

That has not happened to me. I am still living. Therefore, I believe I have complied with what was required of me. While I am alive the sun, earth and oceans know whether anything bad will befall me. I have not made my life an exhibit for people (i.e., he never before has revealed such details about the gift Kieri gave him). I hope they enjoy it."

Soliciting favors from a Kieri, Esteemed as the Incarnation of Our Elder Brother

Many Huichols have warned me never to eat Kieri. I feel compelled to emphasize that eating any part of this plant may well be hazardous to one's health. Traditionally, prayers and offerings to it initiate a pact that must be adhered to scrupulously with salt fasting and sexual purity. Kieri can punish, with serious illness or death, all those who fail to abide by their vows. When transgressions against Kieri are committed, forgiveness or atonement is virtually impossible.

In September of 1986 I was guided by the shaman I called Serratos and my compadre to a very old female Kieri growing in a pine forest at about 2000 meters above sea level. That Kieri is home to a divine spirit (*mara'akame*) that Serratos calls Tamatsi Paritsika or Maxa Tewiyari (Deer Person). Although that Kieri is not visited by temple officers from Santa Catarina both the k*awiteru* (whose songs I cited in my 1985 dissertation) and Serratos had made offerings to it. Serratos told me all Huichols know about this particular Kieri but most of them fear involvement with it because it punishes people who fail to comply with their vows. He warned me that both the seeker and his/her spouse must be sexually faithful to each other. Otherwise either of them may be punished by death, (which will appear to be an accident).

Late in the afternoon when we arrived at this Kieri I noticed it had received only a few offerings, none of which appeared to be recent. We placed our offerings and candles beside the Kieri (See Figs 2, 3, 5) and then Serratos and my compadre started a fire a short distance away. Serratos told me that before I prayed to Tamatsi Paritsica I should confess all sexual experiences I had prior to getting married. I dutifully wrote down all their names, repeated them, and burned the paper in the fire. Then I ate some peyote and prayed in Huichol and Spanish to Tamatsi Paritsika. What happened during the rest of that evening as I sat beside this Kieri is too amazing to reveal. In fact, Serratos advised me against discussing the experience with anyone except my wife.

Fig. 2. Votive arrows we left before I confessed to Grandfather Fire.

Fig. 3. I solicited aid from Tamatsi, associated with this 1.2 meter-tall Kieri.

Serratos' warning illustrates Juan Negrín's explanation of the Huichol practice of hermeticism, including mutism, which means—'do not declare anything esoteric to anyone unless they already know it' (Negrín 2001, 34-36). My quest to acquire wisdom from this Kieri evidently convinced Jesús to divulge his childhood experiences with Kieri to me. In publishing Jesús' biography, I

Fig. 4. The Kieri to which Felipe Sánchez introduced me in 1976.

Fig. 5. Kieri leaves I photographed in 1986.

hope to increase reverence for the divine spirit manifested through the Kieri plant, and respect for those Huichol, like Jesús, who worship our Elder Brother in spirit and in truth.

The true value of Kieri in Huichol culture has never been fully understood. To better enable readers to appreciate how essential Kieri must have been to ancient Huichols, in Chapter 4 I will interpret Jesús' chronicle of how their culture hero, the Deer Shaman, Tamatsi Kauyumari, was created. Here is a brief summary:

A Huichol couple wanted to have children. They were instructed on how to have a child, without having sex, by the Ancestor Deity known as Buzzard Person. He showed the woman the Kieri pollen she would need to create the child and warned her to carry out fully all his instructions. The husband and wife placed the Kieri pollen inside their god house and made the necessary prayers and offerings. Five days later a boy appeared in their god house. The boy grew up rapidly, became an expert marksman, and learned to turn himself into a deer. In deer form he was enticed into the temple of the Animal People. Their lead singer, Wolf Person, wanted to sacrifice him, but he escaped with the help of a small mouse, Tuamurutsi (probably an honorific title for the mouse). Tuamurutsi stole the *takwatsi* (an oblong basket containing the shaman's belongings) of Wolf Person and handed it over to Tamatsi (our Elder Brother). The Animal People began chasing the divine Deer Shaman (Tamatsi), and eventually they killed him, but he was soon resuscitated by Buzzard Person, who followed the advice of our Spiritual Mother (Tatei Werika Wimari). Today, Huichol singers and healers are allied with Tamatsi because he took over the powers inherent in the *takwatsi* of Wolf Person.

This myth establishes that Kieri pollen is holy, being the foundation for the divine deer who became, thanks to the efforts of Buzzard Person, the tutelary spirit of Huichol healers and singers. This chronicle also explains central elements in Huichol deer hunting, namely the ritual use of Kieri pollen and the hunter's firm commitment to sexual purity (Fikes 1985, 216).

Beyond Peyote

CHAPTER 2

Jesús Overcomes Illness by Becoming a Shaman

Translated by Vicente González

"My wife and I were suffering from an illness, but had no idea why we were sick and we suffered for some time. There was a person that I regarded as my brother (his name was José Contreras). He was a very wise shaman. I asked him to investigate our case (diagnose the illness) and he replied, "All right, because you are asking me brother and because I admire you I will do my best to take care of you and your wife. But you will need to be patient with me because I am not going to heal you right now. That will happen after I diagnose your problem" (in his dreams).

He did exactly what he said. He never healed us. He only discerned the cause of our problem in his dream and told us what we were required to pray to ask Tamatsi (represented by the *takwatsi*) for forgiveness. (The sickness was sent because Jesús was not using the *takwatsi* to summon Tamatsi to help him heal and sing.)

Ten days later José Contreras returned. He then told us what was causing our illness. He ordered me to make a miniature drum, an arrow, and a *yakwai* (small gourd for carrying tobacco) and my wife to make a tiny gourd bowl just as he instructed us. After that we were completely healed. The gourd bowl that my wife made depicted five lines of foam from the ocean. We made all the offerings like that, by ourselves, in our village and then we returned to Tuxpan de Bolaños. When we were prepared to go to the ocean we left on a Thursday and delivered our offerings (to the ocean) that same day. We were completely healed, and went back.

In another five days José Contreras returned to ask if we had fulfilled all our obligations. If we had done what he prescribed he would be satisfied and freed from any further commitment. He found us totally content. When he arrived we greeted each other and he asked me if I had carried the items that he ordered me to take as an offering. I told him that everything had been accomplished. He described all the consequences of our illness and of our pilgrimage to the ocean and what there was left to do. He said: "All right my brother, I am very sorry but you will have to appear before Tamatsi (the *takwatsi*). From now on when you plant corn and you finish clearing the cornfield you personally will have to perform the ceremony for the cornfield. That is the way Tamatsi Kauyumari Tukimarika (Kieri pollen manifesting Our Elder Brother Kauyumari), Grandfather Fire and the Sun Father want it to be. It is a miracle you are still alive because your illness is chronic." I responded to him: "All right then, I will do my utmost. After all, it is my pleasure insofar as I am the one to blame for having caused all this in the first place. Everything has a purpose but I never discerned it in the beginning when I started to practice these things. (This refers to the gift he received from the child and the old man after he ate honey containing Kieri nectar.) At this moment I am suffering from the punishment. Well I have no other choice. I must comply."

Immediately after we planted the corn and finished clearing brush from the cornfield, I did it exactly as he ordered me; I started to sing. I got through that night but I never comprehended anything, nor did I see anything. The second time, I sang at the ritual performed after the cornfield is cleared and planted, and I was able to understand something; those must have been the voices of our ancestors. The third time I celebrated the ritual of the First Fruits (Tatei Neixa); by then I was almost an expert. The fourth time I sang it was the ritual of the *atole* (maize beverage). I believed I was nearly a singer because everything was so different compared to the first time.

During our celebration of the ritual of the *atole*, an event occurred that brought an improvement in our lives. An illness struck our granddaughter, and my wife confronted me by saying,

"What good is there in what you are doing? You sing but do not heal. Now that our granddaughter is sick you must heal her." It was for that reason that we made such sacrifices, in order to gain the knowledge of how to save our relatives from diseases. My wife persuaded me to do my first healing, and to my surprise our granddaughter got well. When I did my first healing I didn't know which ancestors to turn to for help. At that moment I turned to Hai Itima (Cleansing Cloud), to Hautsi k+puri and Tatei Werika Wimari (on which, see below).

I put my faith in these mothers, all of whom are proficient: Hai Wenima, Hai Itima, Hautsi k+puri, Tatei Werika Wimari (she that holds the *wikuxa,* threads of life) to Tatei Ut+anaka, Xuturi Wieka, Tatei Xapawiyeme, Tatei Nia'ariwame, Tatei Tsakaimuta, and Tatei Haramara, principally to you Haramara because you have those spirits to whom I have entrusted myself. [The Mother who dwells in the Pacific Ocean, Tatei Haramara, is the figure most closely connected with Jesús. She is the earthly counterpart to Tatei Werika Wimari (the Celestial Mother who holds the threads of life, the Mother who Jesús calls upon to help him heal)]. I implore all of you because you created yourselves by your own efforts. You all can help me make this healing successful." That is how I did it. I healed my granddaughter. That is how I located those divine spirits I just mentioned.

I was able to prove myself. I said to myself, "it is assumed that these divine spirits are the ones most in charge of human diseases." I was thinking to myself and talking to these divine spirits, "in the end all of you are diverse but are united (or are one)." When I voiced these words to those divine spirits I said to them, "what we are doing seems like a white lie that is connected with the truth when the illness is extracted from the person (If a person gets well they attribute that to his skill as a healer).

When I accomplished my first healing I summoned only those divine spirits I just mentioned. Later I added Buzzard Person and Xuturi Wename (the One Who Wipes Away Illnesses).

Calling on them was new for me. Now in my declaration

I state that this is the way I started to heal and sing and now I continue doing it the same way for my family and my rituals. But practicing as a shaman was not my decision in the beginning, nor was it my intention. There was someone else who intervened at the start. [The child and the elderly man that summoned him after he ate the honey containing Kieri nectar.] The one who intervened had a reason. Previously I perhaps was unable to understand that reason. Given my present functions (as a healer and singer) I trust that the one responsible selected me after much deliberation. That is why, up to now, no severe problem has troubled me. I am therefore grateful for what occurred when I was a child. Now I realize that those events blessed me. These days I put into practice what I received when I was a child.

At this moment I am not that certain that I am obeying or not. Only my gods know how they understand my prayers. Whatever I do or don't do, it is always done in order to comply with what I am ordered to do and to do it without subtracting or adding anything.

This is the way they [the child and elder he saw after eating the psychoactive honey] instructed me at the beginning. I don't go to sing at various villages, nor do I heal many people, just my family members and people I trust. I celebrate the rituals at my home with my family. But with the passage of time I began healing mestizos.

I don't know what I am. It is possible that I am confused because I believe that I am infected by my Elder Brother Kauyumari. [The word *kauyumari* means one who goes everywhere boldly]. Up to now I have never been bitten by any rats or any snakes, nor has anything tragic occurred to me. For that reason I believe I have fulfilled the objectives (required by my gods) and that I have used my gift properly.

Now you (Fikes) are asking me what you want to know, and what (Huichol) words you want to understand I have explained a little to you, and this I can tell you. You want to know how I started to heal and to sing. From now on you know how it happened that I began. If in truth you are enthusiastic about these events and you intend to make your pilgrimage I hope you achieve your goals pertaining to Huichol culture. What I disclose to you is something that is possibly prohibited, but I do not fear for the words I speak to you because you are helping me. Everything that I have revealed is all that I know pertaining to the beginning of my singing and healing. And because you asked me I gave you my words and my knowledge and my heart (soul). I put all this in your hands. I hope it is worthy of your inquiry."

(After translation of the foregoing material, Vicente explained the following:)

"José Contreras advised Jesús that to remain healthy he and his wife would have to go to the ocean to leave specific offerings. This would induce Haramara (the Pacific Ocean) to pardon him for not using his gift (from the Kieri). Returning from the ocean, Jesús started to sing. After his singing and performing rituals were well underway, he began to heal, starting with his granddaughter. The granddaughter he healed was born on July 22, 1976 and she soon got sick. Thus Jesús started to heal in Tuxpan de Bolaños the first few months of 1977. And so his singing started by 1975 or 1976."

Jesús Speaks About Becoming a Shaman

(Asked about what sickness Jesús and his wife had when they consulted José Contreras, Jesús replied:)

"Today I am being asked (by Fikes) the question of how our sickness was discovered. I believe what happened was a revelation. We had started making annual pilgrimages to the Pacific Ocean; my second wife was the one that insisted that we go to the ocean. We completed many pilgrimages, fifteen in all, to the ocean. We had two more pilgrimages to complete when we fell ill and we were surprised when my relative, José Contreras, arrived in Tuxpan. I asked him to do us the favor of examining us to learn what was making us sick. After listening to what I had to tell him, José responded immediately, "I am going to fulfill the request that you made of me. But I am not going to heal you until after I investigate the cause of your illness." The next day at about four or five a.m., when we were standing beside the fire, he told me: "Your illness involves something that you both already know about. I believe you two already have a *takwatsi* (oblong basket containing the shaman's sacred paraphernalia) and that is what is causing your illness." After the sun had risen, we left for our village to make confessions and ask for forgiveness from our *takwatsi*.

Five days later José Contreras came back again to see us. At that time he spoke to us, directing his words to my wife: "Sister-in-law, you need to make a gourd bowl to offer to the Pacific Ocean." So we went to the ocean, to the place where we left our offerings; after that we felt much better. On the day when we returned from the ocean José Contreras arrived at Tuxpan de Bolaños. [He knew how long it would take them to make the pilgrimage.] He then told me, "when you celebrate the ritual for planting corn you must sing; by singing your sickness will disappear. As soon as you have finished clearing the brush from your cornfield, when you are ready to consecrate the corn, you must sing." When the time came, I sang at the planting ritual. After singing, I understood that each and every action has a consequence.

That is how I managed to overcome my illness, by complying with what he ordered me to do. I felt totally liberated, and I gradually realized why we made our pilgrimages to the Pacific Ocean. We became familiar with our *nierika* (the visionary ability symbolized by a small round mirror) and then with our *muwieri* (prayer feathers used to summon ancestors when healing or singing) and we then collected all the sacred paraphernalia. We have remained faithful until now. I now comprehend almost everything.

I did not solicit my knowledge. It was granted according to the decision made by my helping spirits, especially Tamatsi Paritsika (Kieri). He selected me, and I am convinced that he blessed me with power. I give thanks to all of you ancestors and ask to be pardoned in order to prevent any misunderstandings between us;

my Grandfather Fire, my Sun Father, and my Elder Brother. All of you are assembled behind Huriwari, the Divine Mountain; you have the power and you have given it to me. May you find no fault with me.

Do not judge me because this is merely a conversation about what I have learned from you; I have never revealed this before, but now I am declaring it. You all are my witnesses if something bad happens to me. That is all for now."

Jesús Explains Why He Made the Drum and
Other Offerings for the Pacific Ocean.

"It was obligatory that I make a drum and carry it to the ocean in order to be free. I made thirteen pilgrimages to the ocean, taking the votive arrow and gourd bowl. We went there every year. Tamatsi Paritsika requested this of us before giving us permission to play the drum. That is how I became authorized (to be a shaman)—it is nothing complicated. Even today I play the drum to please my gods. Every year I play the drum to celebrate the First Fruits ritual, showing our children the spiritual road [upon which children journey to Paritek+a.]

For our gods it is like entertainment, like a guitar that is heard along the road to the altar where they encounter Our Mother—the mother of our children and of us. Once they arrive at the altar, they receive their chocolate (*yurari*). By playing the drum and making offerings in that way, the gods receive life and strength in the same way we receive life's blessings from them [that is, via the enduring partnership that binds people with Ancestor Deities]. [Jesús carried a tiny bow, a tiny gourd bowl, a *nierika* (mirror for communicating with ancestral spirits), a *matsua,* (wristguard), a tiny drum, and tiny gourd (*yakwai*) in order to ask for permission to become a singer and healer. Tatei Haramara saw these votive objects and gave him permission to become a singer.]

Jesús Praises Our Mother's (Ocean) Foam

"It was you that I asked, and you that gave me your foam that represents *uxa*, a generation, that has five steps with foam. All of this represents only you, for any person that arrives (at the ocean) with you in order to seek wisdom. That was how I obtained a *muwieri* (prayer feather) from you, and a *nierika* (mirror used to see the spirits). That was perfectly good because you gave me your foam, *uxa*, and now I still have your power, just as much as does Our Elder Brother. He is truly engaged in communication with all of you gods, responding to your petitions, ready to serve you day and night, because he is the one that knows the symbols that represent each thing that I acquired from you. [Tamatsi interprets the shaman's dreams.]"

Secrets of Huichol Healing

"When they bring me a sick child, man or woman, how do I diagnose their illness so I may heal it? This is not done according to one's whims. It depends on the person's beliefs in the gods and their relationship with them. The principal senders of the sickness appear in dreams. Upon awakening one tells the sick person the reason that they became sick. When it is true—when the shaman is not lying—sometimes the patient wakes up healed. In these matters the Virgin Mary (Tanana) or Santo Cristo (Tatata) are responsible for sending the sickness; in these cases it is called 'God's will'. In other cases our Huichol customs (namely the gourd bowl, the arrow and our ancestors) are the agents that cause illness. This depends on the spiritual qualities each person has, and in which god the person trusts. [Sickness depends on which god a person relies upon and which they have offended. After a child is born, its relatives dream to determine which *uxa* a person has, and to which god the child is most closely related. Sometimes two or three gods work in unison to give the child his spiritual sign, *uxa*. The name a child receives must correspond to the *uxa* that child has been given by a particular god or gods.] By means of Tamatsi's wisdom the father of the family comprehends which name is appropriate for the newborn child. The goal is to determine which ancestor, e.g., Tsakaimuta, Haramara, Nia'ariwame, owns the *uxa* of the girl or boy (see Chapter 5).

That is the way it is; it is not haphazard. One must be extremely conscientious when attempting to heal and dream, because these matters involve great Mysteries, and we must not complicate matters. I am speaking the truth with respect to how I heal.

I am not allowed to suck out sicknesses but I know a way of closing the wounds made by the intrusion of spiritual objects. That is something I can do. I can stop the cut from expanding by closing the four cardinal directions and then standing guard in the intersection until the person gets well. [When the singer stands guard in the intersection for five days, he/she dreams to determine if the patient is going to recover. Sometimes it is necessary for both the patient and shaman to fast from salt.]

One can only try to heal each of these illnesses: *natuárika* (malaria), *tapari xiya* [ovarian cancer sent by the maize mother], *yakwai xiya* [a sexually transmitted illness, either gonorrhea or syphilis, common among men], *awa xiya* [another sexually transmitted disease.] Whatever I do to heal, our Elder Brother is ultimately the one who decides the patient's fate.

To a particular patient a shaman would say, for example, "you need to take some offerings to Tukisata (the Huichol temple at Ratontita), or to Tuamuxawita (the sacred site with caves near San Sebastián)." After depositing the offerings at those sacred places you must seat your child among the *tuwainurixi* [children who are fasting during the First Fruits ritual.] The same remedy would apply for my wife or me [for adults or children the remedy is the same.] The shaman gives this advice to whoever is responsible for the patient, declaring that, by following this advice, the patient will be safe, healthy and alert. This is said when the shaman is certain that the patient is recovering, that the healing is effective. The prognosis is mentioned in this manner while gradually telling the patient what offerings he/she must make and what they must do. For example, taking votive gourd bowls and arrows as offerings to sacred sites such as Tuamuxawita or Nia'ariwameta (a sacred cave near Santa Catarina).

(Addressing a hypothetical patient, Jesús states), "Upon returning from these places you must seat your child among the *tuwainurixi* [children who fast during the First Fruits ritual.] This is how one should speak to the person responsible for the patient. The patient must do whatever the shaman orders.

Sicknesses are very common. One may not know where, when or why they arrive. When someone realizes that they are sick they are already malnourished and then that person runs to consult a shaman. The shamans tell that person which sickness he or she has, and these patients are miraculously healed in accordance with our ancient customs and practices. [Today in Tuxpan de Bolaños more young people consult doctors than shamans.]

In itself, the life of a Huichol is based on ancient beliefs and traditions. Changes in our way of life and thinking have caused some negative results. That is why some Huichols have personal shortcomings and doubts about which path to follow. [Some Huichols now have doubts about complying with traditional customs, especially those that require money, such as animal sacrifice. Sometimes they get depressed and feel confused about doing what is expected of them. Then the conflict between traditional Huichol ideals and their actual behavior may provoke psychosomatic illness.]

The first time I tried to heal mestizos (mixed bloods) was in Mexico City. I put myself to the test by seeing if I could heal them or not. I had been healing Huichols for between fifteen to twenty years but never mestizos. I was successful with them and I was not punished (by the gods). Later, when I went to California, I did the same thing, healing American men and women, and I was never punished."

How Jesús Counsels Patients

"You have come to me requesting that I heal you. In light of your remarks I will attempt to heal you." Whenever I try to heal a patient I tell them, "your illness exists for this reason and whatever I tell you to do you must do. You must follow precisely the directions that I am going to give you if you want to get well. You need to tell me that you are going to obey in order for me to be able to heal you. If you are not going to obey we should not bother." That is how I do my healing.

I say, "I am going to heal you but Our Maize Mother is causing your illness. When you perform the ritual of the bean, or for clearing brush to prepare the cornfield for planting, you must follow my instructions. In that manner I will be able to cure your illness. You will receive a pardon and will be healed if you comply when I advise you to sacrifice a ram for Our Maize Mother or for Our Mother Earth (Yurianaka)."

Speaking clearly I say to the patient, "this is the cause of your illness. Your son or your family members have the same illness and it has the same cause. Because of the intervention of our Elder Brother Kauyumari who prayed for you, they (the gods) have granted you health. During the next five days you will gradually improve, provided that you take the offerings to the place I told you to take them (for example, to the sacred caves such as Tuamuxawita and Nia'ariwameta) and from a particular sacred site you must bring back sacred water (Hay+rime). When you sacrifice the ram you must anoint all your relatives with sacred water in order to receive a blessing and good health."

Huichol Shamanism: A Brief Summary

"If someone receives sickness as a punishment from the Kieri I am not authorized to intervene. Nor am I permitted to cause damage with witchcraft, nor to heal victims of witchcraft. The majority of illnesses occur as a result of somebody's transgression.

In the beginning, *uxa* was the pollen of the Kieri that transformed Tamatsi into a living being. If one wishes to obtain this *uxa* one must complete the periods of fasting that are ordered by Tamatsi. If one cannot comply then it is better not to start because acquiring *uxa* is very exacting. One may not heal or sing before completing these periods of fasting, otherwise that person may be killed or go insane.

In the beginning, when Buzzard Person transformed Tamatsi into a living being, he asked the woman who had no children (Tsakaimuta) to follow his instructions in order that the pollen, *uxa*, could be transformed into a living being. I have feathers (a *muwieri*) from Buzzard Person and a covenant with him. I shall not explain more than this because other people won't be doing this type of healing. Our Elder brother, Buzzard Person, managed to resuscitate our Elder Brother, who was in deer form, because Buzzard Person was the original owner of the *uxa*.

I have healed many children, women and men but only I know exactly what I am doing. In my prayers I summon Tatei Werika Wimari (Our Celestial Mother) to perform the healing and Tamatsi who lives at the summit of the divine hill called Huriwari. With the information that I am giving you now I don't know what will happen to me but, as I have told you, I have already fulfilled the obligatory periods of fasting and sacrifice. When the marriage to my wife was consummated I was fifteen or sixteen years old and by then my pact with the Kieri had already been fulfilled. That is why I had no problems."

CHAPTER 3

HONORING ANCESTORS, TEACHING DESCENDANTS

(Jesús González continues dictating his life story:)
"My father was born, they say, in the village of La Mesa (the Table). My grandfather and my grandmother were born in the same village. They lived together for a long time, but later went somewhere else.

My mother was raised in the village of The Little Squash. My mother's father was raised in the village of The Tree Stump; my great-grandparents and grandparents grew up there. They left that village and went to live at the village of the Little Squash. The Mexican Revolution began while they were living there. They fled from the village The Little Squash and went to live at the village of La Mesa (near Tepíc, in the Huichol community of Tuxpan de Bolaños). [Because of the Revolution they fled from these two villages, Tree Stump and Little Squash, located within the indigenous community of San Sebastián.] From La Mesa they fled to a place called Las Guayabas and then to the place of *pedernales* (flints). It was there my mother became separated from us.

Because food was so scarce, they went back to La Mesa. They were able to return to La Mesa to continue planting their cornfields. I was born soon thereafter at the place called La Labor (in the cornfield), where I grew up.

My mother explained to me that I was born at the village La Labor (labor in the cornfield) two kilometers from La Mesa (the village of the Table), where I grew up. I was born while my family was fishing. My mother was just about to fall into a pool in the river (she was looking for a place to give birth).

When I was seven years old and living at La Mesa, I remembered my birth. At Iparita [A village named after the trap used to catch mice or rats, which Huichols once ate.] I remembered the details of my birth. In those days my father accepted the cargo of policeman-messenger (*topilli*) at Tuxpan. Because he was a *topilli*, we were obliged to stay in Tuxpan de Bolaños during ceremonies.

My father and mother were poor. In those days there were many bandits and that is why we moved from La Mesa to another village. I remember vividly that the parents of my father decided to abandon that village. We moved in the direction of Bolaños, settling near Coco Asco ('nauseating coconut') and La Cienaga ('the swamp'). We fled from the violence of the Revolution. In those days it was difficult to obtain food and clothing. Many more people arrived there; all refugees of the Revolution. Some time passed and we had to go back to another village called Iparita. I remember that we went there to live, and that my brothers and sisters were born there. Iparita was my home at a time when food was scarce and we had to struggle just to survive.

I am grateful to my parents for the tremendous efforts they made so we could survive in spite of all the obstacles. We had to eat wild plants and because we had no clothes we looked like orphans, my siblings and I grew up having to endure many hardships. Nowadays I have my own children and for me it was also quite difficult to provide for their needs as they were growing up. I could not give them everything necessary but I did everything in my power to raise them well. My parents were so poor that they did not leave me anything [e.g., cattle or sheep] to sustain me in life. In those impoverished conditions I had my children who are now adults. My sons have experienced life and they also have children, who are my grandchildren and great-grandchildren.

Today what remains for me is to speak about how I suffered and managed to persevere through many misfortunes such that today everyone sees me still living. That is why I am thankful to all my ancestors. For all that I have, I repeat my thanks to them because I believe they have safeguarded my life and health and that of my family. I believe that they are the only ones that can give us life, experience and wisdom. They are the only ones who know if what we do is right or wrong and they determine whether we deserve good health, prosperity, and the blessings we have been enjoying until now.

I spent my childhood at Iparita where I participated in clearing brush from the cornfields in preparation for planting. In those days, that was the only work there was. We left Iparita when I was a young man and fled from the Cristero leader, Juan Bautista, to the village of El Banco in the mountains east of Tuxpan. While we were living there they killed Juan Bautista in the community of San Sebastián where he grew up. From El Banco we left for the village of White Earth where I hunted. I killed deer for the ritual of the Parched Corn and other rituals. According to my father, as time passed he complied with all the traditional customs required to obtain a wife for me, he went to her parents to get their permission for marriage from my wife's father, Senon Romero. We became husband and wife when I was thirteen or fourteen years old.

We moved around a lot until we came back to the village of Stout Pine whose name today is Barranquilla (Little Canyon). That is where we had our first child. It is well known that in that phase of life one has many things to do. Above all else I was dedicated to deer hunting and to clearing brush from the cornfields. This was to insure the welfare of my first son (who was murdered, see Chapter 7). There I learned to be a husband and father, abiding by our traditional rules.

In the days of my youth, people thought about things differently. My parents decided to arrange a marriage for me. According to them I was able to work and provide for a wife, so they decided to marry us. That is how we came to have the children we have today. We are still together, completing the days of life that are allotted to us. I am still alive as is my wife. As I told you previously, my family has increased tremendously. We have numerous descendants. Well I don't know how and when I will leave them (die) but because of my numerous descendants I earn (or gain) life. [The gods give life to his descendants and by caring for them he receives long life as a consequence.] Only God knows what will happen to me. All my descendants still see me.

During the Cristero rebellion some of my relatives were killed. They killed my paternal grandfather and also my mother's father. My mother survived, though she almost died, but finally managed to save herself. That is why we are alive, my siblings and I. The Cristeros killed the parents of my mother and my father's father was hung. There was no peace during that era; any kind of tragedy was possible. Today it is different, more tranquil and peaceful, but during that time life was difficult. Only those of us that managed to survive know how horrible those times were (circa 1927-1938).

Being a child I could do nothing about it. All I could do was to collect dry branches (for firewood). I grew up obediently and devoted my energy to making arrows. As I got older I was able to use a machete and an axe. Later I could clear brush to prepare the cornfield for planting and run just like a man. At that point I became involved in hunting deer with other deer hunters who invited me to hunt with them. By then we had maize and food to eat, I was working, and life had improved somewhat. But that was still an era of great poverty, quite unlike life today. We grew up like orphans, not with no parents, but without enough food.

Eventually we returned to La Mesa (the Table) where my grandfather was living. There we renovated the god houses (*xirikite*) and built a village fit for performing our rituals. My father and mother told my siblings and I, "now you have returned to your home. This is the place we shall bequeath to our family. You were born here and this is your home. This village is ancient—the first established in this region. Your grandfathers and great-grandfathers have lived here and were from here. This is why this village is indispensable for all of you." Thus today we continue living at this place, conducting our ceremonies to comply with our traditions.

I have had many children who are still living and I proclaim the same thing to my numerous descendants that my father told me: "Be sure you never forget our way of life. Be sure you do not abandon or disobey our traditions."

Today I tell all my relatives that I won't live with them forever.

I tell them that, when the day of my death comes, that they should remember everything I advised them to do. Whether or not they do everything I advised, I have fulfilled my responsibility by telling you all this. I am a mortal man. I am not eternal.

While I am alive all of you will live for the benefit of your children. You need not worry about whether or not I have struggled for your benefit. I am the only one who really knows what I am doing on behalf of all of you. Whether it is based on reality or illusion, until today everything has turned out well. On the day of my death you will suffer some negative effect. At that time you will comprehend what it was that I did. Today we are living together. I see all of you and you see me and your grandmother Maria Micaela (my second wife) is alive and so is your other grandmother Maria Jesucita Romero (my first wife). The grandchildren are living and I, their grandfather, am alive. We are all living in harmony.

I will eventually go to the spirit world. My *takwatsi* shall remain among all of you and speak to you about various subjects. [They will remember him via his *takwatsi.*]

Whether or not these statements are prohibited I make them to respond to the questions. I give my reply because it is said that as time passes my descendants, those who shall never see me, those who come after I die, will hear my voice and my words, and so I am encouraged to make this known.

In the end, nobody can steal what I know, and what I have in my heart. The day they lay me in the grave everything will go with me. Only my words will linger in the wind. What I reveal now comes from my heart. Henceforth you all will decide what to do about it.

At present I am giving thanks to my gods in whom I believe. That is why I utter these words. I hope I will not receive any punishment or illness because of anything I disclose. I am asking for mercy from the Sun Father and from Mother Earth, where I play and place my feet. I ask for mercy from all my spiritual fathers and spiritual mothers."

Entering the Mexican's World

"Some time passed and they transported me to Bolaños, to attend a boarding school. When I was seven years old I entered the school. [This was a boarding school exclusively for Huichols.] I never fought with the mestizos. I ate beans and tortillas. My teachers punished me by hitting me with a belt because I was unable to understand their language and for being disobedient. Most of my other classmates have died. My first wife, Maria Jesucita, also attended that school in Bolaños. She was about five years old then, and there were other Huichol girls there too. They gave us five cents, two cents, or one cent to spend. The oldest children were getting ten cents and the youngest children two or three cents; that was enough in those days. Every Sunday they gave us mangos, *guayabas*, sugar cane and bananas.

We suffered there, but I learned to speak some Spanish. My parents never paid anything for my education. That school, exclusively for Huichols, was opened in 1935 by President Lázaro Cárdenas. There I learned to sign my name and to comprehend Spanish. [Jesús probably left the school because he felt homesick. Sometimes Huichol students ran away from that school but were often taken back.]

During a whole year there we didn't master Spanish. We took one year just to be able to respond to the mestizo teacher. When my confinement there began I was afraid of the mestizos. Eventually a close relationship developed between my mestizo teacher and I. That is how I learned to speak Spanish.

You are already familiar with how mestizos behave; they were treating us badly. I returned to my home from the boarding school. I never learned enough but I tried to do well before I quit studying forever and I became devoted to household tasks. It was impossible to continue studying at that time because we were still unacculturated Huichols. That is the way it was then.

If I didn't learn enough I hold myself responsible. I don't blame anybody else because in those days Huichols were ignorant [Non-acculturated due to the lack of money and schools.] Nowadays schools are set up here in Tuxpan. That is how education was established in the beginning. Today my grandchildren attend classes in their own community; now they know how to read and write. They are not the way I was. They know better than I did how to profit from schools. Even now I struggle whenever I receive a letter. I have to search all over with the letter in my hand to find someone to read it to me. It is as if I never had received an education. Today my grandchildren know and comprehend what is taught to them.

They also have plenty of fruit and vegetables, something that we never ate before. I hope that everyone who studies, whether they are in my family or not, will never do what I did. I hope they learn to respect and love one another, treating others as their fellow brothers and sisters and respecting their teachers, their government and their people. Nowadays I live humbly. As I mentioned when a letter arrives I must turn to my grandchildren for help in reading it, due to the amount of Spanish that I learned."

Serving Our Ancestors and People

"Although I don't know much Spanish I still help my people. This is how I reply in the mestizo language. When we are asked to participate in public meetings as experts and counselors, to explain how things were in the beginning, when Tuxpan was established, I help in this way with the issues in my community. I was a temple officer five times [each term lasts for five years], I was assistant governor four times, I was judge three times, I was a *mayordomo* twice (custodian of a Catholic saint), I was the *comisario* (commissioner) many times, and I was a *topilli* four times. I was a temple officer five times and now I serve the governor as an elder counselor.

The first *cargo* I held was *mayordomo* of San José, and then I was the *topilli* of the sheriff, then the *topilli* for the judge. I was a *topilli* in Tuxpan four times. I was a *mayordomo* twice. I was the governor's assistant four times. I was the judge three times. I was the gourd bowl holder for Yurianaka twice. I served Tatei

Xapawiyeme once and Tatei Yurianaka for the fourth time. I was a gourd bowl holder four times (that is, for twenty years total as a temple officer) and in that way I helped my people in Tuxpan. I never went to Wirikuta (to collect peyote).

When I was judge I had to advise people but I did not try any case involving theft of cattle. When somebody presented a complaint we had to order that the offenders be brought to Tuxpan de Bolaños. After that the judge gets involved in the case, unless it is a serious crime. In that case one must ask for help from the *ministerio publico* [Mexican authorities must punish such offenders.]

The Huichol *topilli* does not receive a salary he eats only whatever his supervisor provides for him. The *topilli* is obliged to cut firewood and bring flowers to elderly people. He must also serve the Huichol political officials and be prepared to arrest and deliver delinquents to them. People who commit serious crimes must be put into the wooden stocks (*cepo*) for punishment. The *topilli* does not earn anything. [the *mayordomo* is responsible for collecting offerings, including money, for the Catholic saints.] No *topilli* or *mayordomo* has a 'staff to command' (*vara de manda*) except the *topilli* of San José.

Every gourd bowl keeper must comply with the orders of the singer in charge of each ritual. The singer may tell a gourd bowl keeper that they must kill a ram, a deer, or a *becerro* (a yearling calf), but it must all be done in harmony with the other gourd bowl keepers.

If I am serving Our Mother Nia'ariwame, I must go personally to deliver her offering to her cave. If I am serving Our Mother Xapawiyeme I must go to her home to deliver her offering. I went three times to Villa Corona to deliver her offerings and to bring back sacred water (from Lake Chapala, where Xapawiyeme lives) and also to the Hill of the Goat (that is also the home of Xapawiyeme). The gourd bowl keeper must also make corn beer for all the rituals each year. The gourd bowl keeper's work is difficult; one that does not work is put into the stocks. He is scolded for failing to perform his duties. [He may be publicly scolded by the elders for not performing well. Anybody who is put into the stocks will be scolded publicly.] Those who communicate well and fulfill the duties of their *cargo* as a gourd bowl keeper have no problems.

I live today among my people because I have served in this way. When we are convened as original *comuneros* (communal land holders) this is what I always announce to people: that in the future when I die I can say that I have helped my people. Nowadays I advise my children and grandchildren to be attentive to the communal property that belongs to our people. When they are needed to occupy some position they should accept it just as I always did. In that manner people will have appreciation for them. That is what I will always tell them because I am living here in Tuxpan, even though I have my village (rancho) over there at El Abandono, where we celebrate the ceremonies of the Parched Corn, the First Fruits and the clearing of the cornfield. I do those ceremonies at El Abandono. Everything that I do is done to serve as an example for those who participate with me in those rituals. Who knows whether or not they will do what I advise them. But as long as I am alive that is what I am going to do."

Deer and Maize Sustain Us

"I was taught to hunt deer by expert hunters. Of course we all understood that we have always performed our rituals with the expectation that they will bring us abundance. With that in mind, I started to participate in rituals and gradually became friendly with the hunters. I eventually learned the secrets connected with using the *winiyeri* (traps for strangling deer). The way they were doing the hunting ritual was to assemble all the various colors of maize, the votive gourd bowls, and the votive arrows before they began chasing the deer. They were accomplishing all this by carrying these offerings into the mountains, to the place where they would be hunting deer. At that particular place they had to erect an altar on which to display the maize. They then took the deer traps and placed each of them at a specific place along the trails used by deer. The hunters stayed at their camp for five to ten days. That is how we killed deer, sometimes two or three. Following a successful hunt, we were able to celebrate the ritual. This is how I gained my knowledge from the expert hunters.

After we finished hunting we had to collect the deer traps and fold them up. The deer traps that proved most effective were marked with blue, green or red yarn or ribbons in order to identify them. [Out of about fifty deer traps only some caught deer, so those traps were identified with yarn ribbons.] The altar on which maize was set was made of wood. There were three or four ears of maize put on the altar. This was sacred seed corn, which had been blessed and given offerings in rituals throughout the year. Certain hills were considered mothers of deer and offerings of votive arrows and gourd bowls were left at those hills, for those mothers of deer. This consecrated corn along with the other offerings, were placed on the altar to help persuade the Maize Mother (or the Corn Spirit) to obtain the deer that were so highly valued. (The Spirit of Maize wants deer more than Huichols do.) Then we went home with all our things and the deer, and, once home again, we celebrated the ritual with the song of *makwixa*. [*Makwixa* occurs after the deer hunt ends. The singer performs this ritual so that all the hunting restrictions (no sex, bathing or salt) are lifted. Thus the deer hunters can resume normal family life again. This is similar to what happens when peyote hunters return to their homes after peyote hunt ritual prohibitions are lifted.] Later each hunter returned to his village to celebrate his own ritual, unless it was communal (as is a Huichol temple ritual) in which case we would perform the ritual together.

Today's hunting rituals differ from what we did in those days, and those rituals had been performed for who knows how long. But even today, in certain villages, we still continue hunting in essentially the traditional way. The old methods of deer hunting have been disappearing due to the use of modern firearms. Nevertheless, we still believe that we are blessed because we continue to comply with our customs. This is why we still follow our traditions, and why we still survive today. Our ancestors followed the same traditions, and perhaps when we die we will retain the same faith (as our ancestors).

Some of us celebrate the rituals of *esquite* (parched corn) of *atole* (maize beverage) of the drum (Tatei Neixa) and others perform the peyote ritual, but the deer is required for all of these. Today we still perform these rituals as we always have in order to receive abundant life and health. As we have always done, we perform rituals under the scrutiny of the Sun, the earth, the fire, the dry season and the rainy season. We ask for approval from all our Ancestor Gods, invoking their presence to carry out everything in conformity with our customs. Tamatsi and Tatutsi (Our Great Grandfather) disclosed the right way to conduct our rituals by showing us the only path (*waiyeyeri*) we must travel. Our maize, just like us, receives the same vital energy from all our ancestors. Thus all of us must be united in following in the footprints (*waiyeyeri*) Our Ancestors left in order to indicate where we must go and what we must do to be blessed by them.

Maize is like our children because from the maize we live and receive life. [Maize must be raised and treated as a child by women.] We also interpret our dreams in order to give names to each of our children; names derived from the moment that corn is born, as a seed, until new ears of corn are harvested. For this reason women have been given the honorific title of *kwewimate* [Women that guard the sacred seed corn in their arms and *nui'akate* (protectors) and *takwaima* (the women who clean the patio in front of the temple or god houses.)] Our women received these names because they are our mothers, the ones that always pray for us. So to them I give thanks and hope our ancestors grant them a praiseworthy life. [The names for Huichol children come by means of the spirit of the corn. Most of these names are revealed in dreams. Our women give us so many things like food and water that sustain life.]

For our Sun Father, our Grandfather Fire and our Mother

Nia'ariwame the deer is their *muwieri* (offering, sacred symbol that summons them). That is why we must kill the deer, whenever they ask us to do it. We also make offerings; the votive arrow and gourd bowl, to take to whichever sacred places correspond to the beliefs of each family. From these sacred sites we must bring back water, water that is sacred to us, that is used in rituals to sprinkle on our votive gourd bowls, arrows, maize and other sacred items. During our ceremonies one must mention all the gods in the four cardinal directions to gather them all together. We must also be sure our celestial Mother, Tatei Werika Wimari, is present. We must be sure she is watching our ceremonies."

CHAPTER 4

The Deer Shaman, Tamatsi, Transforms Society

The narrative presented below was dictated in Huichol by Jesús González Mercado and translated by Vicente González in Tuxpan in October 2001. It is typically recited during the Peyote Dance in May or early June, but González wanted me to tape record it for his descendants and for my benefit. He informed me that this was part of his endeavor to aid me in becoming a shaman, something I dreamed of achieving even before I first met him and other Huichol in 1976 (Fikes 2011). Working diligently with his son, Vicente González, we translated his chronicle of the first shaman into Spanish. I alone assume responsibility for translating it into English. After many years of studying Huichol myths, and after my wife and I completed five pilgrimages supervised by Jesús González to sacred sites in and near the Pacific Ocean, I finally feel confident enough to interpret and share his narrative of the first shaman. His words at the end of this saga have special meaning for me, his protégé: "my interpretation is not something that I invented by myself. It is simply what I learned from my parents and grandparents. I finally came to understand that what they had been telling me is true."

Although many themes discernible in this narrative describing Tamatsi's transformations from a pollinated Kieri flower, to a boy, to a deer and, ultimately, to the first shaman deserve comment, the theme of compassion takes precedence over all of them. It is both the character trait essential to enable Tamatsi to reform society (as he becomes the first shaman) and a cardinal rule of conduct for Huichol shamans. Compassion is the crucial catalyst that makes possible Tamatsi's birth, his rescue from the Animal People intent on sacrificing him, and Buzzard Person's regeneration of him after he is killed by one of those Animal People. Actions inspired by compassion are indispensable to enable Tamatsi to fulfill his destiny of reforming society by becoming the first fully human shaman. The first demonstration of compassion occurs after his human mother admits feeling, "pitiful and dependent because I have nobody to help me" (see paragraph 1 in myth). Buzzard Person (the elder who is an Ancestor Deity) comes to her aid, first by asking her why she is sad and lonely (paragraph #3 below). Her confession, that she wanted children, prompted Buzzard's first compassionate act; i.e., guiding her to a bunch of Kieri flowers (#4, 8, 9). She selects the blue Kieri flower and then, in order to fulfill her wish for a child, complies with all of Buzzard's instructions, thereby creating her divine son (#9-11). She and her husband's collaboration in creating Tamatsi illustrate the asymmetrical partnership forever connecting Huichol with their Ancestor Deities (Fikes 2011).

The Animal People, led by Kam+kime, (the principal singer prior to Tamatsi)[1] wanted to obtain great benefits by sacrificing the deer, Tamatsi. Because Kam+kime's goal is antithetical to Tamatsi's mission to reform society, a conflict erupts (#32-35). With Tamatsi as their captive, the Animal People and Kam+kime prepare to sacrifice him, expecting to gain "more abundant life" (#32). Their plan is foiled when a clever and compassionate mouse (Tuamurutsi) intervenes just in time to rescue Tamatsi, thereby preventing Kam+kime from executing the future deer-shaman (#33-37). The mouse becomes Tamatsi's ally by gaining control over his belongings and telling him, "we can carry out" our plan (#33-34). Our kindhearted mouse frees Tamatsi by deceiving his captors, and also gives Tamatsi power over those Animal People: power symbolized by stealing Kam+kime's *takwatsi* (medicine basket) (#37). This mouse shows sympathy for Tamatsi and a commitment to aid him in carrying out his plan.

After Tamatsi escapes from the Animal People's temple, they keep trying to kill him. One of them, Horned Toad Person, shoots him with an arrow (#41) but Tamatsi "dropped dead" in a place where they did not find him (#43). After Buzzard sees the dead deer his initial urges are selfish (flying away or eating Tamatsi's eyes) (#44-45). His adviser, Tatei Werika Wimari, Our Mother, exemplifies compassion and wisdom. Thus she intervenes to dissuade Buzzard from eating the divine being he had helped to create (#45-47). Her encouragement induces Buzzard to obey her orders. Then "he began feeling compassionate," empowered to restore the uxa (spiritual nucleus) to Tamatsi, thereby bringing him back to life (#50). Our third act of compassion is thus the "miracle" Buzzard performed in resuscitating Tamatsi (#51). Tamatsi was then able to fulfill his life's purpose, becoming the first male deer as well as the first fully human shaman.

Once Tamatsi became a shaman (singer) he established god-houses (*xirikite*) and led rituals (sang) such as the Peyote Dance (#55). Demonstrating compassion, or at least forbearance toward his former captors and would-be murderers, Tamatsi allowed them to participate in that Peyote Dance (#56). As we shall see (in Chapter 5, note 4) although the Animal People lost power to Tamatsi, their chiefs were incorporated as subordinates, guardians of Tamatsi, in the improved world Tamatsi helped create.

Tamatsi Transforms Society (recited by Jesús González)

1. A woman was living and thinking to herself: "I am alone. I am pitiful and dependent because I have nobody to help me." She was living on top of a rocky hill and thinking such thoughts every day. That woman was never aware that somebody was passing by her and watching her everyday. She had no idea that the unidentified observer was divining her thoughts and sorrows.

2. Suddenly she heard a noise, the rhythm of a musical bow (stringed instrument). Without turning in any direction, she asked

herself who could be coming, because she was certain there was nobody else nearby. When she concentrated her gaze on the place (from where) she was hearing the music, she saw an old man. That elder was coming toward her while playing on the bowstring of his bow with an arrow.

3. When the elder reached her he asked her: "What are you doing here so sad and so alone? Aren't you afraid of falling off this cliff?" The elder was laughing loudly because he knew something about the woman that she did not know he knew. The woman answered the elder: "I am always here, looking at the other side (of the gorge), where it is so beautiful." The elder said: "Today I stopped by here on my way to those peaks over there. I want to know why you are so sad and so lonely." The woman replied (with a lie): "I am not sad nor am I worried. There is only one thing missing. I have no children. We (she and her husband) live by ourselves."

4. To that the elder responded: "Is that all you were thinking about? Is that the truth? If those are truly your thoughts and that is what you want, that can be arranged. I am going to do it." The woman questioned him: "Is it certain that you can make that happen? Are you telling the truth?" The elder declared: "I told you I can. Do you see that patch of rocky ground over there? There are children over there. If you truly want children, then tomorrow we will meet again right here. The only thing you need to do is to make a *takwatsi*, (shaman's prayer basket), today, right away. Bring that basket with you and we will meet here again tomorrow." The woman responded to the elder, "If that is all that is required I will gladly make it."

5. Then the elder left, playing his musical bow. At that moment the woman realized who the elder was. He was Wir+k+ Tewiyari (Buzzard Person). Remembering that insight about his identity, the woman returned to her home.

6. After arriving at her house she spoke to her husband: "Listen

to this. I met an elder who was somewhat peculiar. He told me he can solve our problem. He can help us have children. All I have to do is to make a *takwatsi*, that he ordered me to make." Her husband replied: "That is great. If that is what he told you must be done, then do it." So the woman began making the *takwatsi*, thinking to herself: "if what he told me is true, then I must make this *takwatsi*." For that woman everything was easy to accomplish. She quickly finished making the *takwatsi*.

7. Night ended and she woke up. She carried the basket and walked back to the place where she was to meet the elder. When she arrived there, she heard the rhythm of the musical bow. As soon as she heard that music she knew the elder was coming. She wrapped the *takwatsi* up in her bandana and placed it in front of herself.

8. The elder appeared and greeted her. "So, you are here already." The woman answered: "Yes, here I am, just as we had agreed yesterday. I have done it all and here is the *takwatsi* that I brought." The elder replied: "Well, that is good. Let's get going." They began traveling until they came to the patch of rocky ground.

9. When they arrived at a huge round rock the elder declared: "This is the place. Do you see the child that is here? This is where the child is." He showed the woman some pollen. Underneath that pollen there were various flowers. The elder asked: "Which flower are you going to choose?" The woman replied "This one." She selected a blue flower and placed it inside the *takwatsi*. "You were thinking that you wanted a child. Well, now that is all arranged. There is one more thing. Be sure you and your spouse do not disregard my instructions. You must do everything I tell you to do. You must carry out all my commands."

10. The woman was committed to complying with whatever the elder ordered. She picked up the *takwatsi* and started to leave. The elder told her: "In the near future you and your husband will have what you wanted (a son)."

11. Arriving at her house, the woman put the *takwatsi* on the altar (*niwetari*) of the god-house (*xiriki*). Her husband lit candles inside the god-house for five consecutive days. On the fifth day the boy appeared there, seated on the altar of the god-house. On the fifth day, as they entered the god-house to make their offerings, they saw the boy seated there. When they saw him, they gave him chocolate. He did not eat any of it.

12. During the next five days the boy began crawling on all fours. The fifteenth day passed. By the twenty-fifth day he was walking. Anything was possible for that boy. On that day the boy began speaking with his father. "I want you to make me a bow and some arrows. I want to go somewhere and shoot." As soon as the boy asked him, his father complied, making everything the boy asked him to make: the bow and some arrows, a *yakwai* (small gourd for carrying sacred tobacco used during the peyote hunt) and a *matsua* (wrist guard for archers).

13. The boy continued to grow. He was never home anymore (except to eat and sleep). Everyday he was shooting his arrows and returning again to his god-house. The only thing the boy liked eating was dark-blue corn mush. His passion was shooting birds. He was returning to his god-house (to sleep). He was focused on shooting birds.

14. He became an adolescent. He was hardly ever at home with his parents. He continued shooting arrows. As he continued shooting, he began imagining someone, while asking himself "How will I be able to do it (have sex)?" He was preoccupied with that subject during his travels. He reached a mountaintop and looked down. There were some foothills and plateaus covered with good pasturage. There were some tall mountains and small hills. On the slope above a plain with pasturage, he observed some girls (female deer). The youth asked himself: "What will I have to do to get there where the girls are? I will shoot an arrow at them."

15. So he shot an arrow at them. They were surprised. They

asked each other: "What could that be? Who could it be that shot this arrow at us?" When they looked up in the direction from where the arrow had come they saw the youth. They told him, "Come here to us." Then they took his arrow and hid it from him. The youth reacted: "Don't hide my arrow." Once he reached those girls, he insisted that they give him back his arrow. "Please don't do this to me. I need you to return my arrow." They never turned over his arrow to him.

16. They tricked him, claiming that they would give him his arrow back if he would accompany them. They also told him: "You must have sex with us. After that we will return your arrow." The youth refused: "I will not do that. That is not what I am seeking, nor what I want."[2] They declared, "If you will not do what we asked of you, then you must come with us."

17. They offered him different plants to eat, including *hariuki*, *taruxixa* and *tsakuxa*. The youth did not consider any of those plants edible. "These are not my foods. I have never eaten such things."

18. As he came to the top of the mountain with the girls he announced: "I better not continue. I will see you tomorrow." He returned to his house troubled, sad and pensive. Despite all that, he never discussed his feelings with his parents. He entered the god-house because, inside it, there was always dark-blue corn mush, chocolate and water. Those were the foods he drank.

19. Night ended. The next morning he returned to the place where he had found the girls (female deer). They told him: "Well, let's go because our father is waiting for you." They took him down to the lowlands (*Watet+apa*, the primordial underworld). At the bottom, where the trail ended, they found a man who was seated. He was obviously the father of the girls.

20. The youth completed a ceremonial circle (by walking clockwise around the fire in the center of the aboriginal Huichol temple, *tuki*). Then they seated him on the chief singer's chair

(*uweni*). At that moment the girls announced: "At last we have brought you the person that you wanted to see." The youth did not stay seated. He was standing when their father proclaimed: "Because of all these events that have transpired (his meeting with the girls and his being brought to the temple), we want everything to occur in compliance with our wishes. It is time for us to put you to the test." So they tested him.

21. For him nothing was impossible. He sat down again on the singer's chair. Then the mother of the girls (female deer) fastened a prayer-feather (*muwieri*) to him. "Let's see you stand up and hop around the four cardinal directions." That is what he did. He passed their test. Rabbit Person (Tatsiu Tewiyari) was there. He was the elder brother of the youth. That rabbit had some antlers that they fastened to the youth because the rabbit was unable to walk or hop with those antlers. The father of the girls took the antlers from the rabbit and gave them to the youth. For him the antlers were a perfect fit. When the youth tried to enter the god-house, his antlers would not fit. When the antlers got stuck in the doorway they told him it did not matter. "Now try them out for yourself."

22. As the youth was leaving, he affirmed: "Well, because you advised me to try the antlers on, I will." He followed the route back to the mountaintops from where he had descended. He ascended to the precipice called Pariya Tek+a (God-house Viewpoint). From there he arrived at his house, where he found his mother weaving. He lay down (having been transformed into a deer) in front of his mother's loom. She was surprised. "What do you want, why are you scaring me?" She hit him on the nose with her *uparu* (brazil-wood baton used in weaving).

23. After being hit on his nose he went inside the god-house, as he always did, to drink dark-blue corn mush. Inside the god-house, he put his snout inside the dark-blue corn mush. That is why we see the dark circle on the deer's snout today. According to our tradition, this set a precedent. In this manner we explain the

events that are essential in creating Tamatsi (Our Elder Brother). This is our record of creation. It becomes very tangible and clear to anyone who commits to becoming a shaman. Anyone whose life is dedicated to practicing according to this history of Tamatsi will understand all this.

24. When the youth drank the dark blue corn mush he departed from that god-house and declared: "What happened to me is amazing. You were saying that you wanted to have children. Who knows why they did this to me" (turned him into a deer)?

25. Pondering that (transformation), he left his parents. Arriving at some plains he proclaimed, "Now is the time." He jumped around the four cardinal directions and into their intersection. When he stood up he had taken the form of a deer. He took a few leaps and then shook off the dust. He looked around in every direction. He looked around everywhere. When the gods witnessed what he had done they told him: "Everything that has been said and given to you has produced a positive result. You look magnificent with those antlers."

26. He went back to visit the inhabitants of the lower part of the world (that connotes *Watet+apa*, the underworld). He completed a ceremonial circle (around the fire in their *tuki*). He was approved as a deer. That is how it happened in the beginning. Our Elder Brother gained their confidence and was allowed to compete with them.

27. He returned to his house, after taking the form of a person. He took his bow, his arrows and his tobacco gourd (*yakwai*). After getting back home, his mother questioned him: "Listen to me, son, you say you are searching for animals in the mountains, well one of them was just here." Her son replied: "Something looking like an animal came here but you didn't recognize who it was. You were unable to comprehend that I was that deer. I was that animal who came here." His mother stated: "I can not believe it." "Well, whether or not you believe me, I was that deer. In order for you to believe me, take a look at me now."

28. His mother responded, "You must know that what we wanted was for you to live here with us. We never expected that you would dedicate your life to being away from us, to always being somewhere out in the country." The youth answered, "So that we have no more misunderstandings I am going to tell you that I will not be with you anymore. This is because I came here with one objective. I have my goals, my life and my thoughts to pursue." That is what he told them. "Well, I must leave now so that I can finish doing what remains to be done. You should watch carefully to see what it is that I am going to do."

29. Those girls (female deer) that he had originally found had remained in contact with him everyday. Acting with full knowledge of the changes he was undergoing, he and those girls were becoming accustomed to each other. Those girls began playing with him, although that made him worry that they wanted to have sex with him. They used a trick to lure him back to the same place (the *tuki* of the Animal People). When they reached their destination there were numerous singers and healers whose forms were both human and animal. Because of what transpired there, things turned out to be the way they are today.

30. When they took him inside their *tuki* their chief singer (Kam+kime), announced: "Everything will occur exactly the way we thought it would. Your younger sisters (the two girls) have brought you to our *tuki*. This was done to fulfill my dream, which revealed to me that you are the chosen one. That is why my supporters won't allow you to leave the *tuki*, because we worked diligently to bring you here. Offering you will bring us great benefits." According to our history this is what occurred in the beginning.

31. To finish doing everything their plan required, many more Animal People had gathered there. Among them were: Yakwai Tewiyari (a small bird that lives among rocks and is sacrificed at Easter Week), Haiku Tewiyari (Cloud Snake Person), Wiexu

Tewiyari (Boa Snake Person), Haitarame (Coral Snake), Tatei Ipau (Boa [or another huge snake]), Xaye (Rattlesnake), Teka (Horned Toad) and Tupina (Hummingbird). They all had human forms, but they were also animals. That was their *tuki*. "Now that all these events have occurred, let us conclude by doing what comes next." With that said, they united to complete their ceremony.

32. Their lead singer (Kam+kime), sat down to begin. While this was happening inside their tuki the youth was held as a prisoner by his younger sisters. They warned one another. "Do not let him get loose. Hold him tightly so he does not escape from you." In the meantime, the singer was singing: "Now we will truly receive more abundant life, our wishes will be fulfilled, our votive arrows, votive gourd bowls and maize will be strengthened by offering this deer blood." Their lead singer continued singing. "It has all been completed. Now the deer will die. Everybody in our family, all our votive arrows, votive gourd bowls, and maize will be blessed with life." While he was singing, Kam+kime questioned those who were holding Tamatsi in custody. "Are you holding him tightly? Be sure he does not escape. In a few more minutes we will make him our offering in order that all of us will, as I stated, be granted more abundant life."

33. While he was announcing all this, a tiny mouse called Tuamurutsi was hiding inside their *tuki*. He exclaimed: "Be very careful." Then Tamatsi's captors began seizing his personal belongings: his tobacco gourd, bow, arrows, and wristguard. They placed all his personal items in the highest part of the altar in their *tuki*. Then the little mouse asserted: "I will be responsible for all these items." This is how Tamatsi's escape was achieved.

34. The mouse secretly brought Tamatsi all his possessions: his sandals, his bow and arrows, his tobacco gourd, and his wristguard. The mouse told Tamatsi, "Now that this is done we can carry out the next part of our plan. We will soon see if they are able to accomplish what they are plotting."

35. In the meantime, the singer was chanting emotionally, "The time has come to complete our offering. The deer must die (as our sacrificial offering)." At the same time, the mouse continued doing his work. For him anything was possible. He arranged for Tamatsi's captors to grab hold of each other, in order to make them think they still had him under their control. Then the mouse climbed up to the altar of the temple, all the way to the top. Up there a branch with *tempisque* leaves was fastened. He cut it and the branch fell into the fire. Ashes and sparks were dispersed in all directions. The fire was extinguished and it got dark. Taking advantage of the darkness, the mouse grabbed the *takwatsi* and all the prayer feathers used by the singer, Kam+kime. Carrying all those sacred things, he exited from the temple. The mouse fled.

36. The Animal People inside the *tuki* complained to each other: "What happened? Who did it? Do you all still have him under control?" The girls replied, "Yes, we are holding him firmly." The singer was satisfied.

37. Just then Tamatsi escaped. He traveled until he arrived at the base of the valley. By then Tamatsi was carrying the *takwatsi* and all the prayer feathers and the *nierika* (sacred mirror) the mouse had taken away from the singer. Tamatsi succeeded in retrieving everything he needed. In this manner he removed that lead singer's power.

38. As soon as they discovered that Tamatsi was missing they declared, "We must follow his tracks." They interrogated those who had held Tamatsi in custody: "Do not profess that you have him under your control when all of you are holding on to one another. Where is he? What did you do with him? Did you release him or what?" "No, we were holding him securely." "If that were true then why are you holding on tightly to each other?" Finally they admitted that the youth had disappeared.

39. They agreed amongst themselves about what they would do next. There was a Fly Person (Xayú Tewiyari) who possessed a

superb sense of smell. All the singer's assistants agreed to appoint him. They told that fly, "You are not like us. You have been blessed with a highly discriminating sense of smell. You shall be our scout to pursue the youth that escaped." They departed with that fly, following Tamatsi's tracks. "We can not allow him to escape. We must make no mistakes. Let's go."

40. The direction they took after departing was uphill. In the meantime the fly had quickly flown uphill. They heard his buzzing as he zoomed up. It took great effort for the other pursuers of Tamatsi to follow his tracks. The one who struggled most was a large ant. As they were ascending they advised each other, "The instant Tamatsi appears, do not be deceived. Do not fail. Our arrow must penetrate him." The finest of their archers was reported to be Yakwai Tewiyari (Bird Person). But his skill was diminished. Because he was falling he was unable to aim well. Among those archers there was also Horned Toad Person (Teka Tewiyari). He was also falling. They were all falling and dragging themselves.

41. They finally managed to reach the base of the valley where Tamatsi was. Just then, Tamatsi suddenly took off running with tremendous leaps. He escaped past them. Then they all shot their arrows. Tamatsi ran as if nothing had happened. Among those archers Horned Toad Person was the one whose arrow struck Tamatsi. Horned Toad Person sensed his arrow had struck Tamatsi. Yet when they arrived at the second slope, at the place where they had seen Tamatsi struggling to ascend, they found no trace of him. There was only a buzzard perched in a tree. That is all they found.

42. They began scolding that buzzard: "You have hidden the one we were chasing. That is our sacrificial offering." After declaring that, they threw rocks at the buzzard, causing him to fly. They repeated their accusation to the buzzard. Again they threw rocks at him. The buzzard would not put up with that. He flew away. Flying high above and far away from them, Buzzard Person circled around and located Tamatsi.

43. Tamatsi's pursuers decided to return to their *tuki*. After arriving there they discovered it was empty. Tamatsi had taken their sacred paraphernalia. That is what happened. Tamatsi had scarcely made it to the top of the second slope. He managed to change course just enough to get off the trail before he dropped dead.

44. Returning to perch again in the same tree, Buzzard Person stretched out his wings. Then he swooped down toward the ground. He took a few leaps on the ground and stopped next to Tamatsi. He thought: "Why is this creature covered with white stuff? What is enveloping him?" When he got closer he realized it was maggot eggs. He recognized Tamatsi was dead. He concluded: "There is nothing to be done. They shot him and he died."

45. Then Buzzard decided to fly away. He was bouncing along, preparing to lift off the ground, when somebody spoke to him. It was his mother, Tatei Werika Wimari. Because he disregarded what she was telling him, she moved toward him, stopping just above him. Buzzard was all set to eat Tamatsi's eyes. Just at that moment he heard his mother, Tatei Werika Wimari, speaking again. "Please heed my words. Do not disrupt what is about to occur, or prevent what is being reborn. You will be to blame if you do that."

46. Buzzard Person, whose name was originally Kuka Iwa, attained a higher status, equal to that of Tamatsi, according to our tradition. Today we still see Buzzard flying. Buzzard contributed to the creation of this world. This is the way events transpired. To this day we have received life and been an integral part of this world's creation, just as it was established in the beginning.

47. Our Mother was warning the Buzzard once more. "Please consider carefully what you are going to do. If you eat him (Tamatsi), you will devour your own descendants and your *muwieri* (talisman, sacred symbol). Didn't you notice that he is your *muwieri* (the divine being you helped create with Kieri

pollen)? Pay attention!"

48. After saying that, our Mother gave Buzzard this revelation: "Do you see what it is that I hold in my hand? This is the w*ikuxa*, (the spiritual umbilical cord, or lifeline, w*ikuxa*, connects each person's head at the place where *k+puri* (the eternal Water Spirit) enters it, with Our Mother, who controls both *k+puri* and w*ikuxa* (which also connotes one's lifespan) (Fikes 2011, 115-16). which you are about to devour. That is why I am warning you not to destroy him (by destroying Tamatsi's w*ikuxa*, now in Our Mother's hands, Tamatsi will die). It will be better for you to put yourself to the test. You are talented. You know more than I do. I ask you for this favor. Try doing what I ask right now."

49. Buzzard felt disappointed, and came down to earth to wait for her instructions. This timid Buzzard became silent because he had wanted to eat Tamatsi. Our Mother resolutely ordered him: "All right now. Do what I tell you. Move his feet, move his head, move his arm, move his other arm, move his wrist and you will find out what will transpire. You are the one who can do it." Buzzard obeyed and replied: "I don't believe I can do it. But because you say I can, I am going to try. We will discover if I can do it."

50. He began feeling compassionate, touching Tamatsi on the right and the left side and touching his wrist. He examined everything that Tamatsi contained in order to be alive. Then he declared, "Everything is intact. The only thing he needs is the *uxa* (spiritual nucleus). His cheeks are dark gray. His *uxa* must be restored in order for him to return to life." While Buzzard was renewing Tamatsi's *uxa*, Tamatsi started moving.

51. Our Mother spoke to Buzzard: "Now you understand what you were about to destroy. Now you know he is alive. You must realize that he is your blood, your *uxa*, your *muwieri*. That is what he is." After Tamatsi moved, he lifted himself. He stood up on all four legs with his antlers, just as it was in the beginning. Today we observe that deer are still like this. According to our tradition,

this is how deer were created. This was, and is today, Tamatsi Kauyumari. This miracle was completed by Buzzard Person, because of what he did, our bequest (from the Ancestor Deities) survives today.

52. The history of Tamatsi Kauyumari includes what he accomplished, the precedents he established for us who sing today. We are all united to Tamatsi because he managed to acquire from the Animal People all the sacred paraphernalia still used by Huichol singers and healers.

53. That instant when Tamatsi stood up he was enlightened. "Now everything has turned out perfectly." He demonstrated that he was a deer in every detail. He leaped four times in each of the four cardinal directions and then ran off, heading for the country. He passed by a plain and then disappeared into the desert. He was not an ordinary deer. He was originally Kieri pollen (*tukimarika*, which may be the verb 'to pollinate,' according to Liffman).

54. So he disappeared into the desert, trying to return to his parents. He had advised his parents, before arriving to meet them, to prepare his food; dark-blue corn mush and chocolate with cookies, because he was coming there. Then the deer appeared there. He headed inside the god-house, where he found his dark-blue corn mush and chocolate with cookies. He got full by eating them. Because his snout entered the dark-blue corn mush it turned black, exactly the way we see it today. That set a precedent.

55. As soon as he arrived with his parents, because he accomplished everything with ease, he started making god-houses. He did that because he was already a singer. As Tamatsi built the god-houses he notified his parents: "After I finish this, I am going to test myself and learn what I can achieve. Now we shall dance the Peyote Dance. We will see if I can do it correctly."

56. The Animal People (*Kam+kikate*) found out about the Peyote Dance. They began asking themselves: "Who will go there to sing? Will it be me? One of them answered, "It had better be

me!" Each of them carried a *takwatsi* as they went to the ritual. Tamatsi was singing when they arrived at the Peyote Dance ritual. They were somewhat surprised. His singing pleased them but it also caused them some regret. To conceal it, they began dancing, each one with his *takwatsi* hanging over his shoulder. This is what happened in the beginning. This is how the *Kam+kikate* lost. This is how we were created, and how we developed ourselves.

Jesús González's Postscript

Jesús González ended his saga about the Deer-shaman here, but continued by telling the Ancestor Deities that he wants, "to continue living all the remaining days of my life" (see #61) He is thereby asking the ancestors not to take offense because he revealed sacred knowledge to me outside the ritual context. (#61, below). González's closing remarks also included commentary on the significance of this myth, a directive to his descendants, and his opinions concerning the past and present states of Huichol shamanism.

57. Today we assert that we are singers. That is not true because we were not the ones that started it. That one was Tamatsi Kauyumari. Today we sing and heal, claiming that we know a great deal about all that. The truth is that we are deceiving ourselves. Only Tamatsi knows the truth.

58. When we do not accomplish an objective in the way Tamatsi taught us, we have failed and we are fakers. That is the reason why so many Huichols die nowadays (as punishment for their misdeeds).

59. Today we say that we are losing our traditions. This is not true. Whatever was created in the beginning still exists today. The problem is merely our lack of determination to continue practicing our traditions. Today we claim that the ancient powers no longer exist. But we say that because we do not fulfill the requirements to

make it happen, as it was done in the beginning. That is the reason why we have almost gone back to the way it was in the beginning, just as it was with the Kam+kikate (Animal People). All are fakers, liars and deceivers. According to our history that is the way our ancestors were (before Tamatsi became the first shaman). Perhaps that is why we are also that way, at least partially. It was that way in the beginning and that is why it is still that way today.

60. Today we try to understand the creation of maize, the creation of humans and the creation of Tamatsi. Whatever happened then is still the foundation for what we practice nowadays. Each one of we singers is united with all the others. Everything that first occurred was done for our benefit. By means of the precedents set by Tamatsi, today we comprehend the voices of our gods; from whom we obtain life and the well being of our children, our maize and our livestock. We want all of them to live long lives and not to suffer from illness in this life. In ancient times people were living, but they were not like us. They followed their traditions. Because of them, today we do too. Not many, but only a few of us practice the same ways our forefathers practiced. They explained to us everything connected to Huichol life. That is why we continue practicing their ways today. That is the manner in which things happened. I believe that each of us singers knows very well what I am explaining.

61. I beg your pardon, all of you gods who surround me. Do not be worried, do not fear or take offense. I declare this in the presence of all of you, my Mother Nia'ariwame, my Mother Xapawiyeme, my Grandfather Fire, my Sun Father, my Mother Earth. I am begging your pardon, humbling myself in body and soul in front of all of you. I ask for you to bless me with a serene spirit because I have placed my faith in all of you. My hope is to continue living all the remaining days of my life. This is what I proclaim to you in order that you stay satisfied in your homes and hold nothing against me. All of you are the beginning, the present

and the future.

62. This is all I have to affirm about what took place from the beginning until now with respect to Tamatsi's birth. For all those people who listen to this recording, I ask that you listen to it without being too critical. I am not certain that my recitation conforms to what is believed by each of those who know this history. Nevertheless, I confirm to all of you that I personally do not fear, nor shall I fear gossip. I only speak about what I live and practice. It may not be the same for all of you.

63. I also want to let you all know, because I believe this recording may reach a large audience, that I realize I have done something that will last for many years. For some of you this history will be good advice. It is a sacred and divine history. For many of you who pay attention and practice in conformity with this history, you will gain a spirit of wisdom, intelligence and something spiritual. What I state publicly here may eventually be heard by you who are now young boys and girls, or young adults. Perhaps I will not be alive when you listen to it for the first time. That is why I advise you not to be unfaithful to the teachings each of you will receive from your parents and grandparents. The good words and good faith that you all obtain from your parents and grandparents is like a necklace, a ring, or a pearl in your heart that illuminates your spirit, your life and bestows blessings upon your future. I feel obliged to repeat that my interpretation is not something that I invented by myself. It is simply what I learned from my parents and grandparents. I finally came to understand that what they had been telling me is true.

Epilog

We will now summarize the crucial plot points evident in this chronicle of Tamatsi's birth and accomplishments, which represent a charter for Huichol shamans (healers and singers). Buzzard Person showed compassion twice, first by helping Tamatsi's mother to have a child and later by reviving Tamatsi, with direction given by Tatei, Our Mother. Because she is the celestial Mother who endows each human with *k+puri* and *wikuxa* (Fikes 2011, 112-116) her supervision was essential to keep Buzzard's conduct benevolent, consistent with their goal of creating the first Deer Shaman. Likewise, after Tamatsi became a deer with antlers, the little mouse saved him, just before he was to be sacrificed by the Animal People. Later, Buzzard Person showed compassion again by reviving Tamatsi, on the orders of Tatei, Our Mother. Being the goddess who endows each human with *k+puri* and *wikuxa* it is fitting she guides Buzzard in reviving Tamatsi. Deeds performed by each of these three benevolent actors were essential to enable Tamatsi to establish a new society, led by truthful, compassionate shamans. To accomplish their goal, Tamatsi and the mouse took shamanic power away from the Animal People led by Kam+kime. This chronicle celebrates compassion and at the same time clearly proclaims that the first Huichol Deer Shaman, Tamatsi, was created from a pollinated Kieri flower (#47, 53).

The benefits that Tamatsi brought to his people can be clarified by examining paragraphs 57-60. Proclaiming, "Only Tamatsi knows the truth" (#57) embodies the hallmark of Huichol shamanism: that only by achieving unity with Tamatsi can we (shamans) comprehend what is true (unknown). In paragraph 58 González tacitly discloses that, "the ancient powers" still exist, but as he taught me, that is true only when aspiring shamans comply with all the original ground rules, such as remaining sexually pure, overcoming fear, and making appropriate prayers and offerings. Conversely, those who fail to abide by their covenants with Tamatsi inevitably become false, deceitful shamans. In paragraph 60 he explains that all the momentous changes, including "precedents set by Tamatsi" have improved Huichol life. González and three other *Wixarika* shamans taught me that honoring world-changing sacrifices made by Tamatsi and other Huichol ancestors means that their annual ritual cycle must be properly performed, not only in order for shamans to "comprehend the voices of our gods" but also because they want their children, maize and livestock to "live long lives and not to suffer from illness." González's message is that compassionate, truthful shamans act as custodians of collective blessings (which include maize, rain, fire and sunshine). All these essential benefits were initially established and are eternally perpetuated by working in partnership with their Ancestor Deities (Fikes 1985, 2011).

We are now prepared to interpret why it is that sexual continence is a cardinal rule of conduct during Huichol hunting rituals (for deer and peyote) and sexual fidelity to one's spouse during those years when one is becoming a shaman (Fikes 1985, 1993, 2011). My two *kawiteru* mentors from Santa Catarina emphasized that sexual fidelity is the fundamental rule for any man (as well as his spouse) seeking to become a "werewolf" (Fikes 1985, 267-271). Sexual purity is especially appropriate whenever Huichol seek the aid of Kieri (see Chapter 1).

Crucial details, revealed here for the first time in González's myth of Tamatsi, suggest why. The first Huichol shaman was not a mere human, a being produced by having sex. Tamatsi was created by prayers, Kieri pollen, and offerings (#9-11; Fikes 2011, 257-58). Although his mother wanted a child, the Huichol goddess, with Buzzard's help, sent her the "embryo" or spiritual nucleus (*uxa*) of the first shaman. Finally, after becoming a deer, Tamatsi proclaimed his calling (paragraph 28). His divine birth enabled him to transcend sexuality—by naming it and hurling it away. When the deer-girls told him he must have sex with them he repudiated it. "I will not do that. That is not what I am seeking, nor what I want." Thus Huichol reverence toward Kieri and deer is displayed in the details of the myth surrounding the selection of blue Kieri for Tamatsi's birth, as well as the creation of deer later in his life.

Sexual continence for priests or nuns is supposed to indicate piety or benevolence, qualities which set them apart from ordinary people. For Huichol shamans sexual purity connotes those virtues while also being indicators of their lifelong commitment to achieving unity with their immortal mentor, Tamatsi. Their inversion or transcendence of normal human sexuality is predicated upon devotion to Tamatsi. Unity with him is manifested in shamans trembling while performing rituals, healing, discerning the meaning of revelations or dreams, and knowing what is unknown to others. Their experiential unity with Tamatsi is predicated upon a "radical identification of self with other" and exemplifies Roy Rappaport's "highest order meaning" whereby life's ultimate meaning is achieved by becoming one with the tutelary spirit (Fikes 2011, 65, 74). Tamatsi's "inversion" of normal human conduct (Blackburn 1975, 80-88) is precisely what distinguishes him as a divine (sacred) rather than ordinary (profane) being. His miraculous birth, exceedingly precocious growth (crawling, walking, talking), nearly always being away from his parents, shunning of sex, transformation into deer form and resurrection (with Buzzard's aid), all indicate that his purpose in life was singular.

Other culture heroes, including Moses, Christ, Muhammad, and Deganawida (Wallace 1994) demonstrate similar signs of super-human status. Like Tamatsi, Moses and Deganawida relied on such gifts or talents to transform their societies and fulfill their destinies. Each of them struggled in order to triumph over adversaries who had a "vested interest" in perpetuating their own power. Only by overcoming formidable opponents were they able to transform, or reform, their respective societies. Further discussion of ways in which Tamatsi differs from and/or resembles such prophets or saviors is a topic worthy of another book.

CHAPTER 5

PRINCIPLES ESSENTIAL TO BECOMING A SHAMAN

Jesús González served as an aboriginal temple officer for twenty years at Tuxpan.[1] He admired his grandfather's great shamanic power and confirmed that his father was also a shaman. González observed them both, and his candid accounts of their acquisition of shamanic abilities illustrates the diversity of tutelary spirits available to aspiring Huichol shamans, as well as the values that should inspire their conduct. In this chapter, González's accounts of diverse aspects of becoming and practicing as a shaman will be supplemented by clarifications provided by his son, Vicente.

My Grandfather and Father Were Shamans

"I heard, observed and saw my grandfather, who was a singing shaman. When I was young I accompanied him when he went to sing [conduct rituals] at various ranchos. By traveling with him [to those ranchos] I was able to observe him. I was watching, with my own eyes, whatever he was doing. Out of affection he called me "My precious little son." I am sure that my grandfather was a great singer because I saw him do certain things, such as obtaining helping spirits. My grandfather knew how to kill the *itauki*.[2] I was able to see him do that in the rancho of Vallecitos. He was a renowned singer. I sometimes observed him receiving a cow or bull as compensation for his singing. My grandfather understood what his helping spirits were saying. He was doing whatever they told him. He thought whatever he was doing was right.

My grandfather sometimes spoke about a pact he had made with the deer in the mountains. Because of that pact, whenever he went hunting he found them…he told me…that he had made a pact with Tamatsi [incarnate in deer] in the mountains. My grandfather explained that this was the way he started learning to become a shaman. First he went to the mountains with Tamatsi. In the mountains, when he went deer hunting, he found a special little doe. From her he received *uxa* [her wisdom and virtue]. That is what he told me. After going to the same [pilgrimage] place in the mountains for five consecutive years he went to Paritek+a. (Vicente added that by taking offerings to Tamatsi at Paritek+a, both the place where peyote is collected and where the Sun Father was born, he fulfilled his promise to Tamatsi). After finishing those pilgrimages, he went to Tsakaimuta, where he received power from our Grandfather Fire and our Father Sun. After having made pilgrimages at Tsakaimuta he had learned enough to be a singer [shaman]. From Tsakaimuta he went to Te'akata to obtain permission to heal and sing.[3]

Sometime later he obtained *uxa* from Imukui (Mexican Beaded Lizard, *Heloderma horridum*) and then [*uxa*] from the *Xaye* [a species of rattlesnake]. To become an expert archer he went to the mountains to find the lizard called *Teka* (this is a "horned toad" a lizard in the genus *Phrynosoma*). From the Teka he obtained blood [which the lizard itself discharges].[4] That [power from the Teka] is what enabled my grandfather to kill the *itauki*; by throwing his *muwieri* [prayer feather] so that it functioned as a little arrow... The gods granted all this to my grandfather. That is the way my grandfather learned to do everything. My grandfather told me: "My son, learn something while you are still young. If you learn how to do these things, you can feel confident about living in harmony with everything. Then you will be able to heal, to sing and to serve people."

The significance of the *uxa* his grandfather acquired from these four virtuous animals is examined in detail below. In addition to Tamatsi, Buzzard Person, and several Rain Mothers (mentioned in Chapter 2), González acknowledges the cormorant as his helping spirit (see below). González sensed he was first given *uxa* at age seven, when Tamatsi summoned him after he ate psychoactive honey imbued with Kieri nectar. Those extraordinary childhood visions induced by Kieri enabled him to realize that the yellow root called *uxa*, which his father used to paint González's face during

First Fruits (Tatei Neixa) rituals he attended during childhood, merely symbolized the original *uxa*—in the pollinated or fertilized Kieri flower—that was crucial in the creation of Tamatsi (as the boy who became the first compassionate shaman and the deer). González' amazing childhood experience with Tamatsi may help explain why he stated (below) that his father did not instruct him in becoming a shaman, although he observed his father doing what shamans routinely do.[5]

"My father was instructed by his father, my grandfather. My father did the same thing his father did in the mountains. His prayers must have been answered. My father captured a deer. That was something I saw when we were together hunting for deer. This happened while we were living at Iparita (see Chapter 3). That is how he started to become a shaman, with the benefit of his father's instruction. Because his father showed him where to go, both of them acquired their power by going to the same place to become singers [shamans].

The only other sacred site they visited was Tuamuxawita [in the community of San Sebastián]. Every time they finished deer hunting they went to Tuamuxawita. After making pilgrimages for several years to Tuamuxawita, they began going to the Pacific Ocean. My father found what he was searching for at the ocean [shamanic power from Mother Ocean.] After returning from the ocean he had to return again to Tuamuxawita. That is how my father did it, following the example set by his father.

I did not ask anybody to teach me what I know today. Nobody taught me. My father was healing and singing but he never played the drum [during the First Fruits ritual]. First he started to heal, then to sing. When I began observing him he was already healing. My father and I made pilgrimages together to the ocean. His mandate [as a shaman] was diminished because one time while we were traveling to Te'akata he almost died. The reason he almost died young was because of his transgression. That is why I declare that if somebody does not comply with all the prohibitions [involved in becoming a shaman] that person will soon be dead. I am convinced that is truly what happens because I witnessed that happening to my father.

I preferred to make pilgrimages to the Pacific Ocean. By making five [consecutive] annual pilgrimages there, I obtained my *muwieri* [prayer feathers] from the bird called *Haramari* [a species of cormorant]. I conduct my ceremonies using that bird's feathers. Today I travel around here using cormorant feathers to heal children and perform rituals such as the First Fruits. That is how I started. I never learned anything from my father. He did not instruct me but I was observing him. I learned on my own, going to Haramaratsie [a sacred site at the Pacific Ocean, near San Blas, Nayarit]. There I found the *nierika* [visionary ability symbolized by a mirror]. I am still using that *nierika* to heal and cleanse people. I think it was an outstanding one. I also sing with it."

Jesús González is convinced that aspiring shamans must get in touch with their spiritual inheritance, which may be accomplished after the ancestors 'summon' their protégé, or when a would-be shaman prays and deposits offerings for an ancestor, either by themselves or with aid from a shaman.

"We are born with everything, including *uxa*. When the Sun Father commands, I must learn how to heal or sing. If I am unable to visit the gods by myself, then I look for a wise person, someone having the knowledge of a singer [shaman]. That person can help me make contact with the gods. To learn how to become a singer or healer that person will take me directly to where I was destined to go from my birth."

González' grandfather used this method when he took González' father to the same place where he had acquired his *uxa* from the deer in the mountains. The same method was used by both González and Serratos, when each of them guided me on pilgrimages to make prayers and offerings to a specific Ancestor

Deity. Thus González took my wife and I on five consecutive annual pilgrimages to Haramaratsie (near San Blas, at the Pacific Ocean). Serratos supervised my pilgrimage in 1986 to a female Kieri growing somewhere east of Pueblo Nuevo (Fikes 2011; see Chapter 1). Both González and Serratos guided me on those pilgrimages according to their assessment of my *uxa*; presumably discerning an affinity between myself, and the specific god from whom I was soliciting benefits. Of course, even though they guided me it was my responsibility to deliver offerings, make my own prayers, and learn how to discern and act upon the Ancestor Deities' response to my requests.

Uxa Inspires Huichol Naming

In daily life, Huichols address each other using kinship terms such as: my mother or father, and my elder brother or sister. Personal names should manifest each person's *uxa*, which connotes that person's spiritual character. Because *uxa* is an index of one's divine origin, a person's name may never be invented or arbitrarily given by the parents before their child is born. Instead, Huichol names must be revealed by the Ancestor Deities because each individual's spiritual inheritance manifests that person's relationship to those Ancestor Deities who bestowed their *uxa* on that baby. Their Ancestor Deities may decide together what a person's divine ancestry will be. Because "gods" make decisions about each person's birth, a Huichol name must be divined, thereby honoring those gods for their bequest, and insuring their good will and protection for their human protégé (see Chapter 2). González declared that his personal name, Yurkame or Yur+kame is linked to germination. His name discloses that he is a descendant of the most ancient Huichol goddess, Great Grandmother Germination, Takutsi Y+rameka. Jesús continues:

"My grandfather dreamed my name. We grow up getting names based upon revelations of our grandparents; in connection with our being descended from our mothers' mothers (*tateiteima*) and our fathers' fathers (*takakauma*). My grandfather's revelations came from my Sun Father and my Grandfather Fire. Those gods intended for me to receive my personal name, Yur+kame.

The purpose of this *uxa* that we are born with is to enable us to grow up healthy, by having something that helps protect us. I believe my name is genuine because I am still alive. Nothing terrible has happened to me because the gods have assisted me. If somebody is named incorrectly they will quickly die. My grandparents named me accurately because I am still alive today, after all these years.

These matters that I am discussing are prohibited. It is possible that my Sun Father and my Grandfather Fire will be displeased with my having explained all this. Yet these are only words to explain how naming must be done."

These last three sentences indicate that González felt compelled to ask the ancestors not to get angry with him for giving me previously unknown information about the Huichol manner of naming, based on revelations.[6]

Huichol frequently have personal names corresponding to stages in the growth of maize, a usage based on their belief that people and maize are married—mutually dependent—as well as spiritually connected. Each year when the ears of corn are ripe, before they can be consumed, a First Fruits ritual is performed. During that ritual called "Dance for Our Mother" by the Huichol, the singing shaman recites the myth describing how Watakame, the first Huichol corn-planter, acquired maize (Fikes 1993, 225-32). This myth sanctifies the spiritual connection, equated with marriage, between maize and humans. According to González:

"The children and the maize are closely related because children are the *uxa* [spiritual relatives] of the maize gods. For that reason our women receive the name of Uxama, white corn. If it is a man he receives the name Uxate. When a child's grandparents prepare to name that child, they must dream to select the appropriate name for the child, in accordance with [revelations from] maize goddesses such as Our Mother Tsitaima and Our Mother Tsakuruma.

We Huichols feel we are related to the maize. The names we receive should be connected with stages in the growth cycle of maize. My firstborn son's Huichol name, Utsiakame, means "seed-corn guarded in the god-house" [something consecrated]. My third child is named Thomas. His Huichol name is Haka Temai [corn with its first leaf visible above the soil.][7]

Our Mother Tsakuruma takes the form of maize that has ripened in the consecrated place in the cornfield. The spirit of maize tells us, when a girl is born, that she should receive the name Tsakuruma. That justifies we Huichol saying we are related to the maize. Our Mother Tsakuruma is a goddess who embodies Hay+rime [everlasting water]. She lives in the ocean. When the shaman sprinkles everlasting water on a child during the Tatei Neixa (First Fruits) ritual, they invoke Our Mother Tsakuruma in the song and the prayer [to ask her to help that child mature, just as she helps her maize children ripen].

There are specific places where our gods dwell. From them we receive the visions that dictate the name each particular person receives. I am guided by such visions every time I name one of my descendants. I have never before explained that the lives of our children are integrally related to Tatei Niwetsika our Maize Mother. For this reason it is forbidden to eat maize and other crops growing at this time; during the rainy season.

Xuturi means an offspring, a blossom or bud that produces fruit or flowers. We too are born in this manner [like flowering plants]. That is why the word xuturi refers to a newly born child. For this reason that child is washed on the fifth day and the grandfather asks the gods from whom this flower or fruit came, which god decided he/she would be born. This is why children and maize are alike. This is why it is forbidden to beat a pregnant woman, or a woman with an infant. Such an [shocking] act destroys the will of the gods; whose decision it was to grant that baby to the woman. We provoke problems when we oppose the good will of the gods, when we attempt to destroy our own descendants by abusive treatment.

The *xuturi* [flower] made of paper [for use during rituals] represents our children. *Kunuari* is a thick candle which has a *xuturi* [paper flower] attached to it. This paper flower represents all the children it has under its protection. It is the foundation of the family. When it is a couple's first-born child, they make a votive arrow and votive gourd bowl to complement the paper flower that is tied to the thick candle. These items become one, like a family in unity, because together and simultaneously they acquire *k+puri*, a resilient spirit exemplified by everlasting water. The votive gourd bowl, votive arrow and thick candle of the first-born child form the foundation for [protecting] all other children that will be born to the couple."

Ecologists assert that maize depends on humans for survival as much as we depend on it. Some 9,000 years ago humans domesticated maize. As a consequence of several millennia of human selection of maize, it can no longer reproduce—survive in nature—without considerable human care. Huichol nurture their corn through ceremonies, as well as by planting kernels some distance from each other, by weeding around the corn and by protecting it from various predators such as crows, rats, badgers and ground squirrels.

Without having corn as the staple of their diet, the Huichol could not have survived. They rightly continue to recognize that production of maize is based on interdependence or mutualism; a perennial partnership between people and maize. This interdependence is illustrated in the myth describing Watakame's "marriage" to the maize maidens (Fikes 1993, 178, 225-232).

González' comments about naming reveal the kinship and spiritual bonds existing between maize goddesses and Huichols. His understanding of xuturi (a flower, seen as a representation of children) suggests he considers human reproduction as a functional equivalent of maize reproduction (or even flowering plant reproduction). Plants produce fruit like humans produce children. Huichol put an emphasis on achieving these same reproductive goals, e.g., producing offspring, even when those goals are achieved by the radically dissimilar methods that plants and people use to reproduce themselves. Their usage of *xuturi* indicates respect for the enduring interdependence between maize and themselves.[8]

Uxa, Ancestors' Gift to Babies and Worthy Shamans

Although we know *uxa* is a word with multiple meanings, its central meaning connotes one's unique spiritual inheritance, as bestowed at birth by specific Ancestor Deities. Because *uxa* is bestowed at birth, often by various gods, naming a child depends upon discerning the sources of that child's spiritual inheritance. Grandparents are expected to divine a child's unique bond with particular deities (see Chapters 2 and 3). Keeping this in mind, we can properly interpret González' assertion: "The purpose of this *uxa* that we are born with is to enable us to grow up healthy, by having something that helps protect us." Thinking about his statement, I remembered Reuben Snake's comments about a person's name providing protection, like a coat of armor (Fikes 1996, 222). Huichol evidently regard a person's name as akin to an amulet that protects a person by evoking the gods who bestowed the *uxa* on that person.

Uxa also refers to the virtue, sensitivity or wisdom some Huichol, such as González' grandfather, are able to gain by making pilgrimages to particular gods and divine animals. *Uxa* is beneficial, whether it is inherited at birth or acquired through alliances with powerful spirits including Kieri, deer, or rattlesnakes. As Vicente González explained, "Singers and healers want to increase their *uxa* by making more pacts or covenants with other gods, to be able to comprehend more and develop their ability to heal or sing."

The myth of the first Deer Shaman recited by Jesús González equates quintessential *uxa* with a pollinated Kieri flower. The fertilized Kieri flower was tantamount to Tamatsi's spiritual essence. Buzzard Person perceived the divine essence in that Kieri flower, and instructed the woman who became Tamatsi's mother about how to transform it into a child. Accordingly, González and many Huichols affiliated with the aboriginal temple at Tuapuri (Santa Catarina) consider Kieri the supreme, but not the only, source of shamanic wisdom. González explains:

"Those of us with *uxa* are singers [shamans]. The *uxa* is from a specific god with whom we have a covenant. Somebody who wants to acquire *uxa* must solicit it from one god at a time. One must not mix them all up together because Kieri is very jealous. It can make you crazy, or cause you to have an accident, like drowning in a river … This same *uxa one obtains from Kieri enables one to see, hear and understand all the gods because uxa is from them.* Once one has acquired *uxa*, all the gods can see that one has *uxa* from a particular god. Having *uxa* is beneficial because it helps one comprehend what the gods reveal in our dreams. If a person does not have *uxa*, that person lacks wisdom."

Kieri is visited and venerated by some Huichol temple officers (Collings 2000, 19-21). It is widely regarded as a vital aid for Huichol deer hunters (Fikes 1985, 2011), and as a patron by some Huichol seeking shamanic power (Fikes 2011). After pilgrimages to the Sun Father's birthplace became an annual obligation for Huichol temple officers, the unsurpassed value ascribed to *uxa* (as the pollinated Kieri flower from which Tamatsi was born) was diminished, at least for some Huichols, such as Juan Real (Zingg 2004, 16-20).

Two causes presumably contributed to the increase in peyote's cultural value, and the corresponding decline of their reliance on Kieri. The first cause concerns the arduous annual on-foot pilgrimages of 700 kilometers round trip, to the Sun Father's birthplace and back again to the native temples located in their homeland. This trek encouraged pilgrims to ingest peyote (perhaps becoming shamans after completing five or ten annual pilgrimages) while gaining prestige by bringing it (as well as *Hay+rime*, the yellow plant pigment *uxa*, and deer) back to their temples in order to celebrate the Peyote Dance. The second cause is based on their expectation of obtaining group benefits—especially rain, by consulting the Cora elite (McCarty and Matson 1975, 215), to whom peyote was presented as a prescribed contribution, like "tribute" (Fikes 1985, 79-81; 1993, 169-170, Weigand 1975; 2000, 26-28).

My conclusion, that shamanic power obtained via Kieri (Tamatsi's *uxa*) predates peyote-facilitated shamanism (after peyote was seen as Tamatsi's *iyari*) will be bolstered by the addition of evidence in a forthcoming publication. However, some evidence of syncretism between Kieri and peyote, as well as my interpretation of the higher status acquired by certain temple officers who complete peyote pilgrimages, is presented below.

The meaning that *uxa* has for peyote hunters is an obvious indicator that attempts were made to make peyote hunting culturally compatible with the Huichol reverence for Kieri. Despite the fact he did not make peyote pilgrimages, González's remarks below accurately portray peyote pilgrims' beliefs:

"*Uxa* is a yellow root that [grows in the water at Tuihapa or Tuimayau] (and) is consecrated to our Sun Father and Grandfather Fire. They [peyote hunters] say this occurred in the beginning, when the votive gourd bowl was taken to the land of peyote. The one who was carrying it was Kawi Tewiyari [Caterpillar Person, a black caterpillar that lives on broad-leafed oak trees]. Kawi Tewiyari [Caterpillar Person] was the one who bested all the other ancestors who were attempting to carry votive gourd bowls. Together Our Sun Father, Grandfather Fire, and Mother Earth selected him to try to take the votive gourd bowl to its final destination, Nataritsie [an altar in Wirikuta]. He did it.

While making the journey to Wirikuta, Caterpillar Person was naming all the places that are mentioned today during our First

Fruits ritual song. When we recite our myths today, we declare that Caterpillar Person was the chief. Everyone who goes to collect peyote interprets it exactly this way, repeating what I stated, that Caterpillar Person did it. Today that caterpillar has the [yellow] designs on his face, designs that are the gods' *uxa*, indicating that he was the chief who carried the votive gourd bowl to the altar, Nataritsie. His reward was to be given the *uxa* of the gods."

Caterpillar Person divined the names of sacred sites en route to the peyote country, thereby setting a precedent still followed in Huichol rituals. He also delivered offerings, exemplified by the votive gourd bowl, to the gods' altar in Wirikuta. As a reward for his effort, the gods bestowed their *uxa* on him. It remains visible today as yellow lines on the face of a species of black caterpillar (unknown to me) found in the Huichol homeland. The *uxa* associated with Caterpillar Person's achievements also denotes the wisdom that Huichol believe has been acquired by their *kawiterutsixi* (plural of *kawiteru*). By making peyote and other annual pilgrimages, these elderly ritual specialists that preside at rituals performed at ceremonial centers attained the highest standing of all Huichol shamans formerly residing in each of the nineteen or twenty native temple districts (Fikes 1993, 169-170). *Kawiterutsixi* were traditionally elderly males who recited the appropriate *kawitu* (myth or narrative describing what ancestors did to create and organize this world) during a specific ritual (Fikes 1985, 330). Their higher status commemorates Caterpillar Person, who made "peyote pilgrimages" to serve the ancestor deities. Their superior ritual oratory—skill in reciting the *kawitu*—is, in part, obtained by completing pilgrimages, as did their namesake, Caterpillar Person. Thus the *kawiteru* is qualified to lead rituals because he has faithfully followed in the footsteps of the ancestors.

As we know, traditional Huichol temple officers were expected to complete five years of annual pilgrimages in order to procure *Hay+rime* ('everlasting' or 'budding' water) at sacred places located to the south, north, west, east and center of their homeland.

Traveling east, they must procure peyote, three types of *Hay+rime* and *uxa*, the aquatic plant containing yellow pigment used for face painting (Fikes 2011).

What I recognize as the original meaning of *uxa*—the divine power inherent in the pollinated Kieri flower that became both a deer and the first compassionate shaman—was expanded and given a new meaning when applied to the yellow pigment for face painting that is extracted from the aquatic plant (*Mahonia trifoliolata*) obtained at Tuihapa. This modified meaning of *uxa* may have helped boost motivation for making those arduous annual pilgrimages to the Sun Father's birthplace. Learning to become a shaman (by eating peyote, and thereby gaining aid from Tamatsi), and perhaps eventually becoming a *kawiteru*, "naturally" became associated with making such pilgrimages. Peyote was gradually becoming the preferred way to increase one's spiritual ability as well as prestige within the community.

Once the tradition of annual journeys from native temples to the Sun Father's birthplace became established, a devout Huichol was regarded as one who systematically and faithfully finished many pilgrimages to collect peyote, *Hay+rime* and *uxa* as well as to various other sacred sites. By faithfully following Caterpillar Person's path, their reward was being granted *kawiteru* status and *uxa* by their gods. Gaining higher prestige required not only completing long pilgrimages but also demonstrating skill in reciting details of oral history, embodied in a *kawitu* (ritual narrative) appropriate for a specific ceremony.

According to González, when pilgrimages to the birthplace of the Sun Father were still made on foot, after completing ceremonies at the place known as "Uru Motiü" (Fikes 2011), the pilgrims kept walking until they came to Uxa Maiyewe (the place where *uxa* grows):

"There they decreed that the *uxa* is from Tamatsi Kauyumari. Being of one mind, the gods decided that Tamatsi should paint himself with the *uxa*. Tamatsi said, "Let me see how I look, to decide if I turned out well or not." The yellow paint made him look good. For that reason, in honor of Tamatsi, we still use that paint today.

I never go to collect peyote. This is what the peyote hunters report. Today people making pilgrimages to Wirikuta get the uxa there. That is why the peyote hunters use the *uxa*, in the same way that *Tamatsi* first did it.

When children journey to Wirikuta in the First Fruits ritual *uxa* is used to paint their faces. They are painted in accordance with the number of times [years] they have made the trip. Their *uxa* is seen by Tamatsi and by Tatei Ut+anaka (Our Maize Mother). All this is explained in the First Fruits and the Peyote Dance rituals. Because maize and children are connected, they must travel together to Wirikuta during the First Fruits ritual. This is because the gods established this custom for the maize in the beginning, to honor Niwetsika Tauteriyari (Maize Person). Because of the precedent set in the beginning [by our gods] we descendants do the same thing today. We singers understand our gods. We acquire their *uxa* (wisdom) and we follow their *waiyeyeri*, [footprints], the trail they left for us in the beginning, in *Watet+apa*. ... we use *uxa* (yellow paint) ... because Tamatsi did it the same way in the beginning. So to honor him we continue using that *uxa*, because it is his *uxa*. We use this yellow paint only for our Peyote Dance, in order to identify the peyote hunters. For the First Fruits ritual we use it for (children making) the spiritual journey that takes us to our Mother in Wirikuta (i.e., to Tatei Matinieri, see Fikes 2011). It is said that the peyote hunters must return from Wirikuta with their faces painted with *uxa* because it was done that way in the beginning, and we must follow in the gods' footsteps (*waiyeyeri*)."

Because we are focused on interpreting the various meanings of *uxa*, we will briefly note that after peyote was proclaimed an entheogen derived from Deer Person, it was venerated as a divine spirit, being called Tamatsi's *iyari* (mind/spirit) (Fikes 1985, 187-192). Attempting to decipher details of Huichol myths, rituals, and ethnohistory led me to conclude that the equating of Kieri, with deer and (later) peyote by the Huichol, functioned to mitigate the disruption caused when their more powerful eastern and western neighbors (Tepecano and Cora respectively) incorporated the Huichol in an annual temple ritual cycle, embedding this ritual cycle into a pan-tribal confederacy (Fikes 1985, 80-84). Encouraging syncretism between Kieri and peyote presumably promoted coherence, or prevented schisms, that might otherwise have been caused by worshipping two biologically distinct plant entheogens.

Such syncretism is manifested in González's comments (above) on *uxa* identified as a yellow root being derived from Tamatsi (which sanctifies the face paintings done in his honor). Syncretism is also evident whenever Huichol exalt either of these entheogens by applying the same honorific title, 'Tamatsi,' which denotes Our Elder Brother, and connotes our mentor. This syncretism is also discernible when Huichols publicly confess sexual misdeeds, symbolized by tying knots on a rope (to be discussed in the next chapter).

Let us now examine Zingg's singular claims; that the yellow root, *uxa*, is called Kieri in Tuxpan (1938, 585), and that it is connected with the acquisition of healing and 'singing' (shamanic) ability (Zingg 2004, 32, 55). Zingg's conflated claim seems to contradict the 'evil' that Juan Real, Zingg's primary informant, attributed to Kieri (2004, 16-20). Perhaps a different Huichol informant provided those positive comments about the *uxa* obtained in Wirikuta. In fact, Aedo (2011, 134) deduced that Zingg's informant was a peyotero who inverted the meaning of words, as peyoteros sometimes do, in order to connect Kieri's yellow pollen with the yellow pigment used for face painting. Be that as it may, it appears anomalous that González uses the word '*uxa*' for the aquatic plant at Tuihapa, thereby linking that desert-dwelling plant (identified as *Mahonia trifoliolata* by Bauml, Voss & Collins 1990), with Kieri, a divine plant in the genus *Solandra*) that grows throughout the Chapalagana Huichol homeland. This bizarre comparison makes me suspect that there was an attempt to transfer the esteem long attributed to Kieri and to the *uxa* (wisdom) aspiring shamans obtain from diverse divine sources to the *uxa* (as yellow pigment) acquired by temple officers during their pilgrimage to collect peyote, *Hay+rime,* and deposit offerings at the volcanic peak where the Sun first emerged.

In his narrative about the first compassionate shaman, Jesús González clearly affirms that Tamatsi's *uxa* is derived from Kieri pollen. Then, in his explanation cited above, the gods encouraged Tamatsi to paint his face with *uxa* when they first arrived at the place where *uxa* was growing. We know that the *uxa* for face painting is produced by pigment from a yellow root, presumably collected by Huichols only at Tuihapa (aka Tuimayau), that perennial waterhole in Wirikuta, where peyote is collected. My translator (Pancho Torres) and I recognize that form of '*uxa*' as essentially symbolic, because yellow pigment has merely conventional value instead of the high status conferred on entheogens such as peyote and Kieri. My analysis of several other myths, which I discussed with Torres, persuaded me (and perhaps Torres) that the extraction of pigment from that aquatic plant called *uxa* became an annual obligation for Huichol temple officers only after they became participants in an annual ceremonial cycle which obliged them to make annual peyote hunts. This arduous pilgrimage was concomitantly an opportunity for acquiring shamanic power from peyote, the only means available for them to obtain essential items (peyote, *Hay+rime* and *uxa*) required to perform the Peyote Dance, and presumably the only way the Cora chief residing at the Mesa del Nayar obtained peyote as tribute. The myths and ethnohistorical data needed to strengthen my conclusion will be provided in another publication.

As González suggested above, Huichol only use *uxa* to paint designs on their faces during their Peyote Dance and on their children's faces when they celebrate the First Fruits ritual; that ceremony when children "travel", via the shaman's song, through the peyote country all the way to the Sun Father's birthplace

(Fikes 1985, 1993, 2011). The *uxa* which refers to the yellow root obtained during that pilgrimage, differs significantly from: a) the *uxa* diverse gods bestow on infants, b) the *uxa* which shamans acquire from various gods with whom they make pacts, and c) from the pollen of the Kieri flower, which González regards as the quintessential or archetypal *uxa*, that was essential in creating Tamatsi, the first Deer Shaman.

Examining the Diverse Benefits of Uxa and Iyari, its Challenger

We now know that uxa has multiple meanings: the birthright contributions each person receives from the gods, the power or wisdom shamans obtain from diverse deities or divine animals, and, as González's myth of the first shaman indicates, quintessential *uxa* is Kieri pollen, produced in the traditional Chapalagana Huichol homeland. Thus when the word *uxa* is applied to an aquatic plant Huichol collect at a desert waterhole some 350 kilometers east of Tuxpan, we should investigate whether semantic tampering or "directed syncretism" has occurred. The redefining of *uxa* discussed above presumably began after the "peyote pilgrimage" tradition was established among a people whose shamans were already using Kieri.

To reiterate, the root of that aquatic plant used only for face painting is a ritual custom. That yellow pigment is not considered by my shaman mentors as a source of protection (which is associated with *uxa* for naming children), or as a supplier of shamanic power of the sort attained by fulfilling a pact with the rattlesnake, deer, or Kieri.

González, as well as his father and grandfather, are shamans who attained more *uxa* by establishing rapport with divine animals and Ancestor Deities who bestowed special abilities upon them. González insists that a person seeking shamanic power must obtain *uxa* from one god at a time, by scrupulously fulfilling obligations intrinsic to one's pact with that particular god. Moreover, having several sources of shamanic power brings superior healing ability. To gain multiple powers, one by one, implies that some, if not most, Huichol shamans are engaged in lifelong learning. González' grandfather's shamanic abilities nicely illustrate the Huichol conviction that getting *uxa* from diverse sources increases a shaman's power and wisdom. González' original power, given to him by Tamatsi, whose spirit (*uxa*) was incarnate in Kieri pollen, was supplemented by his efforts to earn the aid of certain Rain Mothers, in addition to Buzzard and Cormorant. Because gods, as well as special animals and plants, have distinct attributes, aspiring shamans attempt to obtain more *uxa* by making pacts with particular divine plants, animals, and Ancestor Deities. As González stated previously, "Having *uxa* is beneficial because then one can comprehend what the gods reveal in our dreams. If a person does not have *uxa* that person lacks wisdom."

There seems to be a striking similarity between Gonzalez' quest to accumulate *uxa* from various sources, to facilitate shamanic or spiritual abilities, and what I learned about seeking the tutelary spirit that Santa Catarina shamans refer to as Ne'akame. According to the *kawiteru*, Serratos:

> "Obtaining a Ne'akame empowers one to sing and heal effectively... One is able to dream more frequently and more effectively because the Ne'akame, or Kauyumari, is providing much aid to the singer or healer. The person without a Ne'akame dreams less because they have no (spiritual) helper (Fikes 2011, 50). ...When one arrives to do a healing, first one must diagnose the patient to discern which gods are punishing that person. Then one knows with which song one must do the healing. If several gods are punishing the patient, one must sing various songs. For that reason it is necessary to obtain many Ne'akame, by going to visit the gods (Fikes 2011, 49)."

For Serratos, because specific songs correspond to specific gods, the scope of a shaman's healing ability is increased by developing rapport with various gods. González's reliance on multiple helping spirits and his grandfather's acquisition of *uxa* from four tutelary animals, also illustrates the presumably pan-Huichol doctrine that gaining aid from many deities is essential to develop greater shamanic ability. Comparable ideas about superior healing ability being based on having multiple sources of power are reported for many Native American societies (Deloria 2006), including the Tohono O'odham, another Uto-Aztecan society (called Pima or Papago by outsiders) related to the Tepecano (Underhill 1946, 263-301).

Reorganizing Huichol Society to include Peyote Hunting

The specifics of Huichol "shamanism" are not forever fixed. Huichol society was undoubtedly influenced by its eastern neighbors, the Tepecanos. Supplementing the syncretism that equated peyote with Kieri was the assignment of extraordinary value to the aquatic plant, *uxa*. Associating this root obtained at Tuihapa with Tamatsi strikes me as an example of "directed syncretism" (discussed in Chapter 6 and in a forthcoming publication). There is sufficient evidence to propose that Tepecanos, who inhabited the more fertile lands east of Santa Catarina and Tuxpan de Bolaños, imposed the "peyote pilgrimage" on the Huichol of Santa Catarina. This hypothesis is supported by myths describing the murder of the greatest Huichol goddess, Great Grandmother Germination (Fikes 1985, 83-84). Seen in this light, the higher status accorded to the *kawiteru* is based largely on having completed numerous pilgrimages as a native temple officer. Annual "peyote pilgrimages" were associated with achieving prestige as well as bringing collective benefits (rain and good health) by performing the Peyote Dance (Fikes 2011, 122-132). Such substantial social change almost certainly reduced Huichol reverence for Kieri by encouraging and rewarding reliance on peyote as an alternative source of shamanic power.

This new preference for peyote was facilitated by proclaiming that access to Tamatsi's *iyari*, or mind-spirit, was acquired by eating raw peyote (Fikes 1985, 1993, 2011). Tuxpan Huichol such as Juan Real went further, by accepting the idea that the Sun Father's birth was predicated upon killing the peyote (derived from deer). In Tuxpan this momentous event, the Sun emerging for the first time, resulted after a fierce battle between groups of rival peyote hunters (Zingg 2004, 34-35). Such violent conflict, evident in myths from Santa Catarina, was "justified" by promoting various benefits that could only be obtained by Huichol temple officers making annual pilgrimages to the Sun's birthplace, near Real de Catorce. Killing the divine deer, incarnate in peyote, to acquire shamanic power and/or help the Sun to rise, also entails bringing back *uxa* and *Hay+rime*, from three distinct desert waterholes, which in turn are required for soliciting rain during the Peyote Dance. Making lengthy and arduous pilgrimages every year was sanctified and justified by the perceived inducements they provided for the Huichol, who had become members of a pan-tribal confederacy.

It is in this context of induced, or coerced, social transformation that we should consider the symbolism, and corresponding ritual, of shooting arrows into a cluster of peyote resembling the shape of the deer (Fikes 1993, 192-95; 2011, 138-39) and the emphasis on eating peyote raw, to follow the precedent set by the immortal Wolf People (Fikes 1985, 1993). The wolves, who are associated by my two Santa Catarina *kawiterutsixi* mentors with the Sun Father, appear more cannibalistic than compassionate. For my two *kawiterutsixi* mentors, earthly wolves were apparently linked to five wolf constellations, whose aid was essential to obtaining deer (Fikes 1985, 328). Although they did not state that stellar and solar symbolism was significant in their peyote hunting ritual, seemingly accurate reports by Zingg (see above) and Preuss affirm that it was (Preuss 1909, 211-12; cited in Fikes 1985, 191).

These differences may reflect regional variation, but I am certain that my two *kawiteru* mentors, as well as the shaman Bonales (Fikes 1993, 193-95, 233-235, 2011, 227-229), were convinced that eating the *iyari*, or heart of Deer Person, manifested in peyote, was essential to gain Tamatsi's shamanic power. The cannibalistic ethos implicit in peyote hunt symbolism that I encountered among my Santa Catarina shaman-mentors reminded me that the Aztec word, '*peyotl*' or '*peyutl*' denotes the pericardium that covers the human heart (LaBarre 1989, 16).

It seems reasonable to deduce that the warrior connotations attached to Tamatsi, who was seen by certain Huichol as both a rattlesnake and as the planet Venus (Fikes 1985, 83, 353-54; 2011, 41), were absent in González' portrait of a compassionate Tamatsi, who was born of Kieri pollen. According to the Santa Catarina *kawiterutsixi*, the Wolves associated with the Sun Father must eat Tamatsi's heart, incarnate in peyote, to gain his wisdom. Following the Wolves' precedent, Huichol must eat the deer's heart (peyote) raw to acquire shamanic wisdom and power (Fikes 1993, 193-95).

Certain semantic shifts related to '*uxa*' and '*iyari*' must mark a change in how the "new normal" of shamanic power was to be acquired: by eating peyote during annual pilgrimages. Although pilgrimages to the Sun Father's birthplace were presumably instituted by intimidation, if not coercion, the benefits obtained from those difficult pilgrimages have proven compelling enough for peyote hunting to persist long after the crucial demise (circa 1722) of the confederacy that connected Coras, Huichols and Tepecanos. Eating Tamatsi's *iyari*, seen as incarnate in peyote (as Deer Person), was an amazing innovation, one that supplemented an older doctrine about acquiring *uxa* by making pacts with Kieri, Deer, and other divine animals. The value attached to obtaining Tamatsi's *iyari* by eating peyote has been reinforced by the belief (held by my two *kawiteru* mentors) that *iyari* (identified as each person's heart or conscience) is bequeathed on each embryo only by the Sun Father (Fikes 2011). For them, Huichol society was properly reformed again by recognizing the Sun Father as the only god who imparts *iyari* and by killing Deer Person (as peyote) as well as leaving annual offerings at the Sun's birthplace (Paritek+a). All this meant that peyote hunting was regarded as just as vital to insure the well being of the Huichol as bringing back *Hay+rime*, *uxa* and depositing offerings at their Sun Father's birthplace.

This recalibration of Huichol ritual life was presumably enabled by directed syncretism, exemplified by calling the yellow pigment '*uxa.*' The old idea about *uxa*—acquired by making pacts with various gods, as González explained—was expanded by extolling the Sun Father's power and "replacing" Kieri with peyote as the favored entheogen. This devaluation of Kieri was implied by Serratos in a mythic episode he recited about the triumph of three divine Huichol singers, led by Venus (Tunuame), who killed Great Grandmother Germination after shooting her with their arrows. These three divine singers gave her a beverage made from Kieri in order to memorize diverse ritual songs she sang for them, after becoming intoxicated by that beverage. These three "mythical" singers, set the precedent for having three singers preside over Huichol temple (*tuki*) rituals. The foremost of these singers is called Tunuame (Venus, or Morning Star by San Andrés temple officers, according to Liffman). He, serving the Sun Father, usurped the paramount status formerly accorded to the old Germination Goddess (Fikes 1985, 83).

The fact that these three divine singers replaced that goddess, Takutsi, after they shot her with arrows is significant. As Brundage recognized (1983, 3, 167, 223), Chichimecs commemorated their conquest of foreign lands by celebrating in "myths" their killing of foreign goddesses. The mythic murder of a goddess is therefore an index of Chichimec subjugation of foreigners and imposition of new tribal leaders. Clearly, two new official positions were created: Venus became the namesake of the paramount *tuki* singer and *kawiteru* was the title for leading ritual orators, or perhaps, as Weigand asserts (2000, 26-31), for powerful members of a ruling elite. Selecting such novel Huichol leaders was possible only after the ancient Huichol goddess, Takutsi, was murdered and replaced. Concomitants of that momentous social change were the devaluation of the contributions that Tatei Werika Wimari and her helper, Buzzard, made to creating and saving the Deer Shaman, identifying Venus with the paramount Huichol temple singer, and making peyote hunting the path to achieving maximum prestige, by establishing its role in becoming a *kawiteru*.

While the traditional belief that *uxa* is bestowed upon each baby by one or more gods survived this social transformation intact, the significance of *iyari* emerged as a result of Huichol interaction with powerful neighboring societies, the Cora and Tepecano, with whom the Huichol became allied for ceremony, trade and mutual defense (Fikes 1985, Weigand 1975, 2000).

The scope and significance of imposing the annual cycle of temple rituals upon the Huichol will be further examined in the forthcoming publication mentioned above. But, for now, it is time to return to Jesús González and his family.

CHAPTER 6

VENERATING KIERI AS A CATHOLIC
SAINT AND A SACRED PLANT

Three of the four shamans who mentored me had a lifelong spiritual bond with Kieri. Of the three who venerated Kieri, only Jesús González felt no need to make any peyote pilgrimages. Although he valued peyote, he did not make pilgrimages to collect it. The other two mentors were Santa Catarina *kawiterutsixi* whose lifelong experiences with Kieri were complemented by the completion of peyote pilgrimages as Huichol temple officers. Unlike his father, Vicente González vacillated in his devotion to Kieri. His report (below) about uncanny experiences with the spirit of Kieri, camouflaged as a Catholic saint, will be examined fully in this chapter. But first, before discussing Vicente's adventures, I will describe the traditional veneration of Kieri.

José Sánchez, the Santa Catarina *kawiteru* who died in 1983 (Fikes 1985, 8-12) was consecrated to a specific Kieri near Huejuquilla soon after his birth. His parents requested that Kieri's aid in making him a shaman (Fikes 2011, 45). Like González, Fernando Serratos acknowledged that Kieri pollen was the source of the first Deer Shaman in part of a myth he allowed me to tape-record in 1987 (Fikes 2011, 48-49). Serratos' remarks about Irumari (another title for Tamatsi) being born from Kieri answered questions I asked him about my 1986 pilgrimage, made under his supervision, to solicit aid from a female Kieri. This pilgrimage (summarized in Chapter 1) took me to a Kieri venerated by Serratos' ancestors. Indeed, Serratos' father took him to that same Kieri plant when he was young. Their pilgrimages to petition for favors from that particular Kieri were unrelated to the annual temple ritual cycle at Santa Catarina. However, their commitment to Kieri did not deter them from making numerous "peyote pilgrimages" while serving as Santa Catarina temple officers.[1] The fact that both of these Santa Catarina *kawiterutsixi*, and several other Huichols who spoke with me about Kieri, revered both peyote and Kieri suggests that among Santa Catarina Huichol, Kieri and peyote have peacefully co-existed for perhaps 1,800 years (Zingg 2004, xv).

In stark contrast, Robert Zingg's myth maligns Kieri (which was misidentified as *Datura*, jimsonweed). Zingg's myth defames the Kieri-shaman as deceitful and harmful, a scoundrel who Kauyumari defeated and replaced with peyote pilgrimages and Peyote Dance rituals (Zingg 2004, 16-20).

Jesús González and his son, Vicente, entrusted me with extraordinary information about Kieri. Vicente's testimony, that Huichol are venerating the spirit of Kieri while praying in front of a Catholic saint, made me realize that they are still practicing their aboriginal religion, rather than blending or syncretizing it with Catholicism. Evidence and testimony provided in this chapter clearly show that Kieri is revered throughout the Chapalagana Huichol homeland, even at the Catholic church in Tenzompa, a Mexican town which was, until almost 1910, an integral part of Huichol territory.[2]

Tenzompa may have been home to the ancestors of Jesús González, but he grew up at various ranchos within the *gobernancia* of Tuxpan de Bolaños (as discussed in chapter 3). The Huichol settlement of Tuxpan de Bolaños, where Vicente lives, is some 80 kilometers south of Tenzompa, the town where the Catholic church is located. According to Jesús González,

"We formerly inhabited Tenzompa, until the time when the Mexican revolution began (1910). We (Huichols) used to live in Tenzompa, but after the revolution started, we all fled to various places. Ever since that time, none of us Huichols have lived there because the mestizos arrived and began living there. People say that we left Tenzompa because of the revolution. Of that I have no personal knowledge (he was born just after the revolution ended in 1917).
The saint (represented by an icon in the Catholic Church at Tenzompa) who was ours remained there. Today we still adore him. That is why we go there to perform ritual consecrations ("baptism") for our children. That is the way we do it. That is how we have always done

it. After the mestizos arrived they took control of that saint. But that saint is ours, even though now we are saying it belongs to everyone. They (the mestizos in Tenzompa) made their chapel and it still exists. Today we only visit that chapel, even though they tell us it is ours. We go there nowadays to consecrate ("baptize") my grandchildren and great-grandchildren. We perform a great ritual to honor our saint, Apaxuki. He is a most demanding god. He is easily offended and does not allow us to delay (in making atonement for misdeeds). The arrow he carries is the scorpion, which he sends to punish the disobedient."

Based upon research done by Aguilar Ros (2008) and Bonales' statement in 1979, that Tamatsi sends scorpions to punish transgressions (Fikes 2011, 27), Apaxuki is clearly a synonym for Tamatsi.

Jesús' son Vicente added that this type of "baptism" is done without any priest. The child's grandparents themselves consecrate the child to the "saint" associated with an icon in the Tenzompa church. To appease outsiders (non-Huichols) this particular saint camouflages Kieri for traditional Huichol, who know this "saint" is Tamatsi, first manifested in Kieri, just as Jesús González' proclaims in his myth of the first compassionate shaman.

As Vicente González revealed during our interview, Huichol from diverse communities throughout their homeland maintain their ancestors' devotion to Kieri. They make prayers and offerings to the spirit of Kieri while non-Huichol assume they are worshipping the saint. The fact that their veneration of Kieri has endured, probably hampering Catholic efforts to replace Huichol ritual practices akin to "baptism" with Christian baptism, is surely an indicator of Tamatsi's enduring importance in Huichol life.

When I (JF below) tape-recorded my interview with Vicente (VG) in Spanish, in October of 2004, he had become a practicing Protestant Christian. I translated our interview into English, and am presenting most of it here, for the first time:

JF: You told me there is a Catholic church in Tenzompa where a saint is venerated and some Huichol secretly venerate Kieri through the image of that saint. You have had some experiences there; can you please explain them?

VG: Yes, I had an experience. We can deduce that the saint in Tenzompa is a Huichol saint. According to our singers (shamans) … that saint is allied to Kieri.

JF: What is the name of that saint?

VG: Asunción (Ascension). They celebrate that saint's day in May, on the day of the Ascension (Catholics are obliged to attend mass on that day every year, to commemorate Jesus Christ's ascension to heaven). It (He) is the saint of the Ascension. I had never, even when I was a boy, gone there. (I became interested in going there) because my grandfather, Pedro, the father of my father, had become a singer (by going) there; as did some relatives of Lucas Carrillo. My grandfather, and José Carrillo and other persons hoping to become musicians had gone to Tenzompa because they wanted to learn how to play music. When they returned they were playing (musical) instruments. They became musicians because that saint, Kieri, gave them the gift.

They did a ritual in my house. I was going to carry the required offerings (from that ritual) to Tenzompa. My father had a rifle, which he still owns today in 2004. I took it with me to Tenzompa to have it "blessed," as they describe it. I took it into the church so that when I returned home I could perhaps kill a deer, or become an expert deer hunter so we could have deer (to offer) in our rituals. I was devout about complying with our customs. I was very pious at that time. So then I went and arrived there (at the Catholic church in Tenzompa). Later I regretted having brought the rifle to that church. For that reason, I did not finish what I had planned to do there.

We returned home in two days. I went to one side of the road, facing (west) toward the mountain, to see if I could find a squirrel or a small bird or something. I did indeed find a squirrel. The first two shots I fired missed it. On the third shot, some gunpowder was discharged from behind the bullet casing. Sparks entered my eyes.

In the afternoon when we arrived home, my eye had become badly swollen. My eye was burning, hurting unbearably. My father asked me, "What happened to you?" (Vicente answered) "I was firing a bullet. I was also thinking that I wanted you to heal me." (His father replied) "Do you know why you are injured? It is because you changed your mind about doing what you were supposed to do. This happened to you because you did not do it." I thought to myself, "What a fanatical saint! How is that possible?"

JF: But we should clarify this. Your father wanted to explain to you that, with only the thought of making a covenant with the Kieri, it knew that you were going to arrive: that you were planning to arrive?

VG: Yes. From the moment we were going to depart (to the church at Tenzompa) my father had already sung to inform the saints in advance that we were going to visit them. Because I failed to do that, I believe the saint became angry (and the shooting "accident" was the saint's punishment). So I returned home and then my father warned me. The ritual was (soon) done. I think we returned there two years later. After that, some 7 or 8 years later, the first bolt of lightning struck me at midnight, while I was asleep in my house. That bolt of lightning struck after passing through the roof. It entered my house and made a hole this big inside. But I believe God was with me then. That lightning turned back to depart by the other wall and it made another hole on the outside. Inside the house everything was covered by thick smoke. I put out the sparks with my blanket. The following year another bolt of lightning struck me and my mare.

I was riding that mare when, suddenly, it did not want to walk. It took refuge from the rain under an oak tree. There was about one meter between the oak and the mare's head. I saw something that looked red arrive and strike that oak tree. I lost consciousness for a bit because of the buzzing noise. When I saw again for a moment, in between opening and closing my eyes, I was falling down with the mare. It was a fierce storm. The mare fell, and so did I. After the mare had fallen to the ground, I dismounted. I left her there with her legs pointing upwards. I did not change her position. I just left her with her legs pointed upwards. I was feeling like something or someone was following me. I tore out of there in terror.

JF: But was the mare dead?

VG: Just about dead. There were some small cliffs nearby, one of which had a little cave. I got inside it and kept looking back there to see if there was somebody following me. Maybe I was confused (paranoid) because of the panic from the explosion. Soon enough, some 10 or 15 minutes later, the rain stopped completely. Then I dashed back to get to the mare. She was still knocked down, with her feet pointing upwards because she was unable to get up. Then I grabbed hold of her feet, turned them underneath her and stood her up. She got up but one of her eyes had turned totally white because it was so badly burned. Upon arriving at my house in the afternoon I poured salt on her eye and she got a little bit better. But after that she did not regain her health. I sold her.

Then I set out to be healed by another shaman. That shaman (discovered and) revealed to me: "There are unresolved issues that go back many years (said the shaman to Vicente). You were going to do this, and that, and the other thing, but you never completed any of it."

JF: So the shaman discerned all that without your even telling him anything about it?

VG: Yes, he found out by means of Irumari (his helping spirit). Then he affirmed to me that: "This is the way it occurred. Everything was this way and that way. From the moment you were injured by the bullet, you should have done this. But you never did." (VG replied:) "No, I never did." (The shaman continued:) "When the first bolt of lightning hit you (I confirmed to the shaman that it had struck me), from that moment you should have taken a candle and a votive gourd bowl with images composed of yarn attached inside it. But you did not take those (as an offering to the saint)?" (VG answered) "No, I never did take those." (The shaman said,) "But now, if you no longer wish to follow through with this pact, nor have any further contact with the saint, you must make your prayer over there. That is what the saint wants, that you make your prayer inside the church. Are you going to continue? Whatever you think, you must make it clear, confess it and ask to be forgiven."

He said that a candle and some animal crackers would be enough. "If you do not want to make votive gourd bowls with yarn drawings inside, then buy candles and animal crackers, or something like that, and give him an offering of money." (VG replied:) "Yes, I will do that."

During that year I was driving a pick-up truck, making trips to Huejuquilla to supply my father's store. I was fearful as I drove (passing by Tenzompa, en route to Huejuquilla). Feeling apprehensive, I spoke to the saint: "This is the last visit that I am going to make to you. From this moment on, I won't be visiting on behalf of either my family or myself." 5,000 pesos from those days (circa 1987) is worth 500 pesos today (about 50 U.S. in 2004). I went there (to the church) carrying a handful of animal crackers, a candle and a lighted veladora (large candle enclosed in glass Catholics often use when praying in church). This is what I told the saint: "Here you go. Take them and these 2,500 pesos that I am depositing now. I will make an offering totaling 5,000 pesos. Of those 5,000 pesos, I am leaving 2,500 pesos right now. Next time I return here, you will have the other 2,500 pesos."

I left, moving backwards, walking backwards until I arrived at the door. Then I turned around. It must have been 15 or 20 days, almost a month before I went back there (to the church). I did not take any candles. I did not take anything. I did not say anything nor even think anything when I addressed the saint: "Here is what I mentioned, the debt I promised to repay. Farewell." From that moment when I stopped there until today it has been at least 15 or 16 years.

JF: and you have not suffered any other attack either?

VG: Not one attack, nothing more.

JF: It was a total, in today's money, of 500 pesos. That was a payment so you could get out of trouble, make atonement.

VG: Of course I don't know if the saint spent that money, but it does not matter. Because if a person is thinking about keeping a promise and then later changes his/her mind after the covenant has been made, the gods already know about it; because they do not sleep and for them there are no nights or days. They are always the same, just as God is constant with each person. The gods are like that. When someone does not fulfill one's obligations that is the cause (for one's being punished). Punishment is sent because of what one did not do. We can call it a sin of omission, for the gods it is a transgression.

JF: Do you think there are many, or merely a few Huichols, who visit the saint inside that church in Tenzompa?

VG: Yes, there are many Huichols from here, Tuxpan, and from San Sebastián and from Santa Catarina. I state this based on the fact that from here (Tuxpan) they are renting trucks and going in groups with between 15 and 20, or (at least) 10 persons during the dry season. They travel there only when they complete the ritual of the bull, and the dance of the neckerchief (bandana). The only restriction (on making pilgrimages) is that they must not go there during the rainy season. They do it from January or February to May. There are always pilgrims going there (during that dry season).

JF: Do you believe that those priests truly comprehend why so many Huichols go there?

VG: I think the priests do not know why those Huichols go there. They only see them there, they see them enter the church and leave some money and … that pleases them and makes them feel glad that their saint is being visited, being adored. They feel good only because they presume the Huichol are very devout Catholics. But I affirm that those Huichols are going there as traditionalists, unconnected to Catholicism.

JF: How is it possible that they are hiding their ancestral god underneath the image of a Catholic saint? How do you explain it?

VG: Look here, they hide their god underneath the Catholic saint because this saint was surely theirs. But after the Mexican Revolution started (in 1910), according to the studies, they left the saint there and did not pick him up. After that the mestizos (non-Huichols) who were living in the areas around Tenzompa arrived there. They took possession of the saint. Those mestizos were humble, but now they are arrogant.
They (Huichols) go to the saint at Tenzompa for a purpose. That is why they connect him with Irumari (as a shaman's tutelary spirit) or with an adult Kieri. That is why I declared that they go there totally unconstrained by Catholicism, because they do it as followers of their ancestral tradition.

JF: They do it primarily to obtain good results in deer hunting, or to gain the power to play the violin or guitar very well.

VG: Yes, they do it for everything. The intention of each person differs. What they obtain surely depends on their faith, on the objective for which they go there (to the saint in the church)

... I think that these are the principal reasons they go: some to obtain money, others to learn how to ride horses, others in order to rope, some in order to tame wild horses and mules, others to be protected from witchcraft, and some to have success cultivating marijuana. They go (to that saint) and promise that if they get good results they will deposit some money. Anyway they go for anything (they desire) because that saint takes very decisive action for anything (requested). That is why they go, for whatever they want. He refuses nobody who makes an effort."

These prayers, offerings and "baptisms" ostensibly invoking protection and blessings from that "saint" at the church in Tenzompa have long concealed their abiding adoration of Kieri, an incarnation of Tamatsi presumably worshiped by Huichol inhabiting the area surrounding Tenzompa for countless centuries before missionaries arrived.

Prayers to Tamatsi, the Deer Shaman, Persist

All available evidence suggests that veneration of Kieri, disguised as a Catholic saint in the church at Tenzompa, has nothing to do with Catholic doctrine. Huichols from diverse communities visit that "saint" in Tenzompa to pray for anything they desire. Modern motives for going there, including the solicitation of success in marijuana cultivation, coexist with ancient aboriginal objectives including deer hunting and protection from witchcraft. This range of diverse goals must not be mistaken for proof of syncretism. The spirit of Kieri invoked in the church is identified with Tamatsi, the Deer Shaman who communicates with all the Ancestor Deities.

As González stated, the "*uxa* one obtains from Kieri enables one to see, hear and understand all the gods because *uxa* is from them." This is a corollary of his conviction that the gods endowed Tamatsi with special abilities inherent in the pollinated Kieri flower (i.e., the original *uxa*). Huichol trust that Tamatsi intervenes with whatever deities are relevant to fulfilling their specific desires, provided they deliver appropriate offerings and prayers to him, even while inside the church at Tenzompa. He functions as a general purpose deity, a mediator between Huichols and their pantheon. González' ancient understanding of Kieri is endorsed by his son, who declared that Huichol request anything they want from that Kieri, "because that saint takes very decisive action for anything (requested). That is why they go, for whatever they want. He refuses nobody who makes an effort."

An indicator of Tamatsi's enduring value is evident in what Jesús González proclaimed about taking his grandchildren and great grandchildren to that "saint" to "baptize" them, without a priest's intervention. All available evidence suggests this is an ancient Huichol practice, presumably one which complements the custom of bestowing a child's name in the presence of the goddess residing at a perennial spring near Te'akata after a child's first haircut (Fikes 2011, 119). Today's consecration of children to Kieri, cloaked by the icon at the Tenzompa church, demonstrates continuity with the tradition existing circa 1880, when the parents of José Sánchez, the Santa Catarina *kawiteru*, consecrated him to a Kieri while requesting aid to make him a shaman (Fikes 1985, 9; 2011, 45).[3]

The continuing adoration of Tamatsi is discernible whenever Huichol implore him for protection against witchcraft, even when mestizos see them praying to a Catholic saint.

Seeking Tamatsi's protection from witchcraft is also evident among San Andrés Cohamiata's temple officers. They are tasked with delivering offerings, praying, and confessing their sins to the Kieri revered at an important pan-Huichol shrine perched on top of a mountain located some 100 kilometers northwest of San Andrés (Collings 2000, 19-21; Benítez 1968a, 282). During his five years of service as a Huichol temple officer at San Andrés, Peter Collings accompanied those temple officers responsible for completing annual pilgrimages to "Utu,Tau,Wita."

Collings witnessed his fellow temple officers imploring a 2.5-meter tall Kieri growing through the roof, but mostly inside, their god-house to protect them from witchcraft, as well as asking for, "permission to hunt the deer before every major ceremony" (2000, 19). Collings' photograph of one officer who revered that Kieri shows him tying knots on a string. Collings explained (2000, 19) that each of an officer's sexual misdeeds, represented by one knot, must be publicly confessed there, in the presence of Tamatsi (Kieri), before making any requests, such as for protection from witchcraft.

Reading Collings' report reminded me that I made similar confessions, casting a paper on which I wrote the names of all my lovers other than my wife into the fire while praying to Tamatsi during my all-night vigil at a Kieri in 1986 (see Chapter 1). Such public confessions of sexual misdeeds, represented by knots, are also routinely made by Huichol peyote pilgrims. Huichols clearly seek purification from "sin" before approaching Tamatsi, whose spirit is manifested in both Kieri and peyote.

Collings' hint of a strong bond between Kieri and deer hunting is substantiated by Vicente, who wanted to have his rifle "blessed" by the Kieri spirit, which was invoked in Tenzompa's church, to aid him in hunting deer more effectively. The unity between Kieri pollen, deer, and the first Deer Shaman was fully explained by Jesús González in his narrative of Tamatsi's divine birth and life (in chapter 4).

We may note in passing that Ututawita, the church at Tenzompa, and the site associated with "White Antler" (which Juan Negrín photographed) are hallowed by offerings made to the spirit of Kieri by traditional Chapalagana Huichol associated with diverse temple officer groups.

Conclusion

The policy I called "directed syncretism" is illustrated when Huichol equate *uxa*, seen as yellow pigment obtained from an aquatic plant that only grows in the peyote country, with two presumably more ancient concepts of *uxa* (one associated with naming children for their protection, and another based on acquiring shamanic power by making pacts with divine spirits). In a future publication I discuss in detail the form and purpose of such syncretism, exemplified by Huichol making references to identical place names they use for distinct waterholes, for example one in the middle of Chapalagana Huichol territory, and another (with the same name) located some 350 kilometers away in the peyote country. Combining that analysis with a scrutiny of anomalies evident when comparing diverse myths concerning Kieri, peyote, Deer Person, Buzzard Person and other "mythic" characters will strengthen the interpretation of Huichol ethnohistory presented in this book.

To conclude this chapter it seems sufficient to contrast such pre-Christian syncretism with the clandestine worship of Kieri we observe when Huichols visit the Catholic church at Tenzompa.

Once Spaniards entered the land that is today Mexico, they confronted "pagan" practices such as human sacrifice and cannibalism. Sacred items, especially "idols" involved in native Mexican religious practices and rituals, were condemned as absolutely evil. Thus, when Catholics noticed shrines where Huichol and Cora worshipped their mummified (high status) ancestors, they burned such corpses, as well as the shrines and temples in which they were being revered (Fikes 2011, 223-24). The first Huichol mummified ancestor that the Spanish missionaries saw was being venerated in a shrine hidden in the mountains near Tenzompa. That elegantly dressed mummy, along with his lavish votive offerings and shrine, were burned in 1650 (Hers 1982, 37).[4]

Similarly, the Spaniards who conquered the Cora removed the bones of their mummified chief, Francisco Nayarit, from his shrine on a hill called Tsakaimuta, above the Mesa de Nayar (see Endnote 3 in Chapter 5). After burning the temple that housed the former Cora chief, as well as other nearby temples, they transported Nayarit's bones to Mexico City in 1723, so his remains, as well as the "idol" of the Sun adored by Coras, could be burned in front of a large crowd (Ortega 1754, 166-171).

Reading descriptions of numerous other Mexican Indian

examples of concealing native "idols" inside Catholic churches, caves or lakes (Brenner 2002, 127-157) convinced me that this ingenious strategy was exactly what was needed to preserve paramount idols and worship of Ancestor Deities. That is because colonizers used the Spanish Inquisition to encourage persecution of native religious practitioners—shamans and priests—and destroy any paraphernalia vital to perpetuating native Mexican religions. The fierce suppression of "pagan" practices carried out by Spanish colonizers meant that secrecy was essential if the veneration of "idols" and ancestors was to continue. The history of Huichol subterfuge, i.e., hiding their traditional veneration of Kieri while appearing to venerate a saint, should not be mistaken for syncretism. As Vicente stated, Huichols visiting the church at Tenzompa, "go there totally unconstrained by Catholicism, because they do it as followers of their ancestral tradition."

Because Vicente became a Protestant Christian sometime after his uncanny encounters with lightning, provoked by his disrespect for the "saint," his generalization does not apply to every Huichol making prayers and offerings to that Catholic saint. Liffman's emails of 9-26-2020 made me realize that some Huichols, especially those affiliated with the *tukipa* group in San José— within the Huichol community of San Andrés Cohamiata—fuse the Catholic saint, "Santo Domingo Apaxuki" (Aguilar Ros 2008), more fully with Tamatsi Paritsika than did Vicente and his father. Aguilar Ros (2008, 105-06) provides some additional information about the return of Apaxuki to Nueva Colonia while focusing on Apaxuki's status in San José.

In 2009 I asked my translator, Pancho Torres, for his opinion about the Kieri that Huichols venerated at the Catholic church in Tenzompa. Here is my paraphrased summation of the most pertinent comments Torres made in Spanish on September 26, 2009 while I tape-recorded him. What González says about Kieri being revered as if it were a saint in the Catholic church in Tenzompa is true. In the past, that church was being visited by many Huichols, but the non-Huichol inhabitants of Tenzompa were frightened because the saint did not want to stay put inside that church. They stated that because the saint was disappearing and suddenly reappearing, their priest decided to hand over that saint to the Huichols inhabiting Nueva Colonia (located some 32 kilometers north of Santa Catarina). Huichols from Nueva Colonia call that saint Xatulumí or Ximuáname. He is linked to Our Sun Father, incarnate in Kieri, and is identified with *tukimari* (Kieri pollen).

Huichol believe that the Kieri ("saint") is miraculous. Thus they ask him for favors such as learning how to read and write, having children, becoming a shaman and being successful in deer hunting. But that Kieri is dangerous, even lethal, to anybody who fails to fulfill vows required by those seeking to become shamans.

I infer that Huichols took possession of the icon of Xatulumí or Ximuáname sometime between 1987 and 1997, based on statements from Vicente González and Pancho Torres. Torres told me that the saint was returned to Huichols because, 'it was theirs.' He explained that because "their" saint did not want to remain inside the church at Tenzompa, it was unexpectedly disappearing, but after two or three days passed, it would always return. Because I have not yet seen it, nor asked the Huichol of Nueva Colonia about it, I must leave it to others to substantiate this update. This information that was provided by Torres in 2009 is consistent with the 2004 report Vicente gave me.

CHAPTER 7

POVERTY, MARIJUANA AND MURDER IN TUXPAN

This chapter illustrates the hazards of marijuana cultivation in Tuxpan, including political corruption and murders of rival marijuana growers. After examining circumstances surrounding the murders of two prominent Tuxpan de Bolaños marijuana growers, I conclude that one of those victims, the son of Jesús González, was definitely murdered by rival growers. The other may have been killed for the same reason, or ostensibly because his killer lacked money to pay his cattle grazing fees. Both issues, marijuana cultivation and the renting of Huichol communal land to mestizo cattle barons, are integrally connected to the poverty afflicting most Huichols. Persistent poverty, mestizos grazing their cattle on Huichol land, marijuana cultivation, murders, mestizo land invasions, and Huichol resistance to such incursions are interrelated topics discussed in this chapter. I hope that writing this will inspire some readers to question the tendency to scapegoat Huichol marijuana growers as "evil drug traffickers"—a meme of our American war on drugs. Overcoming this bias requires an acknowledgment that Huichol marijuana cultivation is usually a reaction to chronic poverty, and a recognition that, for more than fifty years, America has provided most of the demand that has driven illicit marijuana growing in Mexico.

Before proceeding further, I must explain the primary sources of Huichol poverty, which include the crucial environmental limitations that have impacted all Chapalagana Huichol for centuries. The brief summary of those restrictions I offer below is rooted in the research of Mexican anthropologist, Alfonso Fabila (1959, 20-27). The rudimentary type of slash and burn horticulture that Huichol have practiced, often on hills with steep slopes, is entirely dependent upon an amount of annual rainfall, averaging 800 milliliters (80 centimeters) annually, which is barely sufficient for maize to grow well. Their traditional homeland contains only about three percent of cultivatable land, and that land's soil layer is thin (30 centimeters on average). As a consequence of such severe constraints, the Huichol would regularly clear underbrush before planting and burn it in order to increase soil fertility for maize cultivation. New land for growing crops was cleared regularly, after using a plot from one to three years.

Although Huichol food production has for centuries been centered on maize, small quantities of squash, beans and amaranth were also grown. Dogs and turkeys, the only domesticated animals Huichol had before the Spaniards arrived, supplied little protein. Dogs were not eaten, and turkeys were consumed rarely. Animal protein came primarily from white-tailed deer, cottontail rabbits, and fish. The consumption of these animals was regulated by the relatively simple hunting and fishing technologies available to the Huichol, and their performance of rituals (Fikes 1985). The rest of the Huichol diet consisted of a variety of wild plants, including maguey, prickly pear cactus and mesquite (Fikes 1985, 13-14).

I know of no valid assessment of the adequacy of the Huichol diet prior to Spanish colonization. However, it seems safe to state that food surpluses were extremely rare given their rudimentary technology and the severe environmental constraints on maize production discussed above.[1]

Using population estimates provided by Fabila, Weigand, and the Mexican government, I concluded that the overall population density in 1966 for the Chapalagana Huichol was between one and two persons per square kilometer (Fikes 1985, 64). Since that time Huichol life has changed drastically as a result of interventions directed by I.N.I. (Instituto Nacional Indigenista) the federal agency responsible for the welfare of Mexico's native people, partially comparable to the American B.I.A., (Bureau of Indian Affairs). The trend has been toward increased population growth, supported mainly by modern medical interventions.

Economic development within the Chapalagana homeland has lagged far behind their population growth. Thus, many Huichol are leaving their homeland to settle in Mexican towns and cities.

Because few Huichol enjoy the luxury of cattle wealth, poverty impacting those living inside and outside their homeland remains an unresolved problem. According to Dr. Paul Liffman (2011, 67): "In the 1990s, the (Mexican) government estimated that 61 percent of Huichols were malnourished, the mortality rate (1,100/100,000) was double the general rate for (the state of) Jalisco, and infant mortality was forty times higher than in developed countries."

It is within this context that marijuana cultivation has, for at least the past thirty five years, been chosen by certain Huichols. They know it is lucrative, and that marijuana can be produced by investing far less money than is needed for buying and raising cattle. Of course, growing marijuana has unleashed a plague of political corruption and homicides inside Chapalagana Huichol territory and throughout Mexico. These problems are central in this chapter and the next, which focuses on the murder of an American journalist, Phil True.

I began hearing rumors about marijuana being grown around Tuxpan de Bolaños in the early 1980s, during my fieldwork in Santa Catarina. In 1996 I began visiting Tuxpan annually, and did so through 2005. During my visits there, I developed a close relationship with Vicente, the son of Jesús González.[2]

Vicente explained details about the murder of his elder brother, Lauro, to me in Spanish on October 2, 2004. A large portion of our taped interview follows, translated by me and altered only with the use of pseudonyms (except for Vicente González), and by my adding of words (in parenthesis) in order to clarify Vicente's meaning.

JF: Who, when, where and for what reason did they kill your brother, Lauro?

VG: They killed my brother Lauro here in the community of Tuxpan. The murderer was a man that my brother had brought back here from Tepic, Nayarit. When they met in Tepic they were friends. After arriving here he eliminated my brother. I had no personal knowledge of the problems my brother was having but I found out who killed him. He was murdered with the pistol that he had purchased himself. I was at my village when it happened, when they told me: "You must go to Tuxpan because your brother has been shot." When I asked if he was alive or dead, somebody said that he was dead. That is what happened.

My brother was born in 1953. He was a leader who had been guiding his people. He began leaving our town (Tuxpan) at about the age of 13, I think. He started to work here in Tuxpan when we were living in our rancho (extended family compound). He began working in the first construction project for the health center that is located in this community. The salary at that time was 15 pesos per week. That is how he began. When that work was finished, the construction of the landing strip (an unpaved runway for small airplanes) for our community began. He worked on that and later on making the road that was built without heavy machinery, connecting Tuxpan de Bolaños with Puente de Camotlán (the nearest Mexican town). After that, in 1971, a project to survey the boundary of the Huichol community commenced. My brother traveled with those engineers that came from Mexico City, from the time they began until they finished. He became familiar with many places and the amount of hectares contained in each region; for both Tuxpan and San Sebastián. That was why he was quick to respond the moment they started a political conflict. He immediately began doing something on behalf of his community. He thought about organizing the community, to achieve power and try to defend our community. Right after that, he was appointed as *Consejo de Vigilancia* (Chief of Security, in charge of armed Huichol tasked with the protection) of the community of San Sebastián. Ever since, Tuxpan and San Sebastián have been entangled in political disagreements.[3] When we, all the residents of Tuxpan, were going to elect my brother as President of Communal Goods (President of all communal land and assets owned by the Huichol community at large), the people of San Sebastián appointed somebody else for that position. For that reason they selected my brother as *Consejo de Vigilancia* (Chief of Security). That was when the community of Tuxpan got disgusted with San Sebastián. Until today there have been no agreements to work together to make progress.

JF: So it has already been 30 years?

VG: That is what happened. After he left his position as *Consejo de Vigilancia* he took over as administrator for Tuxpan, here in the municipio (a political jurisdiction similar to a county) of Bolaños. He served in that position for three years. After that he worked nine or ten years as an employee for the I.N.I. (Instituto Nacional Indigenista) in the agricultural and livestock sector.

JF: So that is why he was in Tepic?

VG: That is right. He was constantly going there. Immediately after that he became Tatuwani, Governor of Tuxpan. After serving as Governor, he was a political leader of our community, in the same manner as Pedro Morales. Pedro, and my brother Lauro were the two persons leading this community for some 10 to 15 years. That was when things changed and we were worse off then than we are today. There were no agreements. Nobody was willing to accept anything. Nobody was willing to make even small changes. My brother was different, when he governed he told the elders: "It was all right that the older people governed according to their ways and means, but we younger people are going to govern now; so give us an opportunity to see what we can accomplish." He was changing things. He organized the first rodeo, which made a lot of money. There was a big band and many *"coleadores"* (men on horseback who pursue bulls, grabbing them by the tails in order to make them fall to the ground) and many good bulls. It was the only year in which we earned some 70,000 pesos (almost six thousand dollars). The amount remaining when he ceased being governor was probably 14,000 pesos (about 1,167 U.S. dollars), which he turned over to the incoming governor. The new Governor could not administer properly, and the money disappeared. Up until now we have been unable to recover even a penny.

JF: For what reason did your brother bring that man from Tepic to Tuxpan? Was he Huichol?

VG: Yes, he was Huichol. Well maybe it is not a good idea to mention it but we can mention it at last because everything has already occurred.

JF: To what Huichol community did he belong?

VG: The man who came here with my brother is from the community of Popotita, from the (place called) Cerro Gordo ("Fat Hill") of the family of Vicente Fernández, who has relatives in Tepic. After my brother had completed all his political work, well he started, as do all politicians, to have contacts with the drug traffickers (*narcotraficantes*).

JF: During that time there was no other way to earn a living?

VG: There was absolutely nothing else. Ever since then, the boss in that business has been Filiberto Sosa. He and my brother began having conflicts. They had a dispute and because Filiberto Sosa has always been proud of himself, proclaiming that he is a shaman, he began trying to use witchcraft against my brother, to harm him by means of the psychic or mystical power of his knowledge. After that my brother was sent to be healed. They (our shamans) told him that somebody had very evil thoughts (intentions) about him. He had conflicts because during the time, when my brother was Governor, Filiberto Sosa was the judge. Later, Filiberto managed to become Governor. That was when he started making trouble for my brother. He (Filiberto) wanted to govern the way he liked to govern. By then he was already a member of the gang of drug traffickers. When he became governor he started using the government; soldiers and *policias preventivas* (police with firearms who deter crimes by standing guard or providing security) against his opponents. Once he became governor that is what he was doing to my brother, to Pedro Morales, and to others.

JF: He wanted to eliminate his competition?

VG: To eliminate his competition in order to gain more money, using his position of being governor. So among them (competitors of Filiberto) the most famous was Felipe Sosa. He was starting to get involved with my brother. Felipe and my brother reached agreement about slaying Filiberto Sosa. They were looking for a hit man, somebody willing to kill. That is why my brother went to Tepic. He looked for and found somebody. He found Juan Ramírez and explained to him what he wanted done.

My brother searched for Juan and brought him here (to Tuxpan) with the objective of killing Filiberto Sosa, because Filiberto was using the law against him.

JF: But what eventually made Juan change, who changed him so that he betrayed your brother?

VG: Juan did not change. It was just that they had to wait until Juan had become familiar with people. He would have to remain here until the deed could be done at the right time. But Filiberto Sosa found out, because rumors always flourish. They told Filiberto: "Did you know that there are two persons that want to murder you?" Upon hearing that, and seeing a stranger arrive in Tuxpan, Filiberto surmised that was the reason the stranger was here. According to information I received, Filiberto Sosa declared: "What have I achieved with my witchcraft? I have not found the solution. Instead of them killing me, it is they who must be killed." So then he, using his shamanic powers, met them face-to-face. It was inevitable that a fight would erupt between them.

They began drinking, as it was their custom to drink together and have discussions. Because witchcraft or spiritualism works gradually to make things get worse, it continued until what he said would happen did occur. "Instead of them killing me, it is they who must be killed." He had already planned the evil he was going to unleash on them.

JF: Did Juan accept a payment from (Filiberto) Sosa?

VG: No, he never accepted a payment from him. It was only by means of the witchcraft (spells) that he was able to get Juan to do it without anybody realizing it.

JF: Was Juan bewitched or drunk or what?

VG: Both he and my brother were bewitched; submerged, lost, blinded by their vices. Somebody who is bewitched does not know it.

JF: Is that why they became angry, or what was it that took place between your brother and Juan?

VG: They did become angry and then Juan killed my brother with the pistol.

JF: But are you certain that the primary cause was witchcraft?

VG: There were two reasons: first because of the politics, because Filiberto started unleashing the law, the government, on them; firstly because of the drug traffickers and then because of the witchcraft. Filiberto Sosa was dressing himself up as a colonel and as a preventive policeman and was going wherever there were marijuana plants. He was aware of what weapons each person possessed because people would inform him that so-and-so has a certain type of firearm. Then the government intervened because he was controlling everyone.

JF: What year was that, about 1985?

VG: Something like that. They killed my brother in 1987.

JF: Yes, I heard rumors that there were many marijuana plants around Tuxpan in those years. People were speaking about that, and for that reason I never wanted to come here.

VG: There is more. When Juan was brought here my brother (Lauro) had a sister-in-law who was raised here from the time she was a girl. When that girl grew up and became a woman she was given to Juan (Ramírez). So he and my brother were *concuños* (Juan became a relative to Lauro by marrying Lauro's sister-in-law). Of course by then Juan was already a murderer. He had killed two more in Tepic. He is free now, but he does not live here.

JF: Did he ever go to prison?

VG: He was in (prison in) Colotlán. From there they moved him to Guadalajara. After he finished serving his sentence for the murder of my brother in Jalisco, they transported him again to Nayarit for the other two homicides that he committed there. I think they released him on bail but I don't know for sure. That is how events transpired.

JF: How did the murder of your brother affect you? Is that when you began drinking a lot?

VG: I already had been drinking for some time before that. It did not affect me that much because we had always been living apart.

JF: He was much older than you?

VG: Yes, he is the oldest one in our family. There were four of us. Now only three of us remain. He helped us, for us he was a hero who fought for the rancho (extended family compound) where we lived. In the past a rich mestizo (mixed-blood, non-Indian) was living there. His name was Pedro Moreno and his children were Manuel, Silviano, and José.

JF: They were living in your rancho?

VG: Yes, there were living there.

JF: invading your lands?

VG: Yes, like others are doing today. But my brother organized some people in order to dislodge the mestizos living there. He went to the *Reforma Agraria*.[4] He went to the state (of Jalisco) government and those people agreed that the mestizos had to leave. They had to sign an agreement in order to get them evicted from the rancho. Nearly half of my uncles and some of my cousins never signed against Moreno because they believed they could not support themselves without him.

JF: Did they do that because of fear or because it was in their interest?

VG: Out of necessity and because of fear. They were working occasionally for Moreno for minimum wages. That is what happened. My brother had difficulties with our own uncles. They got disgusted because they were not in favor of the mestizo (Moreno) being forced to leave. After my brother died, now they are happy living there.

JF: So when your brother was governor he filed a lawsuit against the mestizo invader?

VG: No, he did it as a private citizen. He was only serving as *Consejo de Vigilancia*.

JF: He managed to force that mestizo to leave the community despite the fact that your uncles were not in agreement with him?

VG: He (Moreno) was able to leave because he obliged the Banrural (a Mexican commercial bank providing various types of loans) to buy his cattle. He raised those cattle (and more) on Huichol territory. Banrural bought from him about 840 cattle. After buying his cattle, Banrural gave them on credit (as a loan) to Huichols.

JF: So that is why all of you consider him a hero, because he learned how to accomplish something that was difficult to do given the fact that he had little support?

VG: Yes, that is why we believe that here in our community we can say that there are two heroes. For us they were the most important persons who were able to lead our community and do something to benefit our community. Of course they also benefited sometimes. But I think they gained less than they deserved because they did so much. Pedro Morales and my brother were companions. Pedro was also murdered because he and others wanted to evict (non-Huichol) people from lands (which they had invaded). Years later, during this administration of Vicente Fox, this problem is being resolved. It is about time that they provided enough resources to regain our land. One should remember that blood was spilled (in an effort to regain our land). Other people died too but they died due to accidents or because of drinking parties. They never accomplished anything. After all (that my brother and Pedro did), there is nobody who honors their memory (of them) for who they were. They were still young, but now they are rotting (as cadavers) because crimes were committed. That is how it is.

JF: What was your brother Lauro's full name?

VG: His complete name in Spanish is Lauro … (omitted intentionally).

JF: It is worth mentioning that at that time when your brother Lauro was working with the marijuana growers/dealers there were no jobs nor cattle that he could inherit or use to sustain himself, only the sale of marijuana.

VG: In those years there was no employment. Nor was the Mexican government paying any attention to us. There was no work here that would enable us to support ourselves. Most people were going to the coast of Nayarit; but only during the dry season, when it was not raining. People survived during the rainy season by eating roots and wild plants. To buy corn they were going all the way to Bolaños or even Villa Guerrero with their burros. That is why it came as something of a surprise when the men who knew how to cultivate marijuana arrived and began distributing the seeds. At that time those (mestizo) men were paying 700 pesos for a kilo of marijuana (about 58 U.S. dollars). That is how high the price for marijuana climbed here. That is why (some of our) people were motivated to grow it. But you should bear in mind that era is over. For example, cattle ranchers were employing people for a very low salary, but those workers were submissive because they had no other work. The rancher had cattle and needed workers but was paying them very little; sometimes only providing them with food, despite the fact that that was not enough (to provide for their families).

JF: It should be mentioned that that rancher was the mestizo that we just discussed.

VG: Yes he was a mestizo.

JF: And your brother did not have his own cattle?

VG: No, we did not have our own cattle.

JF: It is important to know the history of Lauro because he is one of the modern examples of a Huichol that realized how to defend his community.

Publishing this interview reflects my commitment to publish the truth, as my Huichol friends and mentors understand it, about unseemly aspects of contemporary life in Tuxpan. Vicente's account may be somewhat biased by the fact that Lauro was his elder brother. Probing his bias to ascertain the whole truth seems unnecessary, given that my primary intention is to make readers aware of the chronic poverty in which most inhabitants of Tuxpan live. For non-Huichols, the most noteworthy truth presented above is that the Huichol have a long history of living in oppression. Silver mining traumatized them, as well as their aboriginal neighbors to the east, the Tepecano, during the colonial Spanish era (Zingg 2004). Mestizo cattle barons have repeatedly invaded Huichol territory for almost a century. From 1910 to 1938 the Huichols of Tuxpan and its neighbor, San Sebastián, were devastated by waves of violent conflict (Zingg 2004). In response, Huichols have long been involved in struggles to defend their homeland, first against Spaniards, especially silver miners, and later, during the Mexican revolution (1910-1917) and the Cristero rebellion (1927-1938). Huichol have continued resisting encroachments into their territory by Mexican cattlemen, logging companies and in their sacred peyote country by foreign mining companies.

Anthropologist Paul Liffman, who first arrived in Tuxpan in January of 1981, has chronicled (2002, 2011) some of this turmoil, while concentrating on the recent efforts of Huichols to defend and reclaim their ancestral lands. His brief but vivid portrait of Pedro Morales complements the narrative about marijuana-related homicide provided above. Indeed, Pedro Morales is the other young leader in Tuxpan about whom Vicente spoke with admiration, while asserting that Morales was murdered because he wanted to evict non-Huichol invaders (i.e., cattlemen) from Huichol communal land. Liffman's doctoral dissertation (2002, 345-346) is my source for the following summary about Pedro Morales.

The Morales family is famous for its shamans, elderly ritual specialists (*kawiterutsixi*), and politicians. Through his powerful extended family network, Pedro Morales gained control over some 2,500 acres of land. This permitted him to produce a substantial amount of marijuana and amass, "hundreds of head of cattle, upwards of 16 wives," and to occupy high political offices. He was about to be installed as judge for the community of Tuxpan when Liffman arrived there. Liffman soon met this "brash, garrulous cacique" native leader, and was invited to accompany him on a horseback tour through much of the community of Tuxpan. After taking Liffman to visit several houses where Morales' wives and relatives resided, Pedro proposed that Liffman demonstrate his good will and prove his commitment to Morales by working to, "arrange a large-scale Huichol folkloric exhibition in Chicago to make him (Morales) about US $5,000." Liffman continues:

A few years later, as the (Mexican state of) Jalisco narco (drug dealers) boom under Rafael Caro Quintero fragmented following the killing of US-DEA agent Enrique Camarena Salazar, *Judiciales* (State Police) apprehended Pedro for his illicit agricultural brokerage activities (marijuana sales), savagely beat him in the Tuxpan village plaza for all to watch, and imprisoned him for a time in Guadalajara. In the early 1990s ... Morales was again powerful ... said to have over 60 children by his many wives.

Given the quantity of marijuana he controlled and his savage beating by State Police, Morales may be considered the first Huichol narco (drug dealer).

According to Liffman's source, Pedro Morales was murdered while making the rounds to collect overdue rent, and perhaps loan payments, from mestizos who were renting Huichol land to graze their cattle. One of those mestizo cattlemen, "asked Pedro to wait outside while he went inside for the money, (and) came out holding a .38 or .357 Magnum pistol, quickly announced 'Now I'll pay you back' ... shot him four times, and disappeared to El Norte (crossing into the USA) to avoid murder charges."

Since there was no trial of Pedro Morales' murderer, we have no conclusive evidence to determine a motive. It is tempting to deduce that the killer was merely what he seemed to be: a mestizo grazing cattle on Huichol communal lands. However, as Liffman noted (2002, 346) Morales also controlled, "a large amount of export-oriented marijuana production." Moreover, in the interview above, Vicente stated that Filiberto Sosa was a marijuana trafficker at the same time he was serving as Governor of Tuxpan de Bolaños. Vicente also claimed Sosa was using his contacts with the Mexican government to make trouble for Lauro, his elder brother, as well as for Pedro Morales. This circumstantial evidence suggests a possibility that the mestizo who shot Morales was a paid hit man.

Huichol Poverty, Mestizo Land Invasions and Cattle Grazing

During the past century, mestizo cattle barons such as Pedro Moreno have exploited Huichols and their communal lands. I will now present facts that may enable readers to properly appreciate the confrontation Vicente's brother, Lauro, had with Pedro Moreno. The 1950 Mexican census confirms the scarcity of arable land relative to grazing land within the Huichol homeland: a mere three percent was suitable for rainy season (non-irrigation) horticulture, while 44 percent was good for grazing (Fabila 1959, 26-27). This fact makes it easy to understand why Mexican cattlemen from several distinct areas including Tenzompa and Mezquitic, have, for decades, been invading Huichol territory and provoking violent clashes with Huichols. After the Cristero rebellion subsided, invasions of Huichol land continued throughout the 1940s and into the 1950s, either despite, or because of, the Mexican army's presence in the region (Rojas 1993, 177-181). Owning many cattle was clearly the best way to become wealthy, especially if one was a mestizo, during the four or more decades before the marijuana boom began.

Alfonso Fabila (1959, 50-58) estimated that 66 percent of all cattle owned by mestizos (non-Huichols) in the two municipios (counties) of Mezquitic and Bolaños were grazing on Huichol land. He calculated that at least 60 percent of all communal lands belonging to San Sebastián and Tuxpan de Bolaños were being invaded by non-Huichol cattlemen. Few of those cattlemen, most of whom were heavily armed, paid grazing fees to the Huichol. They got richer while the vast majority of Huichol remained poor. This wealth disparity was interrupted after mestizo cattlemen from Huajimic (among them several judicial police) came to illegally possess some 50,000 hectares: land which they had hoped to annex from the Huichol. In August of 1959, 152 Huichol armed with bows and arrows managed to expel those invading mestizos. This victory brought together for the first time, Huichol from San Sebastián and Tuxpan de Bolaños. Together they defeated their common enemy. Nevertheless, Huajimic soon gained 24,755 hectares, in 1961 (Rojas 1993, 179-192).

Another bittersweet victory was produced by the combined efforts of Huichols from San Sebastián and Tuxpan de Bolaños. In response to mestizo cattlemen from Puente de Camotlán being provisionally awarded 13,580 hectares of land in 1947, land effectively appropriated from San Sebastián and Tuxpan de Bolaños, those two Huichol communities united on September 15, 1948 to defend their homeland. They succeeded in court, after almost five years, thanks in large part to the efforts of Pedro de Haro and Guadalupe de la Cruz, who fought a land war against overwhelming odds (Benítez 1968a, Weigand 1969). On July 15, 1953 San Sebastián (and its annex, Tuxpan) won title to 240,447 hectares (Rojas 1993, 179-183; Fabila 1959, 29-30). Nevertheless, Puente de Camotlán managed to gain 5,020 hectares in the 1951 court settlement (Rojas 1993, 179).

Even when the Huichol have resisted invasions, achieving legal settlements with mestizos takes much time and money. Sadly mestizo cattlemen have gained land at Huichol expense several times, as illustrated by the chart Beatriz Rojas provided (1993, 179). Comprehending the obstacles the Huichol face should make it easier to value their efforts to defend their ancestral homeland. Nevertheless, some outsiders may find it difficult to honor the memory of Huichols such as Pedro Morales and Lauro, Vicente's brother. Clearly, some Huichol regard Pedro Morales and Lauro as their defenders and heroes.

Tuxpan continues to be a difficult place in which to live. Most Huichols must survive there with few or no cattle, and income from marijuana cultivation is considered too risky by most Huichol.

Mexico is infected with corruption. The government's complicity in the torture and murder of DEA agent Enrique Camarena is paradigmatic. One well-informed student of the Huichol gave me what I believed to be reliable information about certain Mexican government officials who encouraged marijuana cultivation in Huichol territory. As more Huichols told me about the harm to them caused by marijuana cultivation, I became convinced that it must become legal both in the U.S. and in Mexico. Some of my justification for advocating legalization of marijuana has been published:

> I am particularly bothered by the harm to Huichols that continues to result from the treatment of marijuana as an illegal substance. One the one hand the Mexican army has invaded Huichol territory, sprayed Huichol cornfields with dangerous herbicides like Paraquat (even where no marijuana had ever been grown) and hassled people who were not even involved in its cultivation. On the other hand, Huichol marijuana growers and their Mexican distributors are believed to have murdered rivals and those they fear might report their illegal activities. Huichols have warned me not to travel to certain areas. In 1986 my pilgrimage to a specific Kieri was considered somewhat dangerous because of its proximity to marijuana growers. (Fikes 2002, 91).

To be sure, since 2002 opium poppy cultivation has gradually eclipsed marijuana growing in many parts of Mexico.

The lack of sustainable economic development in Tuxpan and the Chapalagana Huichol homeland remains a chronic problem. Modern medicine has contributed to a rapid population increase in Tuxpan during the past four decades. Neither agricultural production nor cattle grazing have improved substantially enough to provide a decent living for the vast majority of Tuxpan Huichol. Factories or other sources of full-time employment had yet to come to Tuxpan in 2005, the last year I was there. Sales of their own art and crafts are helpful in augmenting income, but hardly sufficient to guarantee subsistence for the vast majority of Huichols. In search of a better life, many younger Huichols migrate, either seasonally to Mexican plantations or permanently, to Mexican cities. A few are involved with marijuana growing. Some Huichol are entering the U.S. to work illegally. "There is obviously an urgent need to develop practical economic alternatives to deter involvement in such illegal enterprises" (Fikes in Zingg 2004, 236).

Conclusion

The power differential between mestizo cattlemen and the Huichol, who rent their communal lands to them (as described above), may also apply to most mestizo buyers of marijuana produced on Huichol land by Huichol growers. Is a Huichol grower who delivers marijuana to a mestizo buyer equivalent to a *narcotraficante* (drug trafficker)? Using such a derogatory word may conceal their true (lower) standing. Drug smugglers are implicitly considered less than human. They are usually called *mulas* (mules) or *peones* (pawns in the game of chess). As Liffman explains, Juan Chivarra, one of Phil True's murderers (see the following chapter) may have been a, *"narcopeon"* working for mestizo *narcotraficantes*. "Such *narcopeones* tend the marijuana or opium patches of mestizo *patrones* (bosses) out of desperate poverty, simple greed or fear of refusing the request." These *peones* are relatively easily captured by Mexican authorities and then, "sentenced to long jail terms in regional penitentiaries"

(Liffman 2002, 401).

I hope reading this summary of murder, marijuana cultivation and poverty in Tuxpan serves as a warning written in large print: the superficial and romantic image of Huichol life that has been popularized since 1965, in part by writers like Furst, Myerhoff and (indirectly) Castaneda (Fikes 1993) may be hazardous to your health. The next chapter, focused on Phil True's murder during his solo trek thru Huichol territory, illustrates the danger of knowing little or nothing about the 'dark' side of Huichol life. My experience (Fikes 1999, 420) taught me that many tourists receive a warm welcome by Huichols living (or working to produce yarn paintings and other crafts) in Guadalajara, Tepic or Puerto Vallarta. But, as in the case of Phil True, hiking into isolated parts of the Chapalagana Huichol territory may be dangerous. Tourists should be aware of, and sensitive to, Huichol history, and know that their careless actions can be (mis)interpreted as a serious threat. Of course the danger is many times amplified should they stumble upon a field of marijuana or opium poppies.

CHAPTER 8

PHIL TRUE, THE INCOMPLETE TRUTH

I first heard the news that two Huichols had just been charged in Mexico with murdering an American journalist, Phil True, from another American journalist, Debbie Nathan, based in San Antonio, Texas. She called me two or three days after Christmas in 1998, asking for my opinion about their motive. I immediately explained that the most logical reason Huichols would have for killing an outsider would be fear of being apprehended for cultivating marijuana. Circumstantial evidence that this was indeed their motive will be offered later in this chapter. I then condensed the argument provided in my expose of Carlos Castaneda (Fikes 1993), telling her that, since the 1970s, Dr. Castaneda's books, as well as Castaneda-inspired tour guides, had stimulated more and more non-Indians to invade the Chapalagana Huichol homeland (and Real de Catorce) in search of peyote and shamans similar to Castaneda's fictional shaman, Don Juan Matus. I described reasons why Huichols had started reacting vehemently against such uninvited tourists—by fining, jailing and evicting them from their homeland. I noted that Huichol intolerance for unknown visitors had been increasing, especially in the past few years. Huichol resistance to such visitors may have played a part in the murder of True, a topic we will discuss below.

After reading her newspaper article (Nathan 1998), I felt slightly disappointed because she neglected to call attention to what I had declared to her about the dangers that discovering marijuana in remote areas of the Huichol homeland might create for outsiders. I was encouraged, however, because Nathan took seriously my criticism of Castaneda's negative impact on the Huichol. However, I felt that she rushed to judgment by blaming Castaneda for True's death without having produced any proof that True had ever read Castaneda's books. Fortunately for her, evidence I obtained in 2006, implies True was significantly influenced—not just by his devouring of Castaneda's first five books (four of which were still in his library in 2006)—but also by attending Dr. Carlos Castaneda's 1972 lectures at his alma mater, and mine, the University of California at Irvine. Castaneda's significant influence on True will be described in detail in this chapter as well.

What I learned about Phil True's life and murder persuaded me that both his life and death were exceptional enough to warrant our undivided attention. Before we examine details about his life and murder, I must point out that I have been mentored by four Huichol shamans (two of whom were *kawiterutsixi* [plural of *kawiteru*] at the ceremonial center of Santa Catarina). They, and the vast majority of Chapalagana Huichol, deserve our respect. As my esteemed colleague, Dr. Paul Liffman reminds us, True's murder marks the, "first time in over a century that a peaceful visitor to San Andrés has been killed" (Liffman 2002: 392).

My investigation of True and his tragic death benefitted greatly by my befriending the Huichol shaman, Jesús González, whose life is featured in this book. In 1999 when I visited him and his sons in Tuxpan de Bolaños, they all asked me about Phil True, someone all of them had known. They too suffered, because their child (or brother) was murdered by marijuana growers. Various people (including my anthropological mentor, Professor Phil C. Weigand) were discussing with me the question of why True was murdered, so I began following newspaper coverage of the case against his murderers (Fikes in Zingg 2004).

My college friend, Rich Heimlich, was employed for many years in the newspaper business. Rich helped me get in touch with Robert Rivard, the editor of the *San Antonio Express-News*, the same newspaper where True was employed as a reporter tasked with covering Mexican news. I first contacted Rivard in October of 2005, and I was soon digesting his book published the same year, *Trail of Feathers*.

I appreciate the care evident in almost all of the interviews and research completed by Rivard, as published in his book. I worked diligently to achieve an accurate characterization of Phil True, especially in those rare cases when my interpretations of True, as well as the Huichol, differed from those of Rivard. Because each of us excels in interpreting certain issues, I believe my report in this chapter supplements his book. I feel well qualified when it comes to explaining the impact of Castaneda's pseudo-ethnography on the Huichol (Fikes 1993, 2011b; Austin *et al* 2007), as well as on Phil True, and interpreting what prompts Huichol "hyper-sensitivity" about tourists carrying cameras and entering their homeland without permission. Both phenomena were especially prominent when True undertook his last hike in 1998.

Rivard excels in reporting the facts, and the probable consequences of True's troubled childhood, including nuances of his blue collar days in New York. Moreover, he examines several topics integral to Mexican criminal justice, such as questions regarding the two autopsies, the criminal investigation generally, and the trial and defense of True's murderers that ensued in the wake of True's murder.

Because the murder of Phil True in December of 1998 may be more fully comprehended by carefully reviewing implications stemming from particulars of his childhood, we will now turn our attention to biographical information surrounding True's first twenty years, mostly based on Rivard's book.

Growing Up Fast in Southern California

Phil True was born on June 18, 1948 in southern California. He was a descendant of German immigrants on both his father's and mother's side (Rivard 2005, 32). His paternal grandfather had established a chicken and vegetable farm in the San Fernando Valley, which is now a suburb of metropolitan Los Angeles. His father, Theodore, married his mother, Christeen, the daughter of German immigrants who resided in West Virginia. Christeen's marriage to Theodore brought her to the True's chicken farm in Pacoima, California, where she made a home for Phil and his sister, Bonnie. (Rivard 2005, 34)

Many details of True's childhood, including the sexual abuse he and his sister endured, are sensitively chronicled by Rivard (2005, 36-39). True's parents divorced in 1960, when he was eleven. A turning point in True's childhood came soon thereafter, when his mother had an affair with a married minister of the local non-denominational Christian church they were attending. Rivard reported that this minister was, "an alcoholic and a predator" who often arrived "drunk and belligerent" at 2 a.m., banging on the True's door. His mother would then order Phil to get up and go confront the delinquent preacher. True's sister declared that Phil, "told me later that having to get up at age twelve, dressed only in his underpants, to run off a drunk man in the dark made him grow up real fast." (Rivard 2005, 42).

Six months of such confrontations with Reverend Gunderson, followed by disdain directed at True and his family by members of that preacher's congregation, left an enduring impression on Phil. Scorn spilled over the True family because the preacher and his loyal wife blamed his affair with Phil's mother on her alone. Branding her an ally of Satan enabled fellow church-goers to ostracize them. It was not long before the True family left Gunderson's congregation (Rivard 2005, 43). Many of True's friends stated that he admitted to them, "I don't believe in God because I caught the minister with my mom" (Rivard 2005, 42). True remained a "self-declared agnostic," disillusioned with Christianity for the rest of his life, as Rivard implies (2005, 42, 73).

True's disillusionment explains why he refused to do what his Mexican in-laws presumably expected for their daughter; "to be married at a mass inside the cathedral," in Matamoros, Mexico. Instead, Phil True and Martha Patricia Perez González exchanged their marriage vows, "in the uninspiring confines of the cathedral office" on June 6, 1992 (Rivard 2005, 73). Phil was being true to himself by not getting married inside the cathedral while also honoring the memory of his "estranged father," who died on June 6, 1977 (Rivard 2005, 73).

Rivard's statement about True's "estranged father" should not prevent us from recognizing his father's attempts to take care of his son, Phil. After his parents' divorce, True's father took him on at least a few camping trips prior to the camping trip to Sequoia National Forest in central California. True's best friend accompanied Phil and his father on that particular camping trip. Prior to that trip, "Phil's problems vanished" whenever he and his best friend were together (Rivard 2005, 45). When those two teenage boys were with True's father, surrounded by huge sequoia trees, the three of them, "had a good time," which contributed to True's desire to continue camping, embraced by nature (Rivard 2005, 45). Several years later, True and Peter Harris, "his college friend and roommate" in 1969, "talked New Left politics, got high" and experimented together with psychedelic drugs, including taking LSD in the desert at Joshua Tree National Monument (Rivard 2005, 55). Harris hiked, hitchhiked, and camped several more times with True, presumably from 1969 thru the summer of 1971.

Without citing examples of True hiking alone during those years, Harris told Rivard, "the more True experienced solitude in nature," the more he evolved "into a wilderness sojourner" (Rivard 2005, 55). Rivard endorsed Harris's insufficiently substantiated impression of True, asserting that, "With each passing year since that first camping trip with his father into Sequoia, pursuing solitude had become a more and more important element in True's life" (2005, 60). Rivard was clearly incorrect when stating that the camping trip to Sequoia (which included Phil True, his father and True's best friend) was Phil True's "first camping trip." According to Phil's best friend, "it was my first camping trip but "it wasn't Phil's first trip." (Rivard 2005, 45).

Claiming True was increasingly dedicated to, "pursuing solitude in nature" is an unsubstantiated, if not false characterization of True, when one considers True's childhood and college years. In fact, considerable evidence provided by Rivard himself shows clearly that True wanted Harris as well as his girlfriends (Cathy Bell and

Bronwen Heuer), and later, his wife Martha, to accompany him on his hikes (2005, 56-58, 78). After marrying Martha in 1992, True intended to make her his hiking partner. Being a novice hiker, her first experience was so unpleasant that she told True, "Go by yourself from now on. I am staying at home." (Rivard 2005, 79). For the next three years, if True wanted to hike, he journeyed alone into Big Bend country in Texas, and the Tamaulipas desert (in Mexico). His wife's best friend, Juanita, declared that True told them that, "such journeys were where he found himself" (2005, 79). His wife's inability to hike with him marked either the start of True's commitment to being a, "wilderness sojourner," or an intensification of what had previously been True's infrequent solo hiking. Thus, Rivard's narrative about True's allegiance to hiking all by himself since his early teens seems slightly overblown, given my reading of evidence he presented in his book. Most of that evidence indicates that True enjoyed hiking (and hitchhiking) with others.

True's Travels, from Tumultuous 1968 to Tragedy in 1998
In the spring of 1968, when Phil transferred to the University of California at Irvine (UCI), after completing two years at a junior college near his childhood home, he was escaping, "his troubled childhood by doing something no one else in his family had ever done," by enrolling in a four year state university (Rivard 2005, 48). At UCI, True majored in the Comparative Culture program, let his hair grow long, smoked marijuana, and engaged in protests against the Vietnam War (2005, 52-54). One antiwar protest took him to a, "rally in Berkeley's Peace Park," a landmark event True described in his first newspaper story, published on May 29, 1969 in the *New University* (Rivard 2005, 53). True's first-hand report of brutal treatment he and more than five hundred other students received at the Santa Rita jail was quoted by Rivard (2005, 54).

Phil graduated from UCI in 1970. During the spring of 1972, True was painting houses while living with his girlfriend, Bronwen Heuer (Rivard 2005, 56-58). Both of them were also listening to lectures given by Carlos Castaneda at UCI.

Bronwen Huer (hereafter BH), who knew Phil True intimately for several years before his marriage to Martha (Rivard 2005, 31), provided me with essential information confirming True's familiarity with Castaneda (e-mail letters dated 1-23-06, 1-15-06, 1-04-06).

Carlos Castaneda taught two classes at UCI (representing his only college teaching experience) in the spring of 1972. Like True, I was then a Comparative Culture major at Irvine, having transferred there from the University of California at San Diego (Fikes 2011, 22, 220). Because I was working part-time during those hours when Castaneda's two classes were scheduled, I was unable to attend his lectures. My childhood friend, Steve Nielsen, kept me informed about Castaneda's lectures. Because Phil True graduated with a B.A. in Comparative Culture in June of 1970, he was not required to attend Castaneda's classes almost two years later. He was obviously interested enough in Castaneda that he and BH attended some of Castaneda's undergraduate lectures in spring 1972. According to BH, Castaneda's writing left an impression on Phil True, and everybody else around them at Irvine. BH recalled that,

> "We were impressed by the narrative of his (Castaneda's) experiences but felt that it had passed through two filters already. And maybe this was our arrogance: our experience in the world of psychedelics made us "riper" for getting to the essence of the peyote worlds. We wanted to have our own conversations with Don Juan (Castaneda's contrived shaman) and at times resented the cipher of Carlos Castaneda."

BH declared they were skeptical about Castaneda's supposed research in Mexico. They felt that most of Castaneda's "research" was about "getting high" with Don Juan Matus That impression is probably the most obvious message conveyed in Castaneda's first two books, published in 1968 and 1971 respectively. In our telephone conversation (1-15-2006), BH confirmed that Phil True read all of Carlos Castaneda's early books (a fact corroborated by Martha True) while they were living together near UCI. BH emphasized to me that True did not need to find a shaman or mentor like Don Juan. After all, they had found psychedelic mushrooms on their own. (After our conversation, BH sent me an e-mail which did not confirm what I thought she had said to me in our phone conversation; that they had eaten psychedelic mushrooms together. Her e-mail stated that she alone ingested those mushrooms in Colombia.)

BH and True met Rosemary Lee through the anthropology department at UCI. As BH told me, Rosemary Lee was Castaneda's, "graduate student and during the summer (1972) when Philip and I hitchhiked to Alaska she lived in our house. She told us 'Don't be surprised if I have a crow living here when you get back.' And sure enough she did." This is an allusion to Castaneda's claim that he was gradually transformed into a crow by Don Juan (Fikes 1996b, 141).

Their relationship with Rosemary deepened, in part because the dogs owned by Phil True and Rosemary Lee had bonded. BH acknowledged that Rosemary's pet crow was keen on antagonizing Alice, True's beloved dog. She then united True's fondness for Alice with Castaneda's acceptance by Don Juan, disclosing that one day True told her, "'You know some people have said that Alice is my familiar.' I mention this because I think it is a metaphor for the way we viewed the teachings of Castaneda." My guess about what True and BH meant is that they recognized a similarity between True's affinity with his dog Alice, and Castaneda's claim that, shortly after eating peyote, he cavorted with a black dog. Their playing together was taken as a good omen by Don Juan (Fikes 1993, 61-62, 106,107) who interpreted Castaneda's frolicking with that black dog as proof the peyote deity (whose familiar was that black dog) had selected Castaneda to receive the secret knowledge that he (Don Juan) had accumulated (Castaneda 1969, 36-42; Fikes 1993; 1996, 136). Without fully understanding True's intended meaning, I deduce that True connected Castaneda, peyote, and Alice (all of whom he liked), in a creative if not comic way.

There was, however, a limit to True's enthusiasm for Castaneda. According to BH, "Don Juan's teachings had some attraction but really, I remember Philip to be much more physical than metaphysical." Of the first five books Castaneda wrote, the only one missing from True's library was the third book, *Journey to Ixtlan*. If BH is correct that True had read all of Castaneda's early books, the fact that *Journey to Ixtlan* was "missing" from True's library years later, confirms BH's affirmation, that metaphysics was not his cup of tea. Because Castaneda's third book is the most metaphysical of the first five books in True's library, I suspect he discarded it. This "missing" third book was truly singular. Castaneda's doctoral dissertation was a "thinly disguised version of his third book" (Fikes 1993, 101; 1996b: 135) and it blatantly contradicted the basic premise of Castaneda's first two books.[1]

Castaneda's first two books were full of adventures associated with taking peyote, jimsonweed and psilocybin mushrooms. Physical feats were prominent in both books. In book one he turned into a crow, caroused with a black dog and discovered differences between places which felt scary and sickening versus comforting and powerful (Castaneda 1969, 19-26). Book two featured many uncanny activites such as Don Genaro's breathtaking climbing and jumping around a large waterfall (Castaneda 1972, 100-103), car headlights which startled Castaneda, interpreted by Don Juan as "lights of death" pursing them (1972, 48-49) and a bright light hovering above Castaneda's head while Don Juan and his companions (at a purported peyote ritual) stared at it with awe (Fikes 1996b, 139).

BH was certain that Phil True never set foot inside Mexico while they were living together near UCI. This was because True was proud of his long hair, tied in a ponytail, and was unwilling to cut it off in order to safely journey into the interior of Mexico (where "longhairs" were rumored to have been routinely harassed in those days). Apparently, Phil had even turned down, "a teaching job he applied for after he was told to go get a haircut."

(Rivard 2005, 58). Evidence reviewed so far (in addition to my own experiences at UCI during that era) suggests Kvinta's (1999, 64) generalization is accurate: "True was, after all, a child of the sixties who devoured Carlos Castaneda's books."

In September of 1973 True left Irvine, hitchhiking alone to New York, but returned to retrieve his belongings in Irvine (still with BH). He then moved to New York in 1974 (Rivard 2005, 58), where BH soon joined him. They lived together in New York until they broke up in 1977. In 1977 True, "organized a 10-month strike by bookstore workers" and then, "started a one-man wallpapering business" (Zarembo 1999, 14). True lived on Long Island and, "for the next fifteen years ... held a succession of blue collar jobs" and "smoked pot every day." (Rivard 2005, 59).

BH agreed with Rivard's conclusion, that True's first contact with the Huichol came in October of 1981, when he and his girlfriend, Annette Fuentes, traveled together by bike to Guadalajara (Rivard 2005, 62-64). From 1965 on, the Huichol became increasingly famous for their colorful yarn paintings and their peyote hunts (Fikes 1993, 1999 and see chapter 9). By 1981 Guadalajara was well known as the place to purchase them. According to BH, True returned alone to Guadalajara in 1984 to vacation, and to buy Huichol yarn paintings. True gave BH a small yarn painting which depicts two deer with a river running through the center. She still has it on her desk at work.

When I asked her what it was about the Huichol that first captured Phil's attention, BH identified, "peyote use among the Huichols as a possible 'hook' that made their art and culture appealing to Philip." I then asked BH if True had tried peyote. She replied that she could not remember if he was with her while she was preparing peyote, which she ate. "I can't remember exactly who was there. I do remember however, that it was a sickening experience for all there." (BH's email to me dated 1-23-2006).

True's blue collar life in New York ended in late 1989, when he accepted his first job as a journalist with a newspaper located in Brownsville, Texas, on the Mexican border (Rivard 2005, 24).

To do so True, "closed down his profitable wall-papering business to take a $7 an-hour job at the local newspaper" (Zarembo 1999, 14). True, then 41 years old, was "reinventing" himself, as Rivard put it, through total immersion in Mexican culture. What exactly catalyzed this 'reinvention,' Rivard does not explain.

Five years before becoming a journalist, True was becoming captivated by the Huichol, one of Mexico's most exotic indigenous cultures, and one which often attracted Americans curious about Castaneda's fictional peyote-using shaman, Don Juan Matus (Fikes 1999, 2011b).

What initially attracted Phil True to the Huichol? Based on what we now know about him, the "answer" probably has much to do with the following factors: a) True's disenchantment with orthodox Christianity, caused by the minister's affair with his mother; b) his distrust of the establishment, caused in part by his protests against the Vietnam War; and c) his first-hand experiences with marijuana and other psychedelics.

Remembering my own frame of mind in 1976, when I first arrived in Santa Catarina, my guess is that True viewed the Huichol as a romantic alternative to his own troubled society. Peyote and yarn paintings presumably played a big part in luring True to the Huichol, as BH and I see it.

True's Newspaper Story Proposal

Rivard was puzzled because True had not published anything about the Huichol, not one story, "about the Huichols or the two previous trips he had made" to Tuxpan de Bolaños, which Rivard conceals by calling it, "their stretch of the sierra" (2005, 181). Kvinta's observation (1999, 59), that True's previous, "journeys to the Huichol sierra were short personal junkets intended to gratify True's longstanding passions for indigenous cultures, noble struggles, and far-flung wilderness." rings true enough for me. The sole document suggesting what True knew about the Huichol, is a 520 word story proposal (Reprinted as Appendix E) that was written to persuade his newspaper editors to permit him to write a feature article, presumably to be based on observing and interviewing the Huichol of Tuxpan de Bolaños. This proposal reveals what he found most appealing about the Huichol, and we can infer from it that, for him, peyote is of considerable importance.

Thus, this document is singularly important for those seeking to understand what Kvinta recognized as True's "fascination" with the Huichol.[2] In his story proposal, True mentions in passing that Tuxpan de Bolaños was just being connected to the electric power grid in early 1998, a time when Huichols were using battery powered boom boxes and hand-cranked metal grinders for processing maize kernels into masa (cornmeal). True's proposal failed to mention their cattle, sheep, goats, pigs, chickens and .22 caliber rifles, because he was more focused on extolling their joyful, less technologically dependent lifestyle, as well as their propensity to, "welcome in strangers" (unlike the highland Maya he knew).

True's unrealistic generalization about Huichol hospitality could easily have been corrected had he consulted anthropologists like Phil Weigand, Paul Liffman, myself or any one of several Mexican researchers familiar with issues (e.g., marijuana cultivation) confronting those Huichol still living inside their Chapalagana River Valley homeland. We would have warned him that in areas where marijuana is growing he would be most unwelcome. But, alas, True stated that, "their life has been studied by anthropologists for decades" without citing even a single anthropologist.[3]

The most logical inference any Huichol specialist would make after reading True's proposal is that he was uninformed, though probably interested in learning more, about land invasions, poverty, marijuana cultivation, alcoholism, and the fact that many Huichol left their homes each spring to earn money doing seasonal labor on Mexican plantations. Although True knew that many Huichols, "leave to work or sell beaded masks" (Zarembo 1999, 13), the poverty prevalent in Chapalagana Huichol life in 1998 was not fully acknowledged by True. He was also evidently unaware of Huichol opposition to uninvited outsiders and confrontations between Huichol officials and outsiders, which had been escalating significantly for several years prior to his solo trek thru their territory in 1998, a topic discussed in the next chapter.

Phil True's story proposal points to peyote twice, first when he stated, "Peyote is an integral part of their worship of native gods." His statement is accurate, and totally consistent with what I've written (Fikes 1985, 1993) about how and why collecting and eating peyote—while abiding by all restrictions for performing rituals inherited from their ancestors—is the proverbial royal road, albeit not the only way, to become a Huichol shaman. However, True's story proposal does not adequately connect peyote pilgrimages and rituals with what he implied was his central focus: discerning ways in which Huichols cope with pressures to modernize—accepting certain elements (e.g., livestock, boom-boxes, metal corn grinders, electricity, pick-up trucks, etc.) while retaining much of their ceremonial life, such as peyote and deer hunting rituals, and maize ceremonialism. True also failed to clarify how his Huichol research would enable him to uncover why, and in what ways, peyote remains important to the Huichol, something he would need to learn in order to write intelligently about how peyote pilgrimages and rituals assist Huichol in becoming shamans, and in turn communicate with their ancestors, who constitute the foundation of their religious traditions. Perhaps True had not yet learned that, because peyote contains the spirit of Elder Brother Kauyumari, it is still revered as a teacher and entheogen, essential to aspiring shamans and to all shamans dedicated to maintaining Huichol religious traditions, despite the formidable pressures upon them to modernize (Fikes 1985, 1993, 2011).

True had first hand experience eating peyote at least once in Tuxpan de Bolaños (Rivard 2005, 28), and was clearly attracted enough to it that he wrote about peyote again at the end of his proposal. Inexplicably, his last reference to peyote was not connected with the Huichol. Instead it referred to a non-Huichol man whom True described as a, "decent PRI (Partido Revolucionario Institutional) politician," whom he met in Bolaños, the Mexican administrative center of the municipio (roughly equivalent to a county) in which the Huichol settlement of Tuxpan de Bolaños is located. "He also eats peyote buttons, of which he had three on a shelf behind his desk when I spoke with him."

It is unlikely that the President of Bolaños municipio would start discussing eating peyote with True, given its illegality for non-indigenous Mexicans. Thus I feel confident speculating that after Phil noticed those peyote buttons he then must have asked the municipal President something about them. What seems perplexing is why True bothered to mention this in his proposal, and why, after writing the sentence about the municipal President eating peyote, he added this final sentence: "There is a beautiful story within all of this. Interested?" Was this a hint that peyote enabled True to bond with him?

True's editor at the *San Antonio Express-News*, Robert Rivard, quotes both passages in which True's proposal cites peyote (2005, 4-8) but does not comment on their significance. It must be noted that Rivard did not know about this proposal until after True's murder (2005, 11). Although Rivard was not personally involved in passing judgment on Phil's proposal, he acknowledged that those who were, had rejected it. True responded to their rejection by sending, "a blunt, challenging e-mail to the managing editor and several others." (Rivard 2005, 11). When True's message failed to change their minds, he decided to take a vacation and hike through Huichol territory entirely unknown to him, without a guide or a permit.

True's history of political activism, having written numerous newspaper reports, including stories about, "Zapatista Mayan guerrillas in Chiapas and impoverished *maquiladora* workers along the Texas border" (Kvinta 1999, 64), was absent in his story proposal. All available evidence suggests that True lacked basic knowledge about the Huichols' political opposition to colonial-era silver mining, followed by their resisting, for much of the past 100 years, invasions by Mexican cattlemen and loggers. Nor did True acknowledge the violence and chaos the Mexican Revolution and Cristero rebellion had unleashed upon the Huichol. Thus it did not surprise me that True's editors rejected his proposal, rightly viewing it as, "unconventional, more of a travelogue suited for *National Geographic* ... disconnected from the biggest stories of the day in his region" (Rivard 2005, 10). Thus the "travelogue" tone in True's proposal was clearly an indicator of his desire to unite his long-standing personal interest in the Huichol with his career as a reporter.

His view of the Huichol as happy inhabitants of a peaceful region, whose life, "remains remarkably intact" despite, "contacts with Mexican mestizo culture," was to a large extent a misrepresentation of them, the inevitable result of his unfamiliarity with anthropological publications which describe Huichol conflicts with mestizos (Fabila 1959; Benítez 1968a; Rojas 1992, 1993). Moreover, by 1998 several of Phil Weigand's publications described Huichol conflicts with colonial-era Spaniards, and, more recently with mestizos, especially during the Mexican Revolution and the Cristero Rebellion.

If True had wanted to craft a more accurate portrait of Huichol life, the resources to do so were available. For that reason, Huichol specialists like myself lament True's lack of historical and anthropological perspective about long-standing Huichol conflicts and their uneasy accomodation to their more powerful mestizo "neighbors." His editors evidently realized that True's proposal did not provide a foundation solid enough for True to fulfill their requirements that his Huichol story would directly connect with, "the biggest stories of the day" about Mexico.

True's challenging hike by himself, deep inside the rugged Chapalagana Huichol homeland, had nothing to do with his proposal, except perhaps his shooting of nine rolls of photos (Liffman 2002, 370). Such images of the Huichol homeland might have helped illustrate another story, one he was not authorized to write for his newspaper. To continue gathering information relevant to his proposal would have required that True remain in Tuxpan de Bolaños, where he could interview Huichols about the thorny issues involved in being bicultural, mostly poor, and relatively powerless vis-á-vis the Mexicans controlling the country. It is possible that True had, "stopped thinking as a newspaper man… and had come to see the trip only as a personal quest" (Rivard 2005, 225). Thus, Phil decided to traverse Huichol territory alone, leaving Tuxpan de Bolaños on December 1, 1998 without even stopping to see his friend, Jesús González. At that moment in True's life he chose hiking alone over studying and living among the Huichols of Tuxpan de Bolaños. His journal contained tidbits about the Huichol, but five days after departing from Mexico City True, according to Rivard, had gone, "without a single sustained conversation with a Huichol." (2005, 231).

When Phil failed to call his wife on December 10, 1998 as he had promised, Martha sounded the alarm. Mexican President Zedillo soon ordered federal troops and police to enter Huichol territory in a "rescue operation." Estimates of their number ranged from a high of 2,000 to a low of 60 troops (Liffman 2002, 368). It would not be long before the search could be called off, and the investigation would begin.

One week after he had been murdered, True's body was found by a Huichol hunter, Margarito Diaz, on December 13, 1998 (Rivard 2005, 200). True was killed near the boundary of two Huichol communities, San Sebastián Teponahuaxtlan and San Andrés Cohamiata. From the place where True's body was first found by Diaz, it would have taken True at least five hours on foot to climb up 3,000 feet from the Chapalagana River to the village of San Miguel Huaistita (Liffman 2002, 362, 367). When Diaz led Rivard and other searchers back to True's body two days later, they discovered it had been moved. Aiding them in discovering True's corpse was a trail of goose down feathers, which had spilled out of True's sleeping bag as the murderers moved it downhill. Following those feathers, the searchers finally reached the Chapalagana river bottom where True's body had been buried in the sand. More particulars of the search for Phil, and the recovery of his body are well documented by Rivard (2005, 135-145).

Regarding the investigation that followed, Kvinta (1999, 141) reports that the, "army was aggressive...rumors of brutal interrogations began to spread through the widely scattered Indian settlements." By December 20, 1998 the Mexican army's incursions into the Huichol homeland had become worrisome enough that:

> "a group of Huichol leaders released a statement to the press. ... 'We ask the press and the public opinion to avoid making gerneralizations that lead people to think that Huichols are violent. Our people ....always will be peaceful people that seek dignity and respect for our ancestral culture, rights and territory....We ask the authorities to investigate and locate the criminal or criminals, be they Huichol or not. But we don't want this to lead to violations of human rights of community members or the framing of individuals merely to keep up appearances.'" (Kvinta 1999, 142)

Possible Motives for The Murder of Phil True

Determining beyond a reasonable doubt what had motivated two Huichols, Juan Chivarra and Miguel Hernandez, to kill Phil True in 1998 is a task I feel ill equipped to undertake. Instead, I will suggest my favored theory as to their motive(s) and then offer alternative theories. In 2002 I suggested again what I had guessed in 1998 (in my interview with Debbie Nathan): that the most likely motive for True's murder was fear that he might make statements, or file a report, possibly even with photos, about marijuana cultivation, and thereby put Huichol marijuana growers at risk for arrest and/or destruction of their cash crop. Of course I have always admitted that, "There is no compelling evidence to support my suspicion that True was murdered by Huichols who were worried that he had discovered marijuana" (in Zingg 2004, 276). Rivard's book (2005) offers additional circumstantial evidence which significantly strengthens my hunch that protecting their marijuana was their motive for murdering True.

Rivard noted that following True's murder, government

investigators assigned to apprehend his killers were unwilling to enter the Huichol mountains by themselves. They rightly feared that marijuana cultivators in the area they intended to investigate were, "heavily armed and could easily overwhelm the outgunned searchers if they stumbled down the wrong path" (2005, 359-360). Speaking specifically about the path to the marijuana, apparently cultivated by Juan Chivarra, one eyewitness (who must, for good reason remain anonymous) told Rivard that he had come across, "Chivarra standing by a barricade that he had built to block the path, forcing locals to detour away from a nearby marijuana plot he was cultivating" (2005, 213). Rivard paraphrased excerpts from that letter, sent to him by a young man whose mother taught school at San Miguel Huaistita, and who himself was, "once a regular visitor and occasional resident in San Miguel" (2005, 213). The teacher's son said he had, evidently in 1997, alerted his contacts in the governor's office in Guadalajara, the capital of Jalisco, of Chivarra's marijuana cultivation and, "Soon an army unit arrived in Amoltita and burned the crop only weeks before the harvest." (Rivard 2005, 214).

This loss of their cash crop escalated tension between residents of San Miguel and Amoltita (near the village of Yoata where the two murderers lived). One year later,

> "It was into this milieu that True walked, oblivious to the heightened hostility toward outsiders. It doesn't take much imagination to wonder if Chivarra and Hernandez attacked True fearing that he had come across and possibly photographed marijuana fields they were protecting" (Rivard 2005, 214-215).

That is precisely what I have imagined, but without ruling out other possible murder scenarios, which are summarized in Appendix F.

Whether or not Rivard and I are correct in deducing—on the basis of circumstantial evidence—that Chivarra and Hernandez murdered Phil True to protect their marijuana, Liffman is right in reminding us that most Huichol, "want nothing to do with any kind of illegal drugs" (Liffman 2002: 401). Readers may remember that peyote is regarded by traditional Huichol as an entheogen and tutelary spirit (Fikes 2011). Using it is legal for the Huichol, who are members of one of Mexico's indigenous societies. A similar exemption from drug prosecution exists for members of the Native American Church, who also venerate peyote.

Trailing True, from Tuxpan Back to Irvine

I visited Tuxpan de Bolaños annually between 1996 and 2005, the year when my wife and I made our first of five annual pilgrimages together to the Pacific Ocean with Jesús González. Kvinta, Rivard and True's widow all acknowledged that True and González knew each other (Kvinta 1999; Rivard 2005, 28, 226), but were unaware of a fundamental fact about González. As this biography of González discloses, González derived his shamanic power from Kieri, an entheogen more ancient than peyote. Thus he has never performed peyote ceremonies. True would have had to locate other Huichols (in Tuxpan?) in order to ingest peyote in a ceremony, as Rivard reported he had done (2005, 28), but without revealing any particulars about where, when and with whom, True ate peyote. Rivard admitted (in his email of Feb. 3, 2006) that True ingested peyote only once, "probably in Tuxpan," without providing details about where and when that event occurred. Before True was murdered in December 1998, he and his wife, Martha, "had visited Tuxpan de Bolaños ... and had been allowed to witness a sacred peyote ceremony. On another occasion, Philip returned and participated in such a ceremony, although he never wrote about his peyote-eating experience" (Rivard 2005, 28).

Martha declared that "When we visited Tuxpan de Bolaños during Holy Week in 1998, we spent three hours with the elders in order to be allowed to watch a peyote ritual." (Kvinta 1999, 64).[4] Although True presumably witnessed one peyote ceremony in Tuxpan de Bolaños with Martha during Easter Week, 1998, we have only hearsay concerning True's return to Tuxpan de Bolaños, without Martha, to ingest peyote at another ceremony (Rivard

2005, 28). Incidentally, several details Rivard attributed to Tuxpan de Bolaños are undoubtedly incorrect, probably because he was unfamiliar with that Huichol settlement.[5]

When True rushed through Tuxpan de Bolaños, at the start of his solo trek in December of 1998, peyote was not specifically on his agenda. To be clear, even though True mentioned peyote twice in his proposal, it was not involved in any way with his last hike. Despite True's having parrot feathers he had planned to give to Jesús González, True never took the time to visit González. "When his bus rolled into Tuxpan de Bolaños at 4 p.m. on December 1, (1998) True immediately got off and began walking out of town." (Kvinta 1999, 62). What True did after leaving Tuxpan and before he was murdered need not detain us here.[6] Our focus now will be to examine the part Castaneda played in stimulating True to visit the Huichol for the first time, and to keep returning to them. Martha True wrote me on December 28, 2005 confirming that my summary of our previous phone conversation (see below) required only one correction: Phil was eleven years older than she. She affirmed in her e-mail to me that the following summary of our conversation was accurate. I have assigned numbers to these items (uncontested facts or inferences) to differentiate them from my interpretation of their meaning:

1. Phil True was already interested in the Huichol when they began dating each other on June 13, 1991.

2. By then True already knew about Real de Catorce.

3. True must have (she deduces) met some Huichol, or people selling their art, during his bike trip to Guadalajara (the capital of Jalisco, a state in Mexico) in October 1981.

4. True had purchased some old-fashioned wool—not yarn—paintings; probably made in the late 1960s or early 1970s.

5. According to Martha, Phil's library did not have any books written by Furst or Myerhoff.

6. Martha stated that True's library contained these books written by Carlos Castaneda: *The Teachings of Don Juan*, *A Separate Reality*, *Tales of Power*, and *The Second Ring of Power*.

7. Castaneda must have had a significant influence on True.

8. Phil True was in Tuxpan on one occasion before the two of them went there together to attend Semana Santa (Easter week) rituals.

9. True's third and final trip to Tuxpan (and beyond) was the one he made alone in December of 1998.

Items 1-3 suggest that Phil True had a general and ongoing interest in certain unidentified Huichols. According to Paul Kvinta, "three dozen works of Huichol art" had decorated True's home in Mexico before his widow, Martha, moved to Brownsville, Texas. One of them was a yarn painting, "depicting sacred deer and peyote buttons" (1999, 142). Sadly, neither Kvinta, Robert Rivard, nor Martha True provided any details to help us understand the human sources as well as the locations (Real de Catorce, or Guadalajara?) essential in stimulating True's initial interest in the Huichol. Martha repeatedly asserted that Phil True, "loved the Huichols so much…He had studied and visited them on and off for fifteen years." (Rivard 2005, 212) Because her claim remains unverified, I should not speculate. Sadly, the five most elementary questions all journalists try to answer: 'who, what, where, when, and why' remain unanswered regarding True's alleged 15 years of contact with certain unidentified Huichols.

Item 2 refers to a small Mexican town, Real de Catorce, that has become the global magnet for non-Indian peyote tourists (Fikes 2011b). Once again, neither Rivard nor Martha True discovered, or perhaps decided not to disclose, whether True had first-hand experiences or merely hearsay knowledge gained from others (in publications or conversations) about Real de Catorce. True would have been able to drive there in eight hours from either Brownsville, TX or Mexico City. Was he there? We simply don't know.

Katherine Ellison, who was evidently the first American journalist to accompany Huichol peyote hunters to Real de Catorce, provides readers with a fascinating glimpse into the world of non-Huichols frequenting Real de Catorce in 1992. She consulted extensively with me and Juan Negrín before publishing her newpaper story, which included snippets from her interviews with non-Huichols seeking contact with Huichol peyote hunters in and around Real de Catorce. Ellison was candid in describing her experiences with Taimarita Huichol peyote hunters (Taimarita is a rancho about ten miles [16 kilometers] north of the ceremonial center at Santa Catarina). She informed readers that her San Jose, CA newspaper, the *San Jose Mercury News*, paid $850 US so she could accompany—and photograph—her Huichol companions from Taimarita (1992, 9).

Ellison, as the Mexico City Bureau Chief for the Knight-Ridder Newpapers, was living in Mexico City in 1992. She recently told me that she did not know Phil True. Coincidentally, part of Ellison's preparation for the peyote journey included, "re-reading Carlos Castaneda's tales of his gentle Yaqui Indian teacher, Don Juan." (1992, 12) Ellison's judgment was that peyote was "foul but edible," and after eating it she soon felt, "calmer and happier than at any time in the past week." She continued, "Later that afternoon, I found myself picking up and saving a great number of rocks that seemed to be exceptionally beautiful, even significant, but which now seem to be just rocks." (Ellison 1992, 29).

Real de Catorce, more than any other place in Mexico, symbolizes the "magic land" of Huichol peyote hunting. True's journal proclaimed: "Huichols are the original trekkers, going to Real de Catorce on foot." (Rivard 2005, 231). Publications by Furst and Myerhoff, anthropologists who described their abbreviated peyote hunts, were not found in True's library (as per list, item 5 above). It is possible True visited Real de Catorce to ingest peyote, given what BH revealed, "We wanted to have our own conversations with Don Juan," and, "peyote use among the Huichols (was) a possible 'hook' that made their art and culture appealing to Philip (BH email to me dated 1-23-2006). Rivard had seen Huichols around Real de Catorce for over 25 years, starting in the mid-1970s, yet he never approached them. He wrote, "Maybe I lacked the anthropological curiosity of True, maybe I was less taken with Carlos Castaneda's New Age fictional writings, but I never wanted to intrude on Huichols during a peyote ritual" (2005, 233).

Item 3 above refers to the bike trip to Guadalajara that True made with Annette Fuentes in 1981. As far as we know, True's first contact with Huichols (or with somebody selling Huichol art) occurred then. True's first impression must have been positive because in 1984 True returned alone, during a vacation to Guadalajara, to buy Huichol wool (the precursor to yarn) paintings. Thus, 1984 was the first of the nearly fifteen years of contact True allegedly had with some still unidentified Huichols, according to Martha True.

Item 4 refers to True's purchase of those Huichol wool paintings, one of which still sits on BH's desk. Many Americans think these paintings are inspired by peyote visions. However, based on my experiences in Santa Catarina and Tuxpan de Bolaños, the majority of Huichol art for sale is primarily a means of earning much-needed money. It is logical to deduce that True valued Huichol art. According to Kvinta (1999, 142), Martha was sure True understood the meaning of the complex motifs depicted in at least 36 works of Huichol art "that once adorned their Mexico City home."

Item 5 suggests that True either found nothing of value in the publications of Furst and Myerhoff, or that he was unaware of them. Either of these inferences is reasonable, given the fact that True never contacted Liffman, Weigand, me or other Huichol experts before going to Tuxpan de Bolaños. The one Huichol specialist with whom True had contact, Dr. Stacy Schaefer (Rivard 2005, 211-212), was not eager to share details of whatever she might have discussed with Phil True (according to Rivard's e-mail to me dated 2-13-2006). Moreover, Rivard (in his email to me dated 2-14-2006) stated that Stacy Schaefer told him in an email, "that she and Philip never discussed peyote...despite knowing her and her work." When I inquired, "which anthropologists True had read or consulted in connection with the Huichol" (in my email dated

1-27-2006 to Rivard), Rivard admitted he had no idea (e-mail of 15 February, 2006 to me). All available evidence suggests that, at best, True's interaction with anthropologists was insignificant. Could such neglect be a consequence of the fact he had already met certain Huichols (including Jesús González), and felt it was more important to confer with them than with anthropologists such as Phil Weigand or Stacy Schaefer?

Item 6 attests to True's longstanding interest in books written by Carlos Castaneda. Four of the first five books written by Castaneda were in his library. The "missing" book, *Journey to Ixtlan*, is the most remarkable of Castaneda's first three books because it retracts Don Juan's earlier emphasis on sacred tutelary plants, one of which was peyote (see note 1).

After reading the third Castaneda book, True was probably unimpressed, perhaps sensing that it clashed with the prominence Don Juan had placed on peyote in the first two books. I deduce that Phil True never knew for sure that the Castaneda books were not authentic. Despite what de Mille and I have done to debunk Castaneda's literary corpus as fiction, some anthropologists considered experts on shamanism still considered Castaneda's work authentic in 2006. One of them, Professor Michael Winkelman (who coincidentally earned his Ph.D. in 1985 from the University of California, Irvine), was interviewed in 2006 for the BBC documentary, "Tales from the Jungle: Carlos Castaneda". His endorsement of Castaneda's work as authentic ethnography illustrated a minority view that has gradually disappeared since 2006, as DeMille's and my judgment about Castaneda's writing being fictional has gained acceptance.

True's knowledge about Mexican indigenous religions and rituals was negligible according to my reading of the available evidence. There is no proof that True ever discovered that Castaneda's books were concocted, and a "transparent fraud" (Fikes 1993, 49, 51).

Item 7 implies that Castaneda's influence was significant enough that it played a substantial part in luring True (and many others, including myself) to the Huichol. Within a week of arriving in Santa Catarina in 1976, I had learned enough about the Huichol to recognize that Castaneda's books were fictional, not ethnographic. I immediately stopped reading them, and I never read any part of Castaneda's fifth book, *The Second Ring of Power,* nor any of his subsequent books. That book, and three of the four previous Castaneda books, were in True's library. In contrast, neither DeMille's two books debunking Castaneda, nor mine (1993) were there. There is simply no evidence to indicate that True ever discovered that Castaneda's first two books promulgated profoundly false information about peyote.

Martha agreed that Castaneda was a significant influence on True. I remember admitting to Martha that Castaneda's books had once also been a significant influence on me. I believe she replied by saying something like: "You and Phil had the same mind set."

Martha's statement about Semana Santa (item 8) corrected what she regarded as Rivard and Kvinta's mistake. She plainly told me that she and Phil attended Semana Santa ceremonies together in Tuxpan. She insisted that they were not together at a peyote ceremony, as reported by both Rivard (2005, 28) and Kvinta (1999, 64). If we take her at her word, that means that Phil's peyote eating occurred during his first (solo) visit to Tuxpan, before Martha accompanied him there. Rivard did not disclose his sources, but backed down a bit on his claim that True had eaten peyote in Tuxpan (2005 28), admitting that True ate peyote once "probably in Tuxpan" (e-mail to me, dated 3 February, 2006).

Item 9 has been confirmed by many people, including Martha True. Having reviewed all relevant evidence, I now offer an inference that I think is reasonable: attending Castaneda's lectures in 1972, supplemented by reading Castaneda's first five books, made a significant enough impression on True that he was attracted to the Huichol. For many Americans, curiosity about Huichol peyote use was a routine response to having read the first two (if not more) of Castaneda's books (Fikes 1999, 410-11; and in the following chapter). In particular, Castaneda's peculiar portrait of peyote rituals played some part in initially luring True and many other Americans to the Huichol (Fikes 1993, 1996b, 1999, 2011b). True, "knew about Real de Catorce," but we must guess whether he was ever there or not.

Communications I had with Martha True and Robert Rivard (in combination with reading Rivard's book) led me to conclude that True's experiences in Tuxpan de Bolaños were positive enough that he decided to return (See item 9). The idealistic misrepresentation of Huichol life contained in True's story proposal suggests that when he embarked upon what was to be his last hike through Huichol territory, he had still not heard any news about the murder (or murders) resulting from marijuana growing in Tuxpan de Bolaños. His solo trek took him into dangers he did not imagine existing in the Huichol homeland. Neither attending peyote ceremonies nor recording interviews with Huichols like Jesus González could compete with what seems to have been his goal at that moment: hiking alone to absorb the splendor of nature. Although the murderers, Chivarra and Hernandez, were finally sentenced on April 27, 2004 to twenty years in prison (Rivard 2005, 351) they remain free (see Appendix F). We can only hope and pray that one day True's murderers will be apprehended and justice will be done.

CHAPTER 9

WHY HUICHOLS ATTRACT AND RESIST OUTSIDERS

During the past fifty years, why have some admirers of Carlos Castaneda's books, including Phil True and a 25 year-old Jay Fikes, been attracted to the Huichol? My research indicates that Castaneda's first two books, in addition to publications on Huichol peyote hunts by two of his UCLA anthropologist-colleagues, Drs. Peter Furst and Barbara Myerhoff, have popularized Huichol peyote use and enticed many Americans to visit Huichols, especially those who reside in more accessible places such as Guadalajara, Tepic and El Colorín (Fikes 1993).

There are several reasons why younger, often disenchanted, Americans eager to try peyote and/or become "shamans" themselves, have sought out potential mentors among those expatriate Huichol. First, unlike the Chapalagana Huichol, the Yaqui tribe Castaneda connected to his fictional character, Don Juan, has never had a peyote hunt nor peyote ceremonies. They were seen as less attractive than the Huichol by young Americans yearning for 'exotic' and 'transformational' experiences. Second, Don Juan, the supposedly Yaqui shaman to whom Castaneda allegedly became an apprentice never existed. Third, the shamans and peyote hunt of the Huichol represented an alluring and readily available alternative to Dr. Castaneda's Don Juan (Fikes 1993, 135, 212; 2011b).

In addition, there was a series of sensational lectures on "hallucinogenic drugs" organized by Dr. Furst (Valley News, 1970), as well as his and Barbara Myerhoff's publications (1972 and 1974 respectively) on the peyote hunt, and, his 1969 documentary film, *To Find Our Life*, depicting a Huichol peyote hunt.[1] Cumulatively, and given that the 'psychedelic revolution' was reaching its peak (Fikes 1993), these efforts of Furst and Myerhoff had a significant impact in captivating the imagination of America's counter-culture.

By 1975 the association between Castaneda and Huichol peyote use had become well established within American popular culture (Fikes 1993, 2011b). Nowhere is this connection more blatant than on the cover of the mass-market paperback edition of the English translation of Fernando Benítez' *In the Magic Land of Peyote.* The first statement, at the top of that book's front cover, sets the psychedelic tone: "A Revealing, First-Hand Report from the World of Castaneda's Don Juan." In his introduction to this book, Dr. Peter Furst, the UCLA anthropologist who produced the 1969 documentary film on the Huichol peyote hunt, reported that:

"There has been a veritable pilgrimage to Huichol land of alienated middle-class romantics, who ... come in search of gurus comparable to Carlos Castaneda's don (sic) Juan and of instant religious revelation via the peyote trip" (Fikes 1993, 135).

My first trip to the Huichol *comunidad indígena* of Santa Catarina, in 1976, was arranged after consulting with Alfonso Manzanilla. When I first met him at his office in Tepic, Manzanilla was the chief administrator of several community development programs that included the building of dirt landing strips, bilingual boarding schools, agricultural "modernization" and eventually medical services (largely immunizations and primary care). These interventions in Huichol life were designed to facilitate Huichol adaptation (or "acculturation") to "modern" Mexican norms. Manzanilla managed parallel programs directed toward members of indigenous groups adjacent to the Huichol, e.g., Cora and Tepehuan, while employed by the National Indigenous Institute (Instituto Nacional Indigenista), hereafter I.N.I, which is essentially the Mexican equivalent of the American Bureau of Indian Affairs. Incidentally, the I.N.I was abolished during President Fox's administration and partially reconstituted as the Comisión Nacional para el Desarrollo de los Pueblos Indígenas (Liffman's email of 9-26-2020).

After I explained my research interests which, in 1976, were learning the Huichol language and studying their pre-Hispanic temple ritual cycle, Manzanilla decided that Santa Catarina would be the best place for him to send me. He arranged for me to take a small government plane from Tepic to the tiny dirt landing strip closest to the ceremonial center at Santa Catarina. He was kind enough to appoint a young Huichol man to guide me after I landed. To return his favor, I promised him I would complete two tasks he requested of me: to discover what items or services the Huichol of Santa Catarina wanted from his government, and to obtain a report summarizing an investigation of what had happened to a shipment of shovels, picks, barbed wire and cement that he had recently sent to them. After one week in Santa Catarina, I had learned what Huichol investigators discovered: that a few Huichol had conspired to defraud the Mexican government.

Manzanilla suspected there was a problem because Huichol officials customarily sent back to him a receipt for goods delivered to them by the Mexican government. Because those officials failed to send such a receipt, Manzanilla asked me to find out why. About a week later, inquiries Huichol made about the whereabouts of that "missing" shipment of goods produced significant information about what had happened. Several Huichol elders and officials briefed me on what they had written in a sealed report that I was entrusted to deliver to Manzanilla, immediately upon my return to Tepic. Their report explained that a fraud and conspiracy had been perpetrated by a few Huichol, one of whom was a teacher at the nearest bilingual boarding school. Those Huichol conspirators had "borrowed" the seal of their community in order to solicit the shipment in the name of their community. They kept the entire delivery for themselves, and neglected to send the customary receipt to Manzanilla.

Felipe Sánchez, one of those conspirators, approached me after he learned I had the report exposing his misdeed. Perhaps trying to befriend me, he offered to guide me to a Kieri growing nearby. When we arrived, he briefly explained that Kieri was considered a divine plant. I was pleased to learn that Kieri was not evil (as claimed by previous American anthropologists), but my lukewarm response to his inquiry about what would happen to him after I delivered the report could not have consoled him.

One year later, in June of 1977, I had my first encounter with an unfriendly Huichol. Shortly after I arrived at the ceremonial center of Santa Catarina, I observed more than one hundred Huichols from numerous villages surrounding Santa Catarina, busily preparing to perform their annual Peyote Dance ritual. One young, tall Huichol man impetuously approached me and accused me of being a miner. With the consent of the Huichol political officers and religious elders present at this ritual, that young man searched all of my belongings. Because I knew Huichol etiquette required having a permit, I had neither a camera nor a tape recorder with me. After confirming that I had no mining nor touristic equipment with me, he calmed down, and I was allowed to observe the ceremony.

It probably helped that Jerónimo Bonales defended my right to visit him, and that I was housed in his dwelling during the ritual in Santa Catarina. Moreover, Bonales had an official position (*cargo*) at the Catholic church there, so it is likely that he considered me an 'official' guest for whom he had some responsibility.[2] To avoid further problems, I was careful to follow Bonales' advice to take notes unobtrusively during the 1977 Peyote Dance ritual.

My next significant problem while doing fieldwork involved Felipe Sánchez, who had defrauded the I.N.I., (see above) in 1976. He noticed me during a First Fruits ritual (Tatei Neixa) performed on October 14, 1979 at the rancho where Bonales' extended family lived. That night Sánchez was evidently drunk when he threatened, to my face, to kill me. He then hinted that nobody would ever find my body in such a remote place. I felt fortunate because my translator and friend, Pancho Torres, whose sister was married to Bonales, was there to defend me. Pancho was the eldest son of that rancho's ritual leader, and he was well aware of my role in reporting Sanchez's illegal actions to the I.N.I. Pancho effectively defended me, being armed with a pistol. Sanchez's death threat was obviously his reaction to my having been the messenger of news that exposed him to Alfonso Manzanilla. I did not have any further trouble with Sánchez.

My fieldwork in Santa Catarina remained untroubled until 1998, when I was expelled after enjoying a grace period of one week. In May of that year, I made what turned out to be my last trip to Santa Catarina. When I arrived at the nearby rancho where Serratos lived, I was quickly alerted to the fact that two Americans had recently been instructed to leave the community because they were attempting to visit sacred sites without authorization. I was also told about an Italian tourist who had, sometime within the past few months, refused to surrender his camera to Huichol authorities. He was quickly jailed, fined, and evicted from Santa Catarina.

Much to my surprise, the day after I arrived at Serratos' rancho, a young Huichol man, who was a *comisario* (commissioner, political official), came to talk with me. He fined me and notified me that I had to leave the next morning. After 22 years of doing anthropological research in Santa Catarina, I was shocked at such unfriendly treatment. Fortunately, some of Serratos' relatives defended me. Taking their advice, I paid more money to that *comisario,* thereby gaining permission to extend my stay in Santa Catarina for one week.

A few of my friends in Santa Catarina suggested that the discouraging of outsiders, including anthropologists, from visiting their community was largely a reaction to the Mexican government's harassment of traditional Huichols during peyote pilgrimages and while hunting deer. Later, in 2006, during the course of investigating possible motives for Phil True's murder, I was able to confirm that at least three groups of Huichol peyote hunters had been mistreated in 1998.

Also in 1998, Santa Catarina Huichol confrontations with unauthorized outsiders, anthropologists included, increased dramatically. Unpaved dirt "roads" had made access to Santa Catarina much easier than it was in 1976, when I had first visited. Between the years 1976-1998, their posture toward outsiders, even those like me, who had been accepted previously, gradually became less friendly.[3]

Kvinta discovered that Huichol apprehension about outsiders was, "particularly high in 1998. In March the military, intent on drug interdiction, stopped two groups of Huichols making the peyote pilgrimage, jailed them for two days, and confiscated their peyote" (Kvinta 1999, 67). Arrests of those two groups of peyote pilgrims presumably contributed to my being expelled from Santa Catarina in May of 1998. Moreover, a third group of Huichol peyote hunters was jailed in November of 1998, barely a month before Phil True was murdered, "when the army busted a large group of Huichols en route to their sacred peyote hunting grounds. The Indians were freed only with the help of the federal Indian Affairs Institute," (I.N.I) (Nathan 1998, 8).

We know now that during 1998 two troublesome trends, which are to some extent mutually reinforcing, were rapidly escalating anxiety among Chapalagana Huichol: the growing Huichol dependence on marijuana as a cash crop and, secondly, the ever-increasing volume of non-Indian incursions into the Chapalagana Huichol homeland, as well as into Real de Catorce, the global destination for most peyote tourists (Fikes 2011b).

As early as 1987 marijuana cultivation around Tuxpan de Bolaños had become so lucrative that it was emerging as a motive for homicide between the Huichol (as described in Chapter 7). Despite the risks, involvement with marijuana cultivation continued to spread throughout the Chapalagana Huichol homeland. In 1997 a Mexican army unit, "arrived in Amoltita and burned the (marijuana) crop only weeks before the harvest" (Rivard 2005, 214). Phil True walked into that already tense area, where he was to be challenged by Juan Chivarra, a Huichol who was already known as a marijuana grower (Rivard 2005, 213). Even if True's murder had nothing to do with Chivarra's marijuana crop, it seems clear that opposition to allowing outsiders to travel within the Chapalagana homeland was growing in direct response to increasing marijuana cultivation. I now suspect that Huichol "hypersensitivity" toward outsiders carrying cameras without permits was, by 1998 (if not before), already at least partially a result of marijuana cultivation and the need for secrecy about their illegal cash crop.

The need for secrecy had also increased because the number of non-Indians curious about Huichol shamans and peyote had steadily increased between 1976 and 1998. During the 22 years I did fieldwork in Santa Catarina, from 1976 to 1998, the arrival of unpaved roads, pick-up trucks, electricity, piped water and modern conveniences made visiting Santa Catarina or Tuxpan de Bolaños relatively easy. At the same time, Huichol access to their traditional peyote sources surrounding Real de Catorce was becoming more difficult—mainly because some Mexican authorities (army or police) were detaining bonafide Huichol peyote pilgrims.

As early as 1981 publications of Castaneda and his UCLA collaborators, Drs. Myerhoff and Furst, had inspired at least three "New Age" American tour guides. Their naïve but romantic portrait of Huichol life has stimulated tourism ever since (Fikes 1993, 1999, 2011b; Fikes & Weigand 2004). Although such New Age tourism has brought money to a few expatriate Huichol families (Fikes & Weigand 2004) it has often caused inconvenience, if not harm, to Chapalagana Huichol peyote and deer hunters. Harassment of Huichol peyote hunters, especially those associated with Anglos, by Mexican authorities began as early as 1986 (Fikes 1993, 133-136) but became particularly acute in 1998. The increasing volume of unauthorized outsiders combined with increased Huichol involvement in marijuana cultivation meant outsiders were more likely to be restricted, jailed, fined or evicted by Huichol officials intent on keeping their ceremonies sacrosanct, and by growers eager to conceal their lucrative cash crop. Sadly, Phil True was in the wrong place during the wrong year.

What do We Owe the Chapalagana Huichol?

When I first visited Santa Catarina in 1976, I probably had an idealistic perspective on Huichol society, not unlike Robert Zingg in 1934, and Phil True in 1998. Over the years I gradually learned more about poverty, alcoholism, suicides, homicides and other manifestations of the "sinister" side of Huichol life. Reflecting on the circumstances surrounding Phil True's murder has motivated me to address such unpleasant realities directly. I do not feel it is fair to readers, or to the Huichol, to focus exclusively on non-controversial topics (such as myths and rituals).

I like to think that my publications about the Huichol reflect my dedication to doing accurate ethnography. Although I have some experience as an activist on behalf of American Indians, I have not been as politically active on behalf of the Huichol as I had, at times, hoped to be.[4] My life has been immensely enriched by having learned from four Huichol shaman-mentors, and three Huichol translators. Because I came to respect them, and other Huichols who hosted or helped me during my fieldwork in their homeland, I feel obliged to disclose details about their plight as members of a relatively powerless "tribal" society. It would be a "sin of omission" to avoid a discussion of problems associated with their having been dominated and exploited by the more powerful Spaniards, and later by Mexicans.

The previous two chapters concentrated on clarifying issues far removed from shamanism, entheogens, ritual and myth: topics that have absorbed most of my scholarly attention for the past 44 years. The dangers that marijuana cultivation poses to tourists visiting Chapalagana Huichol territory should be obvious to anybody who has read this far. It is my hope that by connecting marijuana cultivation to the chronic poverty afflicting most Chapalagana Huichol, this book may promote dialogue about the legalization of marijuana, as well as sustainable economic development of Huichol resources. Huichol health and prosperity depend on resolving these issues, as well as gaining greater legal protection for peyote, especially in the area around Real de Catorce, where it is rapidly becoming extinct. The need to protect peyote for future generations is urgent (Guttman 2016).

Huichol myths and their annual temple ritual cycle are firmly rooted in enduring adaptations to their Chapalagana homeland. The mutualism between maize and the Huichol, their reverence for deer, Kieri, peyote and *Hay+rime* (everlasting water), and their temple officers' devotion to honoring precedents set by their ancestors (Fikes 1985, 1993, 2011), are all elements embedded in their tradition which can inspire us to rethink and reform our own ecologically unsustainable way of life. The past 44 years of steady population growth also makes imperative the need to significantly improve the Huichol education system, to build a sustainable economy, and to more effectively protect their homeland and its natural resources from degradation and outsiders intent on quick profits gained at their expense.

I have long regarded the Huichols as a source of ecological wisdom (Fikes 1985, 1993, 2011), and I feel honored that Jesús González selected me to publish his narrative of Tamatsi for his descendants, and for the world. Outsiders, including anthropologists, demonstrate our compassion when we act like the mouse who rescued Tamatsi, in order that he could complete his calling, to sustain harmony between the Huichol, their Ancestor Deities and all the flora and fauna with whom we share this planet. One simple way we can support much needed reforms that "balance" traditional Huichol rituals and practices with wisely managed responses to the unceasing encroachments of the "modern" world, is by contributing to non-profit organizations with a track record of producing results beneficial for most Huichol. Information about some of them is posted on my website: www. jayfikes.com

POSTSCRIPT

Some 30 years ago I came to value traditional Huichol and Native American spirituality more than anthropological theories. This preference deepened as I moved beyond the anthropological mainstream, through intense collaboration with four Huichol shamans and Reuben Snake, a Winnebago (Ho-Chunk) political leader and Roadman (ritual leader) in the Native American Church. While attempting to understand Huichol spirituality through my scholarly research as well as personal experiences during rituals and pilgrimages to sacred sites, I came to recognize that at least one-third of publications about the Huichol by American anthropologists and their supporters prior to 1979 were tainted by ethnocentric, superficial and sometimes defamatory statements.

To honor Reuben Snake and my Huichol shaman-mentors I became committed to preserving the authenticity of their sacred traditions. Thus I devoted myself to a few worthy causes. In 1993 my book exposed Carlos Castaneda's books as fraudulent. In 1994 I was honored for my efforts in passing federal legislation to protect the religious freedom of members of the Native American Church. Joined by Phil Weigand and Juan Negrín, I challenged the American Anthropological Association in 1992 to live up to its pledge to adjudicate complaints about unethical conduct, by investigating our allegations of professional misconduct by Dr. Peter T. Furst. I also served as an expert witness in 2006 in our successful defense of religious freedom of ritual ayahuasca users, members of the American branch of the *Centro Espírita Beneficente União do Vegetal*. In all these endeavors I honored Huichol and Native American religious practitioners and complied with my obligation to do honest ethnography.

This book is the sixth I have written or edited, in addition to a documentary film I prepared on Huichol (Wixarika) rituals. Jesús González, the shaman whose biography is presented in this book, empowered me to proclaim that Kieri (a psychoactive plant in the genus *Solandra*) is a divine plant, revered for centuries before making "peyote pilgrimages" became an annual obligation for Huichol temple officers. I hope our book serves as an antidote to the false and defamatory view that Kieri is evil and persuades anthropologists to heed Gordon Wasson's advice to select the best possible informants, especially when seeking to discover the truth about entheogens. I will be pleased if readers of *Beyond Peyote: Kieri and the Huichol Deer Shaman* gain inspiration from the profoundly spiritual view of nature evident in the words of my mentor, Jesús González.

The end of Jesús González's narrative of Tamatsi's victory over the Wolf People provides an ideal place to interpret this book's essential implications: "This is how we were created, and how we developed ourselves." We know that cooperation between animals, humans, plants and Ancestor Deities was crucial, from Tamatsi's birth to his emergence as the Deer Shaman. Instead of a creation story managed by the one God familiar to Jews, Christians and Moslems, Tamatsi's success depended on the benevolent efforts of diverse contributors. Together, what Tamatsi and his allies did made him a more compassionate leader. This and other Wixarika "myths" I was privileged to record clearly indicate that the partnership between Huichol and their Ancestor Deities has long been fundamental to improving their way of life, and to insuring their survival as a distinct people.

Most anthropologists view enculturation or socialization in a particular society as the essential path we humans must take to develop ourselves, following a universal learning process that "edits" or gives a particular form to the potential that our nature provides (Spiro 1984). Whether we humans become conquerors of non-Christians, like the Spaniards who invaded what is today Mexico, or the followers of Tamatsi, the benevolent Deer Shaman to whom Jesús González dedicated himself, depends on choices we make as individuals and as societies.

After decades of studying human societies it is clear to me that we have a profound obligation to choose who we are to become with great deliberation. As Vine Deloria puts it,

"We are then, in a real sense, co-creators with the ultimate powers of the universe because in striving to fulfill our destiny, we make the changes that help spiritual ideas become incarnate in the flesh. In the spirit world, there might be a wonderland of possibilities, but until an idea takes on flesh and demonstrates its significance, the universe does not appear at all." (2006, xxx)

Thus, as we struggle to overcome the horrific consequences of global warming and the COVID-19 pandemic, we must face the reality that our decisions and actions as humans, and as members of distinct societies, radically impact both our physical, mental and emotional health, and the health of our planet.

I entered a remarkable society upon arriving in Santa Catarina in 1976, and, 20 years later, in Tuxpan de Bolaños. However far I have come since that time in comprehending the lessons taught by my Huichol shaman-mentors, translators, and hosts, it was not far enough for me to become a practicing shaman. In 1976, on the first day Jesús and I met, by 'coincidence,' at the airport in Tepic, I was impatiently waiting for my first flight to Santa Catarina. Jesús instinctively calmed me down, declaring that my anxiety about the plane being delayed was damaging to my health. My wife, Dr. Tosuner-Fikes, remembers Jesús as being the most helpful of the four Huichol shamans who aided me in my quest to become a shaman.

At times, I recall translating for Jesús while he healed non-Huichols and shared his personal experiences in the lectures we gave in California to people of all ages, during two educational tours we made together in 2003 and 2005. Shortly thereafter, he sympathetically guided my wife and me during five consecutive annual pilgrimages between 2005-2009. He wanted to aid me in establishing rapport with Tatei Haramara, the Pacific Ocean Goddess that was essential to him and his wife. Jesús and I made a final pilgrimage to the Pacific Ocean with his grandson in 2010.

To begin practicing as a Huichol shaman, I should have publicly celebrated the completion of our pilgrimages by performing a traditional ritual in Tuxpan de Bolaños for the Ancestor Deities and relatives of Jesús González. During that time, between 2011-2012, fulfilling obligations to my family, both in California and Istanbul, as well as earning a living, prevented me from accepting his invitation to be ordained a shaman. Jesús died in February of 2016, while I was teaching my final semester in Istanbul.

I am consoled by the fact I have conscientiously interpreted and written this biography of Jesús González. I intend to continue applying insights gained from him, and from many momentous experiences I had throughout my 44 years of fieldwork among the Chapalagana Huichol. I pray that our Ancestor Deities will guide me in interpreting several more unpublished Wixarika narratives in a way that honors them and the Huichol who are their partners.

In completing that task I am reminded of what Jesús proclaimed to his people during their community business meetings in Tuxpan de Bolaños, "that in the future, when I die, I can say it can be said that I have helped my people."

Fig. 6. Offerings to White Antlers Kieri. Photo by Juan Negrín, 1976.

170

Appendix A

Notes On Kieri, A Divine Plant in the Genus Solandra

Kieri has long been misunderstood and superficially studied by outsiders. My goals in this appendix are to offer information that is reliable, and to follow this with guidelines to promote more conscientious research on Kieri. First, we must review what we know about this divine Huichol plant.

Both Serratos and González permitted me to tape-record myths that proclaim Kieri was the incarnation of the pan-Huichol tutelary spirit, Our Elder Brother (also called *Kauyumari* or *Irumari*). However, not every Kieri plant is venerated as a vessel of a divine spirit (Benzi 1972, 175; Yasumoto 1996, 240). Those Kieri that are revered are given unique names, in addition to prayers and offerings. For example, *Ututawita* is the name of a place near Huejuquilla where the Kieri called Ututawi grows (Benítez 1968a, 282; Benzi 1972, 174-75). Huichol temple officers from San Andrés regularly pray and make offerings to the spirit manifested in this tall Kieri (Collings 2000, 20-21). Benzi recognized (1972, 175) that various gods, including *Kauyumari*, and other semi-divine beings may become incarnated through the Kieri plant.[1]

Juan Negrín (1975, 1977) has published a photo of a yarn painting with the Huichol artist's explanation of the feasting and consecration of a specific divine Kieri, named "Our Elder Brother White Antlers." Benzi (1972, 176-77) and Benítez (1968a, 283-84) describe a deer hunter's discovery of a divine Kieri growing in a canyon near Pueblo Nuevo, some 16 kilometers northeast of Santa Catarina. Because that divine Kieri disclosed to a shaman that it was controlling all of the deer in the vicinity, the shaman decided to name it after the place where it was growing. The round shape of the rock on which that Kieri was growing reminded him of the round-shaped comal on which tortillas are toasted. Its name "Ratumuyéve" means "the place of the comal." After the shaman named and consecrated that Kieri by leaving offerings, an elderly relative of the narrator determined that cattle were protected by it (Benítez 1968a, 283-84). This anecdote about that Kieri named "Ratumuyéve" was acknowledged by Yasumoto (1996, 240-41) as exemplary of a Kieri that embodies the Ancestor Deity he calls "Kieri Person," the same being I refer to as Our Elder Brother or the Deer Shaman (see chapter 4).

Although the Kieri where I did my all night vigil in 1986 has a special name, it has always been my policy not to disclose names or precise locations of sacred sites connected to Kieri unless others have already done so. My conversations with both Peter Collings and Juan Negrín led me to conclude that they respected Kieri enough to refrain from collecting samples for scientific analysis. Instead, all three of us only photographed Kieri growing at the various Huichol pilgrimage sites we visited.

None of my three shaman mentors allied to Kieri, nor several other Huichol with whom I discussed Kieri, ever recommended that it be ingested (see Chapter 1). Yasumoto agrees (1996, 254), declaring that whenever anybody makes, "a vow directly to Kieri, one just takes offerings." Negrín and Collings concurred that the ingestion of Kieri was both unnecessary and hazardous to one's health.

González's first-person account of being selected to become a shaman, while still a child, was stimulated after he ate psychoactive honey containing Kieri nectar. Given the taboo on ingesting Kieri, this extraordinary episode is remarkably valuable. Serratos dictated a narrative about the ancient goddess of germination, Takutsi, having been given Kieri to drink by three Ancestor Deities who intended to learn from her. After becoming intoxicated with Kieri, she began singing her sacred songs in order to teach them. These three Ancestors represent the foundational charter for the three singing shamans that are still required to perform all Huichol temple rituals (see introduction and Chapter 5). Having absorbed Takutsi's wisdom, which she expressed in the songs, they murdered her after first wounding her with their arrows. Then they established the Huichol temple ritual cycle (Fikes 1985, 83-84).[2]

The momentous events embedded in this myth will be discussed again in chapter 5. Without more evidence we can only speculate whether this mythical occurrence of Kieri-drinking exemplifies a now obsolete Huichol practice, or if it was part of those ancestral singers' campaign to defame her, or perhaps both.

Yasumoto (1996, 254) and I (in chapter 1) acknowledge that both salt-fasting and sexual purity are essential for anyone committed to making Kieri their ally. Punishment of aspiring shamans who breach their covenant with Kieri, or of anybody who fails to abide by their vows to Kieri, may be severe or even lethal. I discuss this topic in chapters 1, 6, and elsewhere (Fikes 2011, 86-87).

The most compelling proof for the divinity of Kieri is contained in González's myth depicting it as central in the creation of the Deer Shaman (see chapter 4), and in details attesting to its veneration at several distinct named sites within the Huichol homeland, as cited above. As we shall see, there is also evidence suggesting that Kieri was worshipped by the Cora and Tepecano, the two "tribes" closely allied for trade, ceremony and mutual defense with the Huichol (Fikes 1985, Weigand 2000). The information associated with the worship of Kieri among Cora and Tepecano should be considered tentative.

The following anecdote includes essential elements I selected from two strikingly similar narratives dictated by the same Huichol (Benítez 1968a, 287-88 and Benzi 1972, 176).[3] This composite chronicle I have assembled indicates that a specific named Kieri, growing in the heart of Cora territory, protects parrots (and perhaps all animals) living nearby from careless hunters like the one mentioned:

A Huichol from San Andrés Cohamiata walked some 50 kilometers west, to the Mesa del Nayar, to hunt a species of parrot with a green body & yellow wings called *kakawame*. After killing at least 15 parrots, he returned to San Andrés to sell their feathers to people living nearby. The next time he went hunting for those parrots at the Mesa del Nayar he was just about to release an arrow from his bow when suddenly hundreds of parrots swarmed above his head making a racket with their wings and shouting, "ka, ka, ka!" The flock flew closer and closer to the hunter's head, creating a whirlwind that caused him to panic. He fled into the mountains and was lost there for three hours. With great difficulty he found his way back to his house. Although he regained his sanity, his normality habitually disappeared whenever a flock of parrots flew overhead. One time, after a flock of parrots caused him to panic and then get lost, he and his parents decided to ask a famous shaman to diagnose the source of his illness. According to that shaman, his ailment was a punishment sent by the god incarnate in a Kieri that was the patron of those parrots living near the Mesa del Nayar. The parrot hunter had killed them without first having brought the Kieri all offerings prescribed by tradition. The shaman told that hunter that, to atone for his misdeed, he must offer deer and bull blood, accompanied by votive gourd bowls and arrows, to that Kieri growing near the Mesa del Nayar. After paying his debt to that Kieri, owner of those parrots, he recuperated his health.

I believe Huichol consider this Kieri divine, because it must be given offerings and because it has a special name, "Reutari" (Benítez 1968a, 287-88). No Cora specialist has published any photo, nor reported an eyewitness account of a pilgrimage to a sacred Kieri. In addition to the narrative above, Yasumoto claimed (1996, 241) that unnamed Huichols told him about a Kieri venerated near the Cora settlement of Santa Teresa. An unverified declaration from a Cora, reported by a Franciscan priest in 1673, about a sacred plant called "*tapat*" (McCarty and Matson 1975, 211-212) may have been Kieri, according to Ted Coyle (email dated July 5, 2020).

Azqueltan was a Tepecano settlement, only 35 kilometers east of Tuxpan de Bolaños, when the anthropologist J. Alden Mason resided there for five months circa 1912 (Mason 1918, Mason 1981). When I first read Mason's "Tepecano Prayers" while writing my doctoral dissertation, I quickly concluded that the divine plant he assumed was *toloache* aka *Datura* must have been Kieri (Fikes 1985, 83). Although the species of *Solandra* that

Tepecanos venerated at the time remains unknown, there are three clues in Mason's data that indicate it was a *Solandra* species.

According to Mason (1918, 138-140, 143-44), that plant typically grew on rocks or on rocky hillsides (a location preferred by *S. brevicalyx*) and was petitioned by Tepecanos for anything they might wish to obtain, which I regard (see chapter 6) as indexical of Kauyumari's status as a general purpose deity. Moreover, they told Mason it had, "a thick trunk of nine inches in diameter" (1918, 139). This reminded me that the tree-like Kieri Peter Collings photographed at *Ututawita* (2000, 20-21) may have had a diameter that size at the base of its trunk. It was probably 2.5 meters tall.

Huichol Venerate Two Species of Kieri

According to Bernardello and Hunziker *(*1987*) Solandra* is, "a neotropical genus ranging from Mexico and the West Indies to South America." Within that genus, ten species have been identified by Bernardello and Hunzinger: *S. boliviano, S. brachycalyx, S. brevicalyx, S. grandiflora, S. longiflora, S. maxima, S. nizandensis, S. paraensis, S. guerrerensis* and S. *guttata.* Two of those ten species, *Solandra guttata* and *Solandra brevicalyx,* have been identified as the Kieri that is widely venerated within the Huichol homeland.[4]

Two indicators of *Solandra brevicalyx* that are most obvious to non-specialists, are its preference for growing on rocky hillsides and its height, which is typically less than six feet. S*olandra brevicalyx* is definitely a Kieri revered by some Chapalagana Huichol (Neurath 2005, 66; Yasumoto 1996, 247-253). In this context the botanists Bernardello and Hunziker (1987, 646) noted that John Lilly's 1971 Kieri specimen, "is clearly a representative of *S. guttata*" and was therefore "wrongly identified by Matuda as *S. brevicalyx*" and also in (Knab 1977).

The Kieri I visited in 1986 was growing in a forested area, at least 2000 meters above sea level. I cautiously identified it as *S. guttata* (Fikes 2003), which links it to the *S. guttata* specimen obtained by John Lilly, at an elevation of 2,200 meters (Bernardello and Hunziker 1987, 646). Incidentally, *S. guttata* is perhaps the most likely of three species of *Solandra* to be the "*tecomaxóchitl*" essential in the "ceremonial practices of the Aztecs" (Bernardello and Hunziker 1987, 646). In addition to *S. guttata*, Bernardello and Hunziker (1987, 650) think *S. guerrerensis* and *S. maxima* could also have been the Aztec sacred plant, *tecomaxóchitl*.

These two Solandra species (*guttata* and *brevicalyx*) are closely related, and both grow at the northern boundary of the genus (Bernardello and Hunziker 1987, 644). The Kieri whose nectar was present in the psychoactive honey González ate is presumably from one of those two *Solandra* species. Because the Kieri that González described in his myth of the Deer Shaman grew on a "patch of rocky ground" at a "huge round rock" (see paragraphs 4, 8, 9 in González's myth, in Chapter 4) it was most likely *S. brevicalyx*.

Guidelines for Obtaining Reliable Information About Kieri

I hope that quoting Gordon Wasson's advice on selecting the most qualified informants (below), as well as my discussion of examples of ethnographic malpractice, will motivate more meticulous studies about Kieri. Analysis of persistent mistakes made about Kieri prompts me to recommend that researchers should strive to cite and acquire narratives dictated by Huichol who actually were consecrated to Kieri as children, especially by their parents or grandparents (see chapter 6), and/or were allied with it as a result of making pilgrimages, or by having dreams or visions attributed to it. The three Huichol shaman-mentors (two of whom were kawiterutsixi) that I rely on regarding Kieri all had such a preferred status. That is, they all typify Wasson's model of "ideal informants."

To minimize the distribution of false or misleading data about Kieri, it seems prudent to select qualified informants, those having achieved rapport with Kieri. Whenever having affinity or a pact with Kieri has not been affirmed by one's Huichol mentors, or when statements about Kieri come from Huichol sources whose status cannot be confirmed by other researchers, one ought to remain cautious about the veracity of such data. All questionable reports require further examination, especially if they are anomalous when compared with information obtained from more qualified informants, such as kawiterutsixi consecrated to Kieri. Wasson's advice on selecting qualified informants is particularly relevant where Kieri is concerned:

> "In the archaic cultures as among advanced peoples, there is a hierarchy of excellence when it comes to the individuals who are the culture bearers. It is not sufficient to rely on the first informants who present themselves, or any shaman who is willing to talk. ... communication must be established with the finest exponents of the old traditions. None of the formidable difficulties of physical existence in those remote regions nor of communication should be allowed to blunt this obligation" (Wasson 1980, 8).

Zingg (2004, 16-20) should never have accepted at face value certain information and myths provided by Juan Real, who was Zingg's source about Kieri. Hence they mistakenly identified *Datura* as Kieri, an error that took some 45 years to resolve. Before publishing those myths, Zingg should have visited the plant that Real described and/or ascertained more about Real's (probable lack of) first-hand experiences with it. Zingg's misidentification of Kieri as *Datura* and the defamation of Kieri as "evil" were ethnographic mistakes exacerbated in the earliest publications about Kieri authored by Drs. Furst and Myerhoff (Fikes 1993).

Given Ramón Medina's appreciation of the protection and the other benefits Kieri provides (Fikes 1993, 117, 150), the story about the evils of *Datura* he imparted to Furst and Myerhoff (1966) seems bizarre. Furst and Myerhoff repeated Zingg's errors: by failing to visit and photograph a single Kieri, they all misidentified it as *Datura,* probably because its use was so well documented among Native Americans. However, given Ramón's consecration to Kieri by his mother (which I will detail in a forthcoming publication) and his knowledge of benefits it bestows on devout Huichols, it is astonishing that Furst and Myerhoff never obtained from Ramón what Fernando Benítez did (1968a, 285-86): an account attesting to musical ability being bestowed by Kieri. Because Furst's protégé, Tim Knab, neglected to specify what, if any, first-hand experiences his unnamed Huichol informants had with Kieri, and because Knab published a singular claim, that a "hallucinogenic effect" was produced when its leaves "were applied anally" (1977, 85), his assertions oblige scrutiny before they can be accepted (Fikes 1993, 117).

In light of past mistakes, rigorous ethnobotanical work is urgently needed on Kieri, the ancient Huichol entheogen still widely venerated, despite the imposition of the temple ritual cycle by the three "mythical" ancestor-singers who killed Takutsi and by the evangelization carried out by Franciscans. Sadly, it is too late for such research among the Tepecano, and possibly the Cora.

Notes

1. According to Benzi (1972, 175), several of Kauyumari's partners or helpers may sometimes be manifested as the plant Kieri, or they might take the form of a child or whirlwind. This statement confirms what Serratos told me: that he saw a child approaching me during my all night vigil in 1986 (at the exact time I heard only a sound approaching me). Moreover, both wind and child were specifically mentioned as surrogates of Kieri (see note four in Chapter 1.)

2. We must note in passing that Brundage's research (1983, 3, 167, 223) led him to conclude that Chichimec narratives of their ancestors shooting arrows to kill a goddess worshiped by foreigners indicates that they had conquered a new land.

3. I translated the Benítez anecdote from Spanish, and Carol Pearson translated Benzi's story from French. José Carrillo, a Huichol bilingual school teacher at San Andrés and the son of the famous shaman Hilario, was the source for both Benítez and Benzi.

4. The ethnobotanist, Dr. James Bauml, has photographed a

Solandra guttata growing near San Andrés Cohamiata (Yasumoto 1996, 246). The results of the analysis done by Evans *et. al* (1972) show that the roots of this species, *S. guttata,* have a high concentration of noratropine, its stalk has a high proportion of hyoscine, and its leaves contain traces of hyoscine, atropine, noratropine, hyoscyamine, and norhyoscyamine, among other chemical compounds. The location of the alkaloids found in plants of this *Solandra* species suggests that its enzyme system is designed to produce these chemicals (Aedo 2011, 132).

In addition to *S. guttata,* which John Lilly and I found growing east of the Chapalagana river, Ángel Aedo (2011, 123) states that two *Solandra* species, (*S. brevicalyx* and *S. guerrerensis*), were well identified within Huichol territory, on the western side of the Chapalagana river. Assuming his identification of *S. guerrerensis* is confirmed on the eastern side of the Chapalagana river, it will be the third of ten *Solandra* species native to the Huichol homeland. Since Aedo's (2011) book does not contain any photo showing offerings to a specific *S. guerrerensis,* one which has been identified as such by competent botanists, it would be premature to claim that species is venerated by the Chapalagana Huichol. To be sure, Aedo's two photos of Kieri (2011, 147-148) do not specify precisely which species of *Solandra* either of these two plants represent.

APPENDIX B

On Revealing Sacred Knowledge

In chapter one, Juan Negrín's explanation of Huichol hermeticism and its corollary, mutism, was mentioned. Jesús González expressed concern, several times, that providing me with his heretofore-secret revelations might bring him harm, as punishment from his helping spirits. Vine Deloria offers a comparable example from the Lakota, who were studied by Frances Densmore between 1911 and 1914. Although Densmore was, in my opinion, an outstanding ethnographer, she pressured her most prolific elderly shaman-informant, Śiya´ka (Densmore 1992, xxvi, 90; Deloria 2006, 212-13), to provide her with complete details of his dream-vision. As Densmore noted, "Śiya´ka was deeply affected by the narration of his dreams. Some men fear that such an act will cause their death. ...In a little more than a year, Śiya´ka was laid to rest in the prairie he loved" (quoted in Deloria 2006, 213).

According to Deloria (2006, 213), Densmore surely knew that by revealing all the details of his vision, which he told her he cherished above all else, Śiya´ka was "bringing his life to a close, his task completed since the vision had become common property." González implies (below) that certain revelations are gifts from the Ancestor Deities to him, their chosen person. Thus they must only be shared with those persons worthy or qualified to receive them. González prays, pleading for mercy, to convince his helping spirits to spare him from a fate similar to that of Śiya'ka.

"What I am explaining here in good faith should not be misunderstood, nor do I wish to disparage what anyone else does, and so I ask to be pardoned. This is only an explanation of the way in which I was able to learn what I know and practice today. I believe that what I have (achieved) today is good, for myself, and all my relatives. As everybody knows, this report is not wrong because it is only a description. As I say, it is not a sin to obey and carry out everything that my helping spirits ask me to do in order to have a good life and to acquire wisdom. Anyway, we have all been well until now. But there is something that I fear.

It may be wrong for me to explain details about my shamanic vocation. I do not know exactly how many people may learn about my life. If something were to happen to me (as a result of disseminating his life's story) I would not have any remedy. All this depends on how and for what reason what I have said will be used, and so I ask my helping spirits to pardon me. They have their rules and their enduring wisdom in order to give me the power to avoid succumbing to weakness. Regardless, I am grateful to them for permitting me to do and be what I am today. Thanks to them I have received what I was searching for and it is because of them that today our life is in full bloom: we have cattle, horses, sheep, maize, great-grandchildren, grandchildren and children [Who are called *xuturi*, pollen from the flower of life.] Because of this abundance, I believe that I am the tree for all my relatives.

Because of all the insights that I received from my helping spirits, you whom I invoke in my songs, you spirits that dwell everywhere: Xapawiyeme, Ut+anaka, Paritek+a, Kauyumari, Tatewari. I invoke all of you, but I beg you to remain tranquil in your homes and do not do anything against me. All of you know that I discovered your footprints in order to understand where you were dwelling. What you revealed to me was freely given so that I could have true comprehension of Huichol customs. Thus I have confidence in myself, and in all of you, that there will be no grumbling and that nothing bad will happen to me. I will be very grateful to you all if you remain wherever you are now. If I am doing anything wrong, I hope that you will show me how I have offended you. Of course I hope that is not the case, but it is better to ask for your blessing and for us all to be united as one family. It is for your sake that I perform rituals that appear to be untrue. I believe, however, that whatever I do is pleasing in your eyes. In your presence I always have the *aikutsi* (large gourd bowl), the *mawari* (ritual offering) and the women (*kwewimate*) whom you blessed and who are attentive and ready to give you all your chocolate (*yurari*). Our women will continue doing this ritual offering because through their efforts the family is raised and strengthened. [Women must make many ritual offerings to revitalize us, to gain *tukari* from our Ancestor Deities.] Whatever I am supposed to offer you all, I offer with a candle and with chocolate. It has been done like that from the beginning.

The person interviewing me (Fikes) wants me to answer his questions. I am answering by paying homage to the source of my wisdom. This is not a detailed explanation. It is enough to tell who I am, and whether I am carrying out my responsibilities in the exact manner I was ordered to do so, having received them as a mandate at the moment I was born to my parents. Inasmuch as I am being questioned about my whole life, I am now giving this narration even though it may be forbidden for me to disclose all my wisdom. For that reason I ask to be pardoned by my helping spirits in whom I believe and who have given me life. Perhaps the gift (shamanic ability) that our ancestors gave me should not be divulged in this type of discussion but I think this is untrue since nobody can take away the memories I guard inside my heart. No one can remove those memories from me except the spirits who gave them to me. Perhaps I will have to suffer the consequences for being daring or disobedient enough to divulge details about which spirits granted me wisdom, but I am convinced that this (problem) will not occur.

I also ask to be absolved by anyone who may read, see, hear or comprehend what I am revealing. I hope that they won't condemn me because each person has a particular ability, talent or gift granted to them by their god or gods. We all know that ultimately each of us thinks and is different from all others. I answer all the questions I am being asked with the hope that it will bring something beneficial for the one that wants to know. If that does not happen, I understand that this is because each person has their own reasons for wanting to use this information.

APPENDIX C

Thanking José Contreras

"Brother José Contreras, what you did for me you did not volunteer to do. You did it because I asked it of you, and because you fulfilled my request I am grateful to you. Because you acted as my defender, today I celebrate my rituals. Because you discovered the source of my illness, we did what you advised us to do. Do not worry when you return to your home. I hope you return safely and well. May you always have success with your helping spirits: Our Elder Brother, Our Father Sun, and Our Grandfather Fire. Thanks to all of them you have discovered the source of my illness. What you said about it is true because it has all been fulfilled.

You were like a stranger who was lost when you first arrived with me. But then I dared to ask you to do me a favor, and you helped by investigating our case. I know that you live at the village El Encino and that you venerate your ancestors, in concert with your family. The only thing that I seek is that everyone serves the good, just as you did with me. Even though I did not go to your house, I took advantage of the fact that you were coming from the village of Jasmines. Even though you did not touch or heal us, you were able to determine what was causing our sickness. Thanks to you everything turned out well so that I now perform rituals in which I always present the *aikutsi* (large gourd bowl) and *mawari* (ritual offering) for my helping spirits. Along with them, I receive life's blessings in the same way that our children are strengthened.

Although it was not your own idea (to heal us) your spirit has been steadfast. Even now I remember you. I did not show my appreciation for everything you did for me by giving you a huge sum of money. I am sure your resolve was much greater than the little bit of compensation that I gave you. Although it was not a payment, it was reward enough for our Elder Brother, who should have it now. [José did not charge a precise amount but for the *takwatsi* it was enough. Evidently the patient's intention to show gratitude is more important than the exact amount given.]

Appendix D

The Animals Around Us

"Wolves and bears once lived here. When I was a boy I never saw any jaguars but only bears, wolves, and mountain lions lived in our mountains. I once met some wolves at the Hill of the Goat when I was carrying some offerings. Four wolves blocked my progress. When we were living somewhere else wolves ate our burros; we saw the wolves eating them near our house. No wolves exist nowadays. Perhaps there are only a few left living well hidden. [Mestizos killed them or scared them away.] Mountain lions still exist and they eat our horses, burros and calves. Lots of other animals such as badgers and raccoons live here. Coyotes eat our chickens, goats and sheep.

I have never had any problems with rattlesnakes. But at the place called Ha Wakuwe (echo of the water) a rattler struck my uncle and he died because of the poison. We still have Mexican beaded lizards that, like rattlers, have lethal venom. The black snake, Haiku, and the coral snake, Haitarame, are also venomous. So is the snake, Uriakai. The horned toad, Teka, and the small rattler, Xain+, are also present. [Teka gives some Huichols excellent marksmanship and can shoot a liquid from its eyes.]

All these animals are dangerous and venomous but the rainy season is the most dangerous time for us. At that time of year people must be more careful because when one has been bitten the results are not pleasant. Sometimes these animals cause infections that can be fatal. However, some—but not all—of these animals are medicinal, and are used to heal people: some for boils (furuncles), wounds or certain infections in the stomach or blood. They don't attack people for no reason, but only when provoked."

Appendix E

Philip True, Story Proposal

3/24/98 8:30AM

I have come across what I think would make a good story; if not for the news side, certainly for one of the Sunday sections.

The Huichol Indians live in Mexico's last true wilderness, the Sierra Madre Occidental of northern Jalisco, Nayarit and Durango. It is John Huston country: a 100-mile wide swath of big-boned mountains and rolling mesas cut by vertical river canyons. In an area of tens of thousands of square miles, there are only a handful of dirt roads. To get anywhere, you most often have to walk or ride horses.

The Huicholes have evolved a cultural expression at least as colorful as the Chiapan Maya. Their white cotton suits are extensively embroidered in red, blue and yellow; they wear beaded necklaces and wristbands; their shamans don hats decked with mirrors, eagle and parrot feathers. Peyote is an integral part of their worship of nativist gods. Their life has been studied by anthropologists for decades.

Unlike the highland Maya, the Huicholes have retained a certain joy in their life. A day near a Huichol community is marked by the nearly constant sound of children laughing and playing. This kind of joy gives them a certain integrity in their being that allows them to welcome in strangers, something the Maya are usually loath to do.

The Huichol lifestyle has been affected by contacts with Mexican mestizo culture, but remains remarkably intact. Outside a handful of small towns, wheels do not exist. A small hand grinder for cornmeal is the usual concession to modernity (although a battery-driven boom box is occasionally seen). Distant communications are still conducted with a column of smoke.

That lifestyle now stands on the cusp of dramatic change. This month, the Mexican government strung electric lines to the town of Tuxpan de Bolaños. After a series of confrontations between Huicholes and mestizo Mexicans living on disputed communal lands last year, other resources (and the government agents that accompany them) are now making their way into the back country. There is a building boom in the 300-person community.

A look at Huichol country as it confronts this influx of modernity would be a fascinating, wonderfully visual piece. The countryside, the people and their ceremonies are breathtaking and accessible. The Huicholes are at once adaptive and open to change, while representing one of Mexico's vanishing indigenous cultures.

At the same time, the jumping off place for Huichol country, the 16th century mining town of Bolaños, is of interest in its own right. Colonial ruins line the town's cobbled streets. The place was nearly abandoned between 1940 and 1970, when the price of silver brought several mines back into production.

It's mayor is that rarest of things, a decent PRI politician. He has a hatful of ambitious schemes to try to bring further prosperity to Bolaños and the Huichol country, few of which will probably fly in this era of reduced developmental resources from Mexico City. He also eats peyote buttons, of which he had three on a shelf behind his desk when I spoke with him.

There is a beautiful story within all of this. Interested?

San Antonio Express-News, 27 December 1998.

APPENDIX F

Interpreting Events After True's Murder

Both Dr. Paul Liffman and Robert Rivard have interpreted forensic evidence and probed several possible motives for Phil True's murder. Liffman is a well-known anthropologist who had worked for six years in the indigenous Huichol community of San Andrés Cohamiata by 2002, the year he finished his doctoral dissertation. True's murder took place near the southern boundary of the *comunidad indigena* of San Andrés (Liffman, 2002, 413). Liffman does not disclose his conclusion about the motive for the murder of Phil True. Instead, he cautions us about the obstacles standing in the way of learning the truth about True's murder. "As is so often the case in Mexico, there was no authoritative interpretation or even certain empirical knowledge on which to base a definitive version of events." (2002, 412). Liffman's doctoral dissertation provides an intelligent analysis of the tangle of opposing interest groups (2002, 358), each of which construed the crime scene evidence, two distinct autopsy reports, and the two murderers' confessions according to its own particular prejudices. After True's body was found, an avalanche of accusations and arguments over what really happened was structured along pre-existing schisms such as Mexican government versus journalists, mestizos versus Huichols, and patriotic Mexicans versus Mexico-bashers (Liffman 2002, 377). To further complicate matters, the federal government ordered a second autopsy. It was done despite (or perhaps because of) the first autopsy, whose results were presented by Dr. Mario Rivas Souza, an eminent and outspoken forensic authority for the state of Jalisco (Mexico). Dr. Rivas declared that True had been struck hard in the back of his skull, perhaps with a rock, and strangled with his own bandana (Rivard 2005, 158-161). Dr. Rivas Souza, a seasoned forensic expert, always stood by his original pronouncement, that True was murdered. He seemed to suspect that the federal government, "may have wanted the second one [autopsy] to blur the first." (Liffman 2002, 394). Investigating all of the results of the second autopsy need not detain us now. The primary effect, if not the intent, of the second autopsy was to facilitate the thought that True died in a tragic accident. Suffice it to say that by contradicting the first autopsy (which is considered more reliable than any subsequent autopsy because doing it inevitably alters the evidence) an ambiguity was created. This uncertainty encouraged each of the various interest groups to justify their favorite interpretation. More such cognitive fog was produced when Mexican authorities developed, "only one of True's nine rolls of exposed film," supposedly for "lack of funds." Liffman continues, concluding that, "It is as if the government wished to keep the empirical field clear for speculation." (Liffman 2002, 370). Put in plain English, if you don't like the truth, make it harder for people to find it. More fog obstructing the truth about True's murder was produced by the two murderers. During the weeks following their arrest by civilian authorities on December 26, 1998, Juan Chivarra and Miguel Hernandez confessed several times. Each version offered different, even contradictory, motives for True's murder. Their first confession claimed they were outraged by True's taking photographs, without permission, of a "sacred spring," a "sacred river," and sacred objects (Liffman 2002, 383).

The fact that True failed to obtain a permit when entering the indigenous community of San Sebastián via its annex, Tuxpan de Bolaños, raised the question of who had sovereignty over Huichol territory, a complex and controversial issue beyond the scope of this essay. Suffice it to say that it has long been customary for outsiders, formerly mostly anthropologists, visiting the Chapalagana Huichol to obtain written permission from the authorities of the specific Huichol community in which they intend to reside. This customary usage affirms the legitimacy of Huichol authorities who were originally recognized, or created, by colonial Spaniards (Zingg 2004). Paul Kvinta (1999), a journalist who retraced, with the help of a Huichol guide, True's solo hike, was sure that True had not secured permission from Huichol authorities in San Sebastián, the community bordering San Andrés, where True was murdered. True clearly failed to pull a permit from Tuxpan de Bolaños, the place where his final journey started after he got off the bus. According to True's journal, a man named Juan (Chivarra) threatened True with jail for having a camera and failing to get permission authorizing him to be in the community of San Sebastián. True identified himself to Juan as a reporter and proclaimed he had obtained permission from Tuxpan. We can only speculate about whether Chivarra called True's bluff on that false claim. Failure to obtain permission from Huichol authorities may result in being jailed, fined and/or expelled from that community (Fikes 1999, and see chapter 9). Liffman concurs, stating that sometimes a payment makes access possible. (2002, 385). He adds that a Huichol, "community usually charges outsiders fees of US $10-20 dollars just to attend major ceremonies." Even if Juan Chivarra were upset with True for not having any permit from Tuxpan or San Sebastián, that alone should not have incited him to murder True—unless there were unusual extenuating circumstances.

The murderers' other complaint about True seems more serious (especially because it was added to his failure to obtain a permit). Huichol sensitivity to being photographed has been observed by all anthropologists. The Mexico City based journalist, Katherine Ellison, expressed sympathy for Huichol sentiment: "Today, aware that foreigners see their culture as a valuable commodity, they have taken the additional steps of banning cameras and tape-recorders in their communities, and have thrown disobedient visitors into their locally run jails" (Ellison 1992, 9). I found it almost impossible to photograph rituals performed at ceremonial centers such as Santa Catarina and Las Latas. However, in those ranchos where I was trusted, I was permitted to take photos. True's taking of nine rolls of illicit photos could have upset Huichols who did not know him. Pondering True's prolific photo taking, I infer True's first-hand experiences were limited to urban Huichols (e.g., in Guadalajara), and more friendly families residing in Tuxpan (such as the family of Jesús González). If True had significant prior experience with unfriendly Huichols, as I did in Santa Catarina in 1977 and 1998 (see Chapter 9) he would have known better than to take a camera, without a permit, on a trek deep inside the Huichol hinterland. Kvinta (1999) cites True's journal on Chivarra's threat to have True arrested, because True was taking photographs (see note 6 in Chapter 8). Still, I find it unlikely that True's unauthorized photography was the sole reason Chivarra and Hernandez killed him.

With results from the second autopsy, and after the two Huichols gained access to legal counsel, the rationalizations they offered on December 29, 1998 for murdering True shifted from the indigenous rights-oriented initial confession, to a domestic self-defense plea, as Liffman described it. They declared True was on drugs or drunk when he forcibly entered the Hernandez's home, "probably trying to rape one of their women or steal one of their children" (Liffman 2002, 395). In another version of their "confession," True had supposedly been, "pursuing Hernandez's wife and naked children into the house in order to photograph them," against their will. True allegedly barged into their house, under the influence of "some drug" while speaking English (Liffman 2002, 395-96). These wicked and wild scenarios starring Phil True may have appeared more plausible because the second autopsy, "found a 0.26 percent blood alcohol level in the decomposing body" (Liffman 2002, 396). Matching their "confessions" with the high blood alcohol level detected in True's decomposing body was, effectively if not intentionally, a strategy for persuading some Mexicans that the murderers killed True in order to defend their families from a crazy drunken gringo. I reject such intoxication-oriented scenarios as fiction, not only because True was a committed family man and veteran hiker (Liffman 2002, 396), but also because four of five forensic experts in the U.S.A. who examined the Mexican second autopsy report had dismissed the, "significance of the blood-alcohol level and attributed the reading to postmortem decomposition." Rivard paraphrased Dr. Peerwani, one of those four experts: "the blood-alcohol test conducted in the Guadalajara laboratory…was meaningless. Rivard continues by quoting Peerwani that the test used was, "totally unacceptable in our legal system." (2005, 314).

Chivarra and Hernandez were arrested and charged with robbery. In police photos taken after their arrest, "True's camera, clothes, boots, tent, first-aid kit, passport and other documents, as well as $4,000 pesos (US $400) in cash" were shown in their possession (Liffman 2002, 397, 381). The photo of Chivarra and Hernandez, with True's belongings, makes its hard to entirely dismiss robbery as a possible cause for the murder. To speculate, perhaps Chivarra's knowledge that Phil lacked a permit and had a camera, emboldened him to murder True at a place far from his rancho.

Some forty eight hours after the first confrontation between True and Chivarra occurred near his rancho, Chivarra, along with his wife, Yolanda, and brother-in-law, Miguel Hernandez, were walking on their pilgrimage to deposit offerings at a sacred cave when they spotted True climbing up the canyon from the Chapalagana river (Kvinta 1999, 140). Kvinta embellished upon another "confession" from the two murderers, asserting that Chivarra again became angry at True, supposedly because he saw True's camera. Meanwhile Chivarra, Hernandez and Yolanda were approaching True from behind and below him. Chivarra then told Hernandez, "Let's kill the gringo," and then pounced on True's back, which caused him to fall, "backward down the slope, where he struck his head against a rock." The two murderers then strangled True with his own bandanna and took True's possessions (Kvinta 1999, 140-141). At best there may be elements of truth in this scenario, but we don't know exactly what they are.

Sometime in 2002, not long after the "defendants" were sentenced to 13 years in jail, yet another motive for murdering True was proclaimed by Juan Chivarra. This new confession came to light in conversations between Rivard and Patricia Morales, a

Mexican advocate of Huichol causes, whose vigorous defense of Juan Chivarra and his accomplice, Miguel Hernandez, was crucial in the judge's decision to free the two of them from prison in Colotlán (Rivard 2005, 331-332, 346-47). Sometime after Morales heard Chivarra's father regretfully tell her (during a visit the two of them made to the prison) that his son had indeed killed True, she may have felt remorseful for her part in persuading the judge to free two guilty Huichols (Rivard 2005, 328-29). Then, after the two killers were pronounced guilty of murder and sentenced to 13 years, she angrily demanded that Chivarra tell her the truth. In response, Chivarra claimed (privately, only to her) that he killed True because he had no permit for himself nor his camera, yet had asked Chivarra to help him find "semiprecious stones that Huichols consider sacred." This "confession" also features Chivarra, his wife Yolanda, and Hernandez making a pilgrimage and heading down the same path that True had already taken after leaving their rancho.

Adding the gemstones to this new plot, Chivarra claimed he saw True, "searching for gemstones along the river." Chivarra then ordered Hernandez to help him kill True then and there (Rivard 2005, 329-330). Rivard and Morales discussed their divergent interpretations of a small bag with a handful of stones found in True's backpack, and a journal entry by Phil mentioned that Juan was complaining that trespassers like True were seeking to steal Huichol mineral wealth. Evidently, what Chivarra told Morales was just what she wanted to hear in order to ease her guilt. Still intent on persuading Rivard, Morales provided particulars taken from the story Juan Chivarra told her (with details never disclosed in any of Chivarra's prior narratives). She was certain that Chivarra's claim was correct, that among the Huichol, "True was persona non grata because of previous forays into Huichol territory made without permission in search of agates and opals to enrich himself. He had been caught trading in gemstones before, she assured me, and on one such trip had been detained and held in a crude Huichol stockades." (Rivard 2005, 332).

Rivard thought Chivarra's allegations about True, as Morales remembered them, were preposterous. Nevertheless Rivard explained what Weigand told him about the traumatic colonial experiences that some Huichol endured, including being forced to labor in silver mines owned by Spaniards. Their mistreatment by miners as well as Spaniards ancillary to mining, helped make Huichols hypersensitive to any outsider displaying curiosity about semiprecious stones (Rivard 2005, 331). Morales admitted that Chivarra's newest "confession" to her did not justify murdering True, but asserted she was sure that True's failure to produce a single publication about the Huichol was a sure sign he had been hiding something. She believed True's supposedly secret gemstone business explained the fact that True had never written a single article about the Huichol (Rivard 2005, 332). Without any corroborating evidence demonstrating True's involvement in selling semiprecious stones, I interpret Chivarra's self-serving statements about True being a gemstone thief as a yarn concocted to justify his murder to a Huichol audience, as well as to ardent Huichol sympathizers such as Morales.

A press conference was held in Guadalajara in 2003, almost two years after the killers were released from the Colotlán jail in August, 2001. Patricia Morales repeated her baseless narrative at that press conference. When she finished, Rivard publically implied that Morales was telling another tall tale, repeating one of many "confessions" and excuses invented by the killers. Rivard included in his statement that, "Philip was murdered by Juan (Chivarra) and Miguel (Hernandez) and nothing can justify what they did" (Rivard 2005, 347).

That press conference was, at least in part, a way of swaying a Mexican federal judge to force the highest court in the state of Jalisco to review and then issue a new ruling on True's murderers. Preceding that press conference, a federal judge had, in February of 2003, set aside their conviction and their sentence to thirteen years in prison—until the Jalisco's high court reviewed their case again. Over a year passed with no new ruling.

Finally on March 30, 2004 another federal judge mandated, "the intransigent state magistrates to issue a ruling." (Rivard 2005, 350). On April 27, 2004, Jalisco's high court ruled that Chivarra and Hernandez were guilty and sentenced them to twenty years in prison (Rivard 2005, 351). Three days after the verdicts and sentences were issued, Mexican President Vicente Fox, through his international press spokesman, telephoned Robert Rivard to wish him well and to acknowledge that the Phil True case was one of the reasons President Fox had introduced a, "comprehensive judicial reform initiative" (Rivard 2005, 352).

APPENDIX G

Remarks about the Wixarika Language

The Huichol (Wixarika) language is most closely related to Náayeri, the language spoken by their western neighbors, the Cora (Coyle 2001, 16). Both of these languages belong to the Sonorese branch of southern Uto-Aztecan" (Valiñas quoted in Zingg 2004, xv-xvi).

While writing my doctoral dissertation Professor Ken Hill prepared me to use a (Huichol) Wixarika language transcription system based almost entirely on the transcription system devised by the linguist, Professor Joseph Grimes (Fikes 1985, 4-6). My ethnographic research was greatly aided by consulting Huichol-Spanish and Spanish-Huichol dictionaries and cassette tapes kindly provided by Professor Grimes. During the process of writing this book I finally acted on advice from Professor Paul Liffman, as did my mentor, Professor Phil Weigand, who wrote, "We have adopted the system developed by the *Departamento de Estudios de Lenguas Indígenas* (DELI) of the *Universidad de Guadalajara* for transcribing Huichol terms, mostly at Liffman's suggestion" (Weigand 2000, 32).

In this context, linguistic specialists will benefit by studying Liffman's (2011, xiii) "A Note on the Wixarika Language." Following Liffman, this book recognizes only five vowels (a, e, i, u, +). The sound I formerly transcribed as ü as in the word *Paritecüa* is now an + as in the word *Paritek+a*. This new transcription system, devised by Professor Iturrioz, has been widely adopted by scholars working with the Wixarika and by the Wixaritari themselves. Of course having dictionaries illustrating that new system would be welcomed by researchers like myself.

For the sake of my non-specialist readers and to continue my prior transcription practice, I am still omitting initial glottal stops, as did Grimes (Fikes 1985, 4). Thus my spelling of *uxa* and *Ututawita* contrast with Dr. Liffman's spelling of *'uxa* and *'ututawita*. I feel compelled to capitalize certain Wixarika words, such as *Ututawita* and *Hay+rime*, because of their centrality in Huichol belief and ritual. I welcome constructive criticism of my mistakes in transcribing Huichol words as well as highlighting nuances in meaning associated with Wixarika words. If I learn this book has many transcription errors, I will correct them on my website: www.jayfikes.com

After reading the manuscript that became this book, Professor Liffman made several suggestions to correct my spelling of Wixarika words and/or interpret their meaning and linguistic origin, in the case of *topilli*. Because researchers may find his comments, and mine in response, useful, I include some of them below. My usages are listed, followed by information derived from Liffman's generous comments.

tukimari (pollen): *t+kimari* This word probably means Kieri pollen. Fikes agrees.

matsua (wristguard): *mats+wa*

topilli (young man serving a governor or other colonial-era official): Liffman notes that *tupilli* is a colonial-era, Nahuatl-based word for that young man, and that in Wixarika the word is *tupiri*.

Yurianaka (moist or fertile earth goddess): Yurienaka

Nia'ariwame (Rain Mother): N+'ariwame

waiyeyeri (ancestral path): *wayeyeri* (spatialized ritual practice)

nuiakate (protectors): *nuiwakate* (those who are being born)

2020 census data from Mexico's *INEGI*, Censo de Población y Vivienda, show a total of 60,263 persons three years and older who spoke Huichol (Wixarika). Almost ninety percent of them live in two Mexican States, Nayarit and Jalisco. A table provided by John P. Schmal (in his email dated 7/4/2021), is posted on my website: www.jayfikes.com

ENDNOTES

Introduction

1. When I met Reuben Snake in Washington, D.C., soon after the United States Supreme Court's landmark 1990 decision to disregard first amendment protections of religious freedom for members of the Native American Church (who ingest peyote during their all-night religious rituals), my goal was to help him overturn that misguided and ethnocentric ruling. Our priority was to persuade Congress to pass federal legislation protecting Native American Church services. We quickly decided to provide vital information Congress (and citizens) needed to understand the purposes and procedures embedded in the religious rituals Reuben Snake had led for almost 20 years as an ordained Roadman of the Native American Church. One vehicle for providing that information was the documentary film, "The Peyote Road" (1992). Later, in 1993, Reuben and I agreed to prepare his biography, thinking it might prove useful in lobbying Congress and inspiring younger Native Americans.

2. His first significant public battle, in 1969, started when news of an alleged rape of a woman in Walt Hill, Nebraska elicited a knee-jerk, blanket condemnation of all Native Americans. That news began "going viral" after a racist, anti-Indian petition was published in the town newspaper. Rather than continuing to suffer the effects of such racism in silence, Snake organized the Winnebago (and their neighbors, the Omaha) in an effective economic boycott of Walt Hill. The media attention Reuben solicited, in addition to the economic damage the boycott soon caused, prompted Walt Hill's civic leaders to meet with tribal leaders to formulate a plan that gradually improved relations between Anglos and Native Americans (Fikes 1996, 110-112).

His final battle, which I joined, was won in 1993, with passage of the Religious Freedom Restoration Act (Public Law 103-141) and in 1994 when President Clinton signed federal legislation (Public

Law 103-344) to protect Native American religious freedoms. In Reuben Snake's biography I interpreted the religious rituals he led as a Roadman from within an historical, ecological, and political perspective. We wanted readers to be conscious of the centuries of injustice and religious intolerance that were exemplified by the Supreme Court's 1990 ruling against the Native American Church, in *Oregon Employment Division v. Smith.*

Chapter 1

1. Tuxpan de Bolaños had about 1,269 inhabitants in 2010. It is accessible by unpaved roads and a tiny dirt landing strip. Electricity brought by power lines is available. Soccer fields, radios, televisions, pick-up trucks and small stores stocked with a variety of Mexican goods represent and amplify the erosion of traditional Huichol culture. Reliance on modern medicine provided by Mexican-educated doctors and nurses, as well as attendance at government schools (from primary through senior-high), are contributing to the development of a bicultural identity. Tuxpan lacks an aboriginal temple, the central element in ceremonial centers, but keepers of the votive bowls (the temple officers) still perform aboriginal ceremonies such as the Dance of Our Mother, Tatei Neixa (Fikes 1985, 1993; Fikes and Weigand 1998, Zingg 2004). Although Tuxpan de Bolaños was not legally chartered until 1885, it retains colonial Spanish religious offices such as *mayordomos* (custodians of Jesus, the Virgin Mary and other Catholic saints), and political offices such as judges, that were imposed on Huichol *comunidades indigenas* (Téllez 2011, 159-172; Weigand 1978; Fikes and Weigand 1998, 19-20; Zingg 2004).

2. 120 years ago there were about twenty ceremonial centers, (whose paramount feature is a round temple some 12 meters in diameter) functioning throughout the 4,107 square kilometer Huichol homeland. Aboriginal temple officers are recruited from numerous villages surrounding a specific ceremonial center.

Considerable evidence suggests that since about 200 C.E. the annual cycle of aboriginal rituals performed at ceremonial centers has controlled vital subsistence activities (i.e., deer and rabbit hunting, fishing, and maize horticulture) and facilitated trade of sacred items (e.g., peyote, conch shells, and feathers) with neighboring cultures. Aboriginal temple rituals are intended to honor, entertain and feed Rain Mothers and other ancestors who personify natural phenomena. Rituals copy the world-organizing precedents set by ancestors and thereby induce them to protect human health and provide abundant sustenance.

3. This story of how he acquired his power years after eating wasps' honey, derived from Kieri nectar is remarkable. As Appendix A (about Kieri) indicates, there is no doubt that Kieri is an ancient entheogen, and one that surely predates peyote (see Chapters 5 & 6). Kieri invokes a mixture of fear and reverence among all Huichols I have consulted, and it is widely considered to be an aid in deer hunting and violin playing (Fikes 1985).

The Kieri whose spirit summoned Jesús is a species of *Solandra*, perhaps *Solandra brevicalyx*. My research in Tuxpan as well as the publications of other researchers, suggest that Kieri is a name that can be applied to various species, including those outside the genus *Solandra*. Particular care must be taken to determine what type of plant is meant when a Huichol uses the word (see Appendix A).

Containing tropane alkaloids such as hyoscyamine, hyoscine/scopolamine, nortropine, etc., *Solandra* is closely related to the genus *Datura*, and is considered a dangerous plant: one that can cause delirium, paralysis, and sometimes death.

4. This is the messenger and passenger of the Kieri plant that lives in one place. This messenger Kieri appears in various places by means of the wind. It sings, shouts, whistles and plays the violin. The child that summoned Jesús represents this messenger Kieri. The old man represents the *tukimarika*, the adult Kieri and the *takwatsi* he received from the old man represents Tamatsi. Liffman infers that *tukimarika* is a verb meaning 'to pollinate'

(email to Fikes dated 9-26-2020). Perhaps an "adult Kieri" is a mature plant, capable of pollinating.

5. The grandfather who fasted for Jesús was actually the husband of Jesús' father's sister. This would make him a *naukixiwi*; we would call him an uncle or an affine. This grandfather was himself a shaman and he knew that the salt fast was required. He fasted one month for Jesús.

Chapter 4

1. In addition to being the chief singing shaman in the primordial underworld (Watet+apa), Kam+kime is the father of the wolves and is capable of teaching Wixaritari to heal and sing. Santa Catarina Huichol shamans held him in higher esteem than did Jesús González (Fikes 1985, 330-331, 2011). González calls him Kam+kikame. He states, in paragraphs 29 & 31, that Kam+kime and his followers have both human and animal forms. Both González and my two kawiteru mentors from Santa Catarina agree that aspiring shamans must refuse becoming allies of the impious yuwitari, beings who remained in Watet+apa, the primordial underworld (Fikes 2011, 107-110). Kam+kime's followers do not want Tamatsi, their intended sacrificial victim, to escape. Their obstruction of Tamatsi's vocation is based on fear and jealousy. Their desire to corrupt Tamatsi with sex, or even murder him, is consistent with their attack on the boy selected by the Ancestor Deities to become the Sun. In his myth depicting the birth of the Sun, the Santa Catarina kawiteru, José Sánchez, explains that the boy's mother as well as many allied Ancestor Deities were waiting to offer foods to the boy (now the Sun) emerging for the first time from Paritek+a. "When the others became aware that the Sun was about to rise they went there to attack him because they were envious. Despite that, he emerged. When he ascended into heaven, the heat he made caused the envious ones to melt and they were transformed into hills. ... All the Serpent People remained there in the underworld." As I understand it, the Animal

or Serpent People (Kukuterixi) have dual forms because they are unfinished or incomplete beings. As a result of having remained in the primordial underworld, they lack the iyari (conscience) bestowed on each Huichol by the Sun Father. Their immaturity explains why they oppose Huichol heroes such as Tamatsi, the Sun Father and Grandfather Fire (Fikes 2011, 108). The word yuwitari (or y+witari, according to Liffman) is a synonym for González's use of Kam+kikate (referring especially to the Wolf People in this myth) as well as for Kukuterixi (Snake or Animal People).

2. These two girls seem determined to corrupt Tamatsi, if not by having sex, then by trying to feed him three plants (unidentified by me) which he found inedible (see paragraph 17). Liffman noted in personal correspondence, hariuki fibers are used to bind arrowheads to shafts. The two girls were clearly serving their father, Kam+kime, who intended to sacrifice Tamatsi before he could fulfill his destiny. To accomplish his mission, Tamatsi needed to become the male deer in order to regain his own sacred paraphernalia and that of Kam+kime, to build god-houses and finally to lead the Peyote Dance attended by the vanquished Wolf People, the Kam+kikate (see paragraphs 51-56).

Chapter 5

1. Because Tuxpan de Bolaños lacks a native temple (*tuki*), it is slightly incorrect to call him a temple officer. Zingg's myth (2004, 40-48) about Tuxpan's keepers of the votive gourd bowls shows that they function akin to the temple officers I observed at Santa Catarina. Thus González served a specific Ancestor Deity during five consecutive years, as did the Santa Catarina shamans who were my mentors. During his period of service to a specific ancestor, he was identified as the keeper of the votive gourd bowl consecrated to that ancestor. According to Vicente, his father served Harianaka twice, Yurianaka once and Xapawiyeme once. Correcting his earlier statement (see Chapter 3), González elaborated on Vicente's summary:

"For five consecutive years I was the votive gourd bowl keeper of Tatei Harianaka. Her gourd bowl was white. I served Tatei Yurianaka for five years. Then I served Harianaka another five years, then for five years I served Tatei Xapawiyeme. I was carrying all their offerings to the sacred sites that correspond to each one of them. To deliver offerings to Xapawiyeme I had to go to the lagoon at Villa Corona. Because of my long years of experience, I know what a votive gourd bowl keeper does."

2. There is, or was formerly, a kind of *itauki* that could be redeemed by performing a ritual (Fikes 2011). That *itauki* evidently differs from the purely malevolent entity that takes possession of certain senile persons. According to González, "The *itauki* is never developed consciously or voluntarily by anybody. It only happens when somebody is moribund and spiritually weak. That is when the evil spirits take advantage of the person and start to bring materials needed to make the *itauki*. That person is not conscious when he/she decides to make the *itauki*. If they were they would consider the harm it will do to their children, cattle, corn and livestock. Nobody would ever want to damage them. But when one's thinking changes as a result of a spiritual weakness, then that person says, "I no longer want to live, to remain in this world. I believe I shall die." That is when the evil spirits, or perhaps the devil, because they say he exists—oblige the person to make the *itauki* in order to destroy one's own family. This evil spirit (*itauki*) will capture the *k+puri* (vital spirit, related to *Hay+rime* and thick human hair located around the anterior fontanelle) of every member of the family.

"In this manner we destroy our descendants, because of our own spiritual weakness. Of course when one is healthy, one is content with one's family and never considers such things. But sometimes, due to tragedies such as homicide and heartbreak, we languish to the point where we obliterate ourselves. Because that person is dying, they are willing to harm their own relatives. For that reason they die in three or four days. The *itauki* … is made unconsciously, by means of dreams. Then the same evil spirit that possesses that (dying) person may impose restrictions on that person. One, two or three years may pass before the family that was captured by the *itauki* begins to sicken, or its livestock begins to die. That is why they say that when somebody does this [creates an *itauki*] that person is rejected at every place [that must be visited in the afterlife]. They (gods) do not permit the deceased to travel [in spirit, after death] with this evil spirit they made."

(Vicente explained that this travel ban refers to the deceased bidding farewell to the gods in order to arrive at his/her final destination in the next life.)

"The children, cattle, corn and everything else connected to that family are sickening and dying because the evil is dispersed through the [air] wind. (Vicente added that the *itauki* has control over the *k+puri* of everyone and travels through the air in the darkness.) That [the *itauki* has stolen people's spirits, *k+puri*] is what we discover when we turn for help to our shamans. The shaman diagnoses the cause of this disease. The shaman tells us if it is caused by an *itauki*. The shaman also proclaims that the deceased person was the one responsible for damaging his/her family...that person did it involuntarily. They are held responsible after they die. The evil spirit used tricks to make that person its accomplice.

I do not know how to kill the *itauki*. If I did know how (to kill it) I would know much more about this issue. Sick people get better because the *k+puri* that was stolen from each of them is returned, at least in a material way."

Because no anthropologist has ever witnessed the ritualized killing of the *itauki*, I asked Vicente to clarify. ["After a Huichol healer kills the *itauki*, the evil spirit that hijacks the spirits of the deceased's relatives, he returns an object, such as a hair, which is taken as conclusive evidence that the *itauki* is dead. The hair recovered by the shaman is a manifestation of the spiritual booty stolen by the *itauki*. After the shaman kills the *itauki* the people who were sick are given *k+puri*-containing water, *Hay+rime*, in order to revitalize their souls."]

3. Vicente added that, because the gods helped his great grandfather get the *uxa* of the doe, he was obliged to express his gratitude to them by making offerings at various sacred sites such as Tsakaimuta and Te'akata. Grandfather Fire and the Sun Father, whose god-houses are at Te'akata, provide essential aid in deer hunting (Fikes 2011). The deity called Tsakaimuta remains virtually unknown to non-Huichols. According to González:

"Tsakaimuta is one of the principal mothers for all humans. She sustains all of us. One can ask whatever one wishes, to become a singer or whatever it might be, when visiting her at her shrine. She is virtuous in every endeavor. If one wishes to become a singer she will grant it, provided one makes pilgrimages to her for five consecutive years. But she is dangerous, because she punishes anyone who fails to fulfill his/her obligations. She is one of our principal Ancestor Deities. I went to that hill where she lives. Those of us who go to implore her aid in becoming singers are obliged to bring our *takwatsi*. If we do not bring it, we will become crippled or emaciated. When one suffers from such sicknesses, sent by her as punishment, we say that somebody has bewitched us. But in truth I "bewitch" myself by being a sinner, by failing to fulfill my pact. We are experiencing troubles today because we are unable to visit Tsakaimuta. We are feeble because we are descendants of Tsakaimuta. Our grandparents relied on (the goddess of) that place too."

Tsakaimuta is the name of a sacred hill and/or a cave at the Mesa del Nayar, which was the capital of the Cora chiefdom, located west of the Chapalagana Huichol homeland. Lumholtz reported (1900, 11-12, 81,142) that the deity dwelling there is an assistant to the Sun Father who is associated with the setting sun and rain. Zingg was puzzled when he learned that Tsakaimuta ordered Tamatsi to provide him with ten candles, twice as many as the five candles Tamatsi offered to Grandfather Fire (1938, 316, 638). Reports by Catholic missionaries, Ortega (1754) and Arias de Saavedra (1673), suggested that Tsakaimuta was among the highest ranking of all ancestors (gods) before Spaniards conquered the Cora capital in 1722. Before 1722, the Cora chief, Nayari, was venerated in mummified form in a temple just below the temple consecrated to the Sun Father. Both these temples were on the hill called Tsakaimuta. The Cora chief, who also performed as their highest-ranking priest, served Tsakaimuta. Tsakaimuta was also the name of a large "province" or theocratic chiefdom ruled by the Cora priest-chief (McCarty and Matson 1975, 198-200). During my fieldwork I learned that Tsakaimuta is represented and served by a Santa Catarina temple officer because Tsakaimuta is a Rain Mother who should be regularly petitioned for rain (Fikes 1985, 155, 355). Thus the temple officer serving Tsakaimuta made prayers and offerings at her shrine on the Mesa del Nayar, as did Vicente González's great grandfather.

4. Obtaining *uxa* from these three reptiles has mythological justification. González declared that gaining the *uxa* of the Teka (horned toad) enabled his grandfather to kill the *itauki*. This feat is consistent with his chronicle about Tamatsi, which asserts that the Teka shot Tamatsi after he escaped, in deer form, from the temple of the animal people. In a comparable myth about Tamatsi, Serratos states that it was Rattlesnake Person (Xaye) who shot the arrow that killed Tamatsi. Jesús González identified Imukui, with the boy whose intelligence and power permitted him to transform himself into the Sun Father. González credits Imukui and Xaye with having sufficient power to protect Huichol singers (shamans) against sorcerers (or 'witches,' whom I treat as identical because they too are anti-social).

5. González' comments imply that aspiring shamans learn primarily by observation and personal experience. This bias toward personal experience differs greatly from the learning style prevalent in most public schools in the United States (Fikes 1978, 1993). The mentoring relationship between González and his grandfather and father (neither of whom were literate) differs somewhat from the less intimate—and more public—kind of instruction presumably associated with participation as a temple officer during a five-year aboriginal temple ritual cycle. Peter

Collings, a non-Huichol, served one term (five years, starting in 1972) as a temple officer in San Andrés Cohamiata. He then observed that the temple officers who have returned with peyote from *Wirikuta* were obliged to publicly, "repeat the names and official positions of the Huichol government and of the temple (*tuki*) as well as naming all the sacred places and the pantheon of gods" (2000, 27).

6. González often asked certain deities to pardon him for divulging secrets to me. On this occasion he stated:

"My Sun Father, my Grandfather Fire and my Elder Brother please do not take offense with me. I know you were the ones who introduced these customs of naming children. I complied with all restrictions required to become a shaman. That is why the power I received may be used in my practice [as a shaman]. Whatever I do is based on the encounters I had with my gods. Our Mothers, Nia'ariwame and Tuamuxawi, forgive me if I interpret your words without respect. Last year [2003] I went on a long trip (with Jay Fikes to California) so I could earn money in order to buy cattle. Because I made that trip, now I am prepared to celebrate the First Fruits ritual. My gods, I think you will be satisfied with their blood. Our Maize Mother (Tatei Niwetsika), you will observe the children accompanied by their toy, the three-legged drum, which we play. I hope all our children will receive good health and prosperity. (Vicente added that his father is pleading for the gods to forgive him.) With this gratitude that we show you [by performing rituals and making offerings] I hope you all will be content. Do not send any sickness because of the questions that Fikes is asking me. According to him it is to complete a book that we started, one that you already know about."

His apology for earning money, by healing and lecturing with me in California in 2003 (and again in 2005), reminds his helping spirits that they too benefitted from his efforts. Thus they have no reason to punish him with sickness.

7. González mentioned that he gave his other two sons non-maize oriented names:

"Soon after him, my second child, named Vicente in Spanish, was born. His Huichol name, Tsauri, means a wise or intelligent person. My fourth child was Manuel. He is called Matsua, which means the bracelet of the gods, the archer's wrist guard. ... Each of their names is derived from one of the gods. My children will notice that they came from those gods. That is why each of them has his own name, on which he can rely."

8. Scientists describe maize reproduction based on their model of external fertilization, noting that maize reproduction requires wind to disseminate corn pollen (which must land on the stigma for fertilization to occur). In contrast, human reproduction depends on internal fertilization that unites male sperm with female egg. Science pays more attention to the fertilization method (contrasting external with internal) rather than the result, i.e., the reproduction of the species (the goal to be achieved). Their model prioritizes evolution, by emphasizing the ways in which humans differ from plants. Such an evolutionary view of nature ranks humans above plants. That view implies our species is superior and is perhaps a concomitant of our profit-oriented mode of production, wherein nature is treated impersonally, and the global ecosystem upon which all humans depend for survival is divided into parcels of "land" or acreage, to be bought and sold as one type of "fictitious commodity" (Polanyi 2001). In sharp contrast to that evolutionary view, modern ecologists may recognize that the Huichol model of nature, with its emphasis on mutualism with maize, as well as kinship with wolves and deer has long term adaptive value. As Roy Rappaport noted, "The criterion of adequacy for a cognized model (of nature) is not its accuracy, but its adaptive effectiveness." (1979, 98).

Chapter 6

1. During the arduous and lengthy pilgrimage Huichol temple officers formerly made on foot, they did procure peyote, which grows some 350 kilometers east of their homeland. However, their

pilgrimage also required leaving offerings at the birthplace of their Sun Father and then returning home with peyote, three kinds of divine water (*Hay+rime*; each of which embodies a specific Rain Mother), and the yellow root (*uxa*) used for face-painting (Fikes 2011). These three indispensable ritual items, in addition to deer, must be obtained each year in order to perform Peyote Dances at Santa Catarina, Tuxpan, and other native ceremonial centers. Thus it is a gross oversimplification to call this a "peyote pilgrimage."

2. Lumholtz (1900, 3, 9-10) observed in 1895 or 1898 that the area surrounding Tenzompa, "has been almost entirely taken by the Mexicans" while Dr. Hers (1982, 35) states that mestizos took control of Tenzompa in 1873 (when the rebel leader, Manuel Lozada, died.) Jesús González and his son Vicente believe that many Huichol remained in Tenzompa until 1910, when the Mexican Revolution began.

3. When Sánchez the *kawiteru* told me this, in 1981, I did not know enough to ask him if that particular Kieri was venerated in the Catholic church. I only knew that his grandparents consecrated him to a Kieri growing near Huejuquilla, a Mexican town some 32 kilometers north of Tenzompa. I now suspect that his grandparents took him to a famous Kieri growing in the middle of the mountains near Huejuquilla. This Kieri, identified by Benítez as "*Ututávita*," is essential for deer hunting, and is located on the pilgrimage path to the Sun Father's birthplace (Benítez 1968a, 282). The Kieri visited by Peter Collings and the San Andrés temple officers (2000, 19) is also called Ututawita (which Collings spelled "Utu,Tau,Wita") and is petitioned for help in hunting deer.

4. The archaeologist, Dr. Marie-Areti Hers, inspected artifacts and structures integral to three distinct hilltop shrines, each located in a pine forest relatively close to Tenzompa, in the Bolaños valley, a fertile region that was inhabited by both Huichol and Tepecano. The third hilltop shrine, at the summit of Calpulalta (at 2,100 meters), contained ruins of several circular structures. It was the most complex of these three sacred sites, and may have briefly lodged worshipers ascending some 330 meters from the

Bolaños valley below. The second hilltop site Hers examined was located at 2,200 meters. This site reminded her of another shrine; one that housed the mummified Huichol ancestor that zealous Catholics destroyed in 1650 (Fikes 2011, 223-24; Hers 1982, 37). According to Dr. Hers, although the little temple (3.6 by 3.2 meters) at this second site was structurally similar to a Huichol *tuki*, it was probably affiliated with a religion other than that of the Huichol (Hers 1982, 36-40). She also concludes that the region surrounding Tenzompa was disrupted and depopulated sometime between 1250 and 1350 CE, at the time when the more dominant and militaristic Chalchihuites culture disappeared (Hers 1982 41; 1989, 39).

Hers speculated that the remote setting of the second shrine she examined was selected primarily to escape Franciscan missionary control (Hers 1982, 39) and that the third hilltop shrine at Calpulalta belonged to a religion that has been erased from the region (Hers 1982, 40). However, it occurs to me that because both shrines are located on hilltops in pine forests they may indicate that Kieri, or Elder Brother Wolf or Wind were venerated. I have found Kieri growing, as well as Wolf shrines, located in pine forests at about that elevation. Lumholtz claimed that the area adjacent to Tenzompa was dedicated to the Wind God (1900, 10), which is also associated with Kieri by many Huichol (Neurath 2005, 66). The most amazing hilltop shrine I visited was dedicated to the ancient goddess Takutsi Y+rameka (Fikes 2011, 43-44). All of these Ancestor Deities are undeniably Huichol.

Chapter 7

1. It is unclear to what extent, if any, nutrition for most Huichol improved after domesticated animals Spaniards brought began to be eaten. Although most Huichol I saw in the late 1970s had a few chickens, most Huichol did not have large numbers of cattle, sheep or goats. Moreover, their most fertile land—in the Bolaños river valley around Huejuquilla and Tenzompa, was stolen by

Spanish colonists.

2. Vicente, who became a Protestant Christian, saw himself as more modern and progressive than his friends and relatives in Tuxpan. He is certainly an intellectual, and is skeptical about the value of traditional Huichol religion and the efficacy of the colonial-era government that still survived in Tuxpan. He also favored Tuxpan seceding from the *comunidad indigena* of San Sebastián (which has defined Tuxpan as its annex).

3. Vicente was incorrect in stating that the land dispute (circa 1971) between San Sebastián and Tuxpan was the start of "political disagreements" which remained unresolved 33 years later, when we recorded this interview. The Mexican Revolution and the counter-revolution which followed (called the *Cristero* Rebellion) were particularly devastating within the indigenous community of San Sebastián Teponahuaxtlan and its annex, Tuxpan. Robert Zingg's Tuxpan informants told him that their "fierce neighbors" from San Sebastián raided and robbed them during the Mexican Revolution, forcing them to flee from their homes to take refuge near the Pacific Coast or to the east, especially in the mining town of Bolaños (Zingg 1938, xlv, 740). San Sebastián *Cristeros* fought against Mexico's federal government from 1927 to 1938 (Zingg 2004, xxvi). Because Tuxpan Huichols were allies of that government, they were targeted by San Sebastián *Cristeros*. Overt hostility between them ended a few years after the *Cristero* leader was killed in 1935 by Huichols from Tuxpan (Zingg 2004, xxvi-xxvii).

4. Because land rights were central to Mexican revolutionaries led by Emiliano Zapata and Pancho Villa, starting about 1920, redistribution of land, from large landowners to landless and/or poor farmers, developed into a national priority. To facilitate equitable land ownership, Mexico's federal government established the Ministry of Agrarian Reform (Reforma Agraria). Land redistribution for poor non-Huichol farmers accelerated greatly during the presidency of Lázaro Cárdenas (1934-1940) while protection of Huichol communal lands lagged behind,

except for that of Santa Catarina Huichols. They still had to wait 19 years before gaining title to 15,843 hectares in 1940 (Rojas 1993, 179). President Cárdenas presumably inspired other Huichol communities to, "make legal claims for restitution of" communal lands recognized first by Spain and recognized again "under the 1917 revolutionary Mexican Constitution" (Liffman 2011, 46, 120-122, 224). Rojas (1992, 1993, 160-192), Téllez (2011, 101-110) and Liffman concur that after 1940 "invasion of Indian lands continued, and the (federal) government recognized mestizo claims to large chunks of Indian land throughout the region long before it addressed indigenous claims" (Liffman 2011, 46).

Chapter 8

1. The most compelling proof of fraud in Castaneda's writing is manifested in self-contradictory statements made by Castaneda and his fictional shaman (Fikes, 2008). The most significant example of such inconsistency is connected to Castaneda's Don Juan proclaiming, and later revoking, the purpose for having Castaneda ingest three species of sacred plants: *Datura stramonium* (jimsonweed), *Psilocybe mexicana* (sacred mushrooms), and *Lophophora williamsii* (peyote). In his first two books, Castaneda (1969, 1972) claimed these three sacred plants were integral to his apprenticeship with Don Juan Matus, who linked using jimsonweed and psilocybin mushrooms, "to the acquisition of ...a (supernatural) power he called an 'ally.'" Peyote, whose spirit supposedly advised Don Juan to accept Castaneda as his apprentice (Castaneda 1969, 39-41; Fikes 2008) was special because it facilitated acquiring wisdom or "knowledge of the right way to live," (Castaneda, 1969: 9). In Castaneda's third book, *Journey to Ixtlan*, Don Juan cancelled the central place he originally attributed to these three sacred plants, asserting that he administered those plants only to eradicate Castaneda's "lack of sensitivity" or stubbornness in clinging to his worldview (Castaneda 1973, 13). In Castaneda's third book, these sacred plants were relegated to

providing the shock-therapy Don Juan needed in order to remove an obstacle which had prevented Castaneda from internalizing Don Juan's teachings about sorcery (Castaneda 1973, 7-9, 13; Fikes, 1996b). By downgrading sacred plant use to a mere tool or strategy required for teaching sorcery, Don Juan annulled the eternal tutelary function he originally ascribed to the spirits contained in peyote, jimsonweed and psilocybin mushrooms.

This dramatic reversal of his original teachings meant that Don Juan, not the three distinct sacred plant spirits, turned into the supreme source of power directing Castaneda. This reversal also enabled Castaneda to receive his doctoral dissertation from U.C.L.A., after adding a 500 word abstract and changing the title from *Journey to Ixtlan* to *Sorcery: A Description of the World.* (Fikes 1993, 101, 252). Years later, in an interview with Keith Thompson (1994, 71, 152), Castaneda contradicted that dramatic reversal made in *Journey to Ixtlan*, declaring that using peyote helped people connect with the joys and sorrows of this world (Fikes 1996b, 140).

2. Paul Kvinta (1999, 59) expressed surprise because True did not begin his proposal by, "admitting his own long fascination with the subject." Kvinta's support for True's 'fascination' with the Huichol was built on the unsubstantiated claim of Martha True: that for fifteen years True had studied and visited the Huichol. Kvinta went further, stating that True had been traveling into, "the expanse of Mexican wildnerness he (True) called 'Huichol country'" since the 1980s (Kvinta 1999, 58-59). Kvinta and Liffman each characterized True's proposal as being an inaccurate representation of contemporary Huichol life. Liffman used words such as 'idyllic,' 'nostalgic,' and 'unspoiled' to characterize True's peculiar portrait of Huichol life (2002, 365-66). Similarly, Kvinta (1999, 59) recognized True was keen on emphasizing the, "Arcadian, transcendental qualities of the Huichol universe," thus alluding to an idealized, simpler time in Ancient Greece, when ancient Arcadian Greeks worshipped Pan as their principal god.

True's two references to peyote in his proposal were presumably indicators of his fascination with the Huichol peyote pilgrimage, as exemplified by this entry in his journal: "Huichols are the original trekkers, going to Real de Catorce on foot." (Rivard 2005, 231). This assertion seems nostalgic because the Huichol tradition of walking east some 350 kilometers (220 miles) one-way from Santa Catarina to Tatei Matinieri (Fikes 2011, 245, 248) to leave offerings and pray, then continuing to walk to the sacred mountain, Paritek+a, had all but vanished by the late 1970s, at least twenty years before 1998. Their traditional round-trip pilgrimage on foot lasted almost two months. All pilgrims were required to make personal sacrifices (e.g., abstaining from sex and bathing, minimizing ingestion of food and water), to bring back holy water, Hay+rime, from three distinct waterholes, as well as peyote and uxa, the aquatic plant producing yellow pigment used for face painting (Fikes 2011, 122). Their trek was no picnic. Over time, their pilgrimage became increasingly difficult to complete on foot as ancient sacred sites and trails were gradually fenced off. The "modern" world was forcing Huichols to change, both inside and outside of their Chapalagana homeland.

3. Two American anthropologists, Robert Zingg and Phil Weigand (accompanied by his Mexican wife, Acelia Garcia de Weigand), managed to do research with the Huichol of Tuxpan de Bolaños and San Sebastián respectively (Liffman 2002, 374). Zingg did a total of twelve months of fieldwork, residing primarily in Tuxpan de Bolaños between 1934-35 (Zingg 1938, xi, xxi). Phil Weigand's initial fieldwork in San Sebastián, "was accomplished from February to November in 1966 and from January to March in 1969" (Weigand 1972, iv). There is no evidence that Phil True had systematically studied Huichol social organization, political struggles or acculturation. His proposal did not cite any relevant anthropological works, such as the publications of Zingg and Weigand.

4. Six years after Kvinta (1999, 64) proclaimed that Martha revealed, "we spent three hours with the elders in order to be allowed to watch a peyote ritual," Martha told me (during our

phone conversation of 12-7-2005) that she had never attended a peyote ceremony with her husband. I leave that apparent inconsistency for others to untangle. Martha confirmed to me that True witnessed a peyote ceremony by himself, on a visit he made sometime before he and Martha attended the Holy Week ceremony together in Tuxpan in 1998.

5. Rivard confused the Huichol settlement of Tuxpan de Bolaños with Bolaños, the mestizo town and former silver-mining mecca. The Mexican town of Bolaños is some fifty kilometers northeast of the much smaller Huichol settlement of Tuxpan de Bolaños. Accordingly, Rivard's description of Tuxpan de Bolaños is misleading and wrong. It is the Mexican town of Bolaños that was True's, "gateway to the Huichol sierra" and Bolaños that is the place where True had his friendly encounter with the PRI mayor, Curiel Mayorga, who was mentioned in True's story proposal (Rivard 2005, 28, 226). Rivard erroneously asserted (2005, 28) that the oldest colonial structures, "built after Spanish soldiers and missionaries arrived" are in Tuxpan de Bolaños. The reality is that those old structures are in the Mexican town of Bolaños. Another error followed when Rivard claimed that Tuxpan de Bolaños is, "a town of several thousand Huichol and mestizo inhabitants" (2005, 29). That description fits Bolaños, the administrative center of the municipio (comparable to a county) in which the Huichol settlement called Tuxpan de Bolaños is located. In 2004, Tuxpan de Bolaños had about 500 inhabitants (not "several thousand"), almost all of them Huichol, not mestizo (Zingg 2004, 234).

6. "After True identified himself as a journalist, Chivarra demanded to know who had given him approval to travel here. ... True hedged, claiming that someone in Tuxpan had OK'd his trip, but Chivarra ... threatened to have True arrested." (Kvinta 1999, 67 citing True's journal). Kvinta's article (1999) makes it obvious that True had no written permit from any Huichol authorities in Tuxpan de Bolaños. True, presumably trying to protect himself, must have lied to Chivarra. But because Chivarra had seen True's camera and complained about it, True asked Chivarra, "If I take

no pictures, can I pass on?" (Kvinta 1999, 67). Chivarra replied "Yes, follow me to my ranch" (Zarembo 1999, 12).

See Appendix F for more about True's camera and unauthorized photo-taking.

Chapter 9

1. My first criticism of Dr. Peter Furst's 1969 film, *To Find Our Life*, was published in my book debunking Carlos Castaneda (Fikes 1993, 80-85). I also published an expanded criticism of Furst's film and reviews of other ethnographic films about the Huichol (Fikes 1993b, 221-240). In both publications, I identified numerous anomalies and contradictions in Furst's film, depicting a highly abbreviated peyote hunt led by Ramón Medina Silva. I faulted Furst for concealing significant information about Ramón Medina's life as an expatriate Huichol, a person who was not qualified to lead a traditional *tuki*-based peyote hunt. Professor Phil Weigand went further, in his letter to the American Anthropological Association's (AAA) Committee on Ethics (dated June 7, 1992):

"This film's staging, from start to finish, implies that it represents a traditional peyote trek and an authentic religious ceremony. This is beyond the misrepresentation of the ethnographic data ... it is fabrication. Dr Furst has paid for the staging of other non-authentic ceremonies as well."

Neither Professor Weigand nor I received any direct response to our severe criticisms of his film from Dr. Furst. Nor did the Ethics Committee of the AAA provide us with any response from Furst to either of our complaint letters about his professional misconduct. The subcommittee of the AAA Ethics Committee established to adjudicate alleged violations of ethics was permanently eliminated by the AAA shortly after our complaints about Dr. Furst were ignored and dismissed. Juan Negrín's complaint letter, dated April 23, 1992, alleging misconduct by Furst was rejected by the AAA

Ethics Committee only because Negrín was not a professional anthropologist.

2. Prior to serving for five years as the custodian (*mayordomo*) of the icon of the elder Jesus Christ, as well as being the singer at rituals performed at the *Teyupani* (Catholic church) in Santa Catarina, Bonales had served two five-year terms as an aboriginal temple officer. When I met him in 1976 he was renowned as a healer and esteemed as a performer of funeral, deer hunting and First Fruits rituals (Fikes 2011, 227-229).

3. Snubbing, resisting and even expelling uninvited outsiders has also been routine among Huichol of the *comunidad indigena* of San Andrés. Benítez (1968a, 276-77) candidly described opposition to his research at San Andrés, and by peyote seekers from the Huichol ceremonial center (*tuki*) at Las Guayabas, south of San Andrés (1975, 42, 65, 71-72). He contrasted that resistance and sabotage of his research at San Andrés, where he was treated as an unwelcome intruder; to the welcome he received by Huichol residing near Ocota de la Sierra (Benítez (1968a, 278-79).

One American anthropologist, whom I first met in 1978, had already visited a village near Santa Catarina by then. He continued making infrequent and brief visits to that village until 1994, when he was jailed and fined because during Easter week ceremonies at Santa Catarina he had no permit for the camera he was carrying.

4. In 1995 I was prepared to accept the position of Director of a ten year long applied anthropology project designed to assist the Chapalagana Huichol. Professor Joe Winter of the University of New Mexico at Albuquerque had invited me to accept the position of Director for various educational, economic and medical aid projects to be funded by grants he was soliciting from six foundations, including Kellogg, Ford, Rockefeller and MacArthur. Later, as a witness in my lawsuit against Peter Furst, Professor Winter provided testimony as well as a notarized affidavit. In that affidavit, dated November 11, 1997, Dr. Winter affirmed that:

"Shortly after the (grant) proposals had been sent to the foundations,

I received a hostile letter from Dr. Peter T. Furst, copy attached. His June 22, 1995 letter not only attacked our proposed project but also stated that he is 'often asked by funding agencies to comment on proposals' such as mine. That letter convinced me that Dr. Furst might interfere with our attempt to obtain funding. ... A few months later we learned that only one of these six foundations was willing to fund our project to aid the Huichols and that it was only for a small planning grant...that did not include Dr. Fikes. ... I decided not to reapply for funding for the Huichol Assistance Project from the five other foundations. It was felt by me that Dr. Furst may have improperly influenced at least one of the funding agencies and that Dr. Furst's anticipated continued interference could make the efforts to obtain funding futile."

Furst's interference with this Huichol assistance project was decisive in my decision to take legal action against him in 1996. I remember my lawyer attempting in vain to get one or more of those foundations to respond to our request for any information about Dr. Furst's possible communications with them. They did not want to cooperate and this part of my lawsuit was soon dismissed in a "summary judgment."

BIBLIOGRAPHY

Aedo, Ángel. 2011. *La Dimensión Mas Oscura de la Existencia*. México, D.F.: Universidad Nacional Autónoma de México.

Aguilar Ros, Alejandra. 2008. "Danzando a Apaxuki, La Semana Santa en San Andrés Cohamiata desde los mestizos visitantes," in *Raíces en Movimiento: prácticas religiosas tradicionales en contextos translocales*. Centro estudios mexicanos y centroamericanos. Open Edition Books edition, Accessed via academia.com on 9-30-2020.

Anonymous. 1970. "Hallucinogenic Drugs Use by Other Societies Studied," in *Valley News* Van Nuys, CA., March 27.

Arias y Saavedra, Antonio. 1990. "Información Rendida por el Padre Antonio Arias y Saavedra, acerca del Estado de la Sierra del Nayarit, en el Siglo XVII [1673]," in *Los Albores de un nuevo mundo: siglos XVI y XVII*, ed. Thomas Calvo. Colección de Documentos para la Historia de Nayarit, I. México City: Centro de Estudios Mexicanos y Centroamericanos.

Austin, N., Seaman, H. & Barrett, M. (Producers). 2007. *Tales from the jungle: Carlos Castaneda* [Television broadcast]. London, United Kingdom: BBC Channel 4, aired January 15.

Basilov, Vladimir N. 1997. "Chosen by the Spirits," in *Shamanic Worlds*. Ed., Marjorie Mandelstam Balzer. New York & London: North Castle Books. pp. 3-48.

Bauml, James A., Gilbert Voss and Peter Collings, 1990. "Short Communications," in *Journal of Ethnobiology* 10 (1): pp. 99-102.

Benítez, Fernando. 1968a. *Los Indios de México*, Vol. 2. México, D.F.: Biblioteca Era.

————— 1968b. *En la Tierra Mágica de Peyote*. México, D.F.: Biblioteca Era.

————— 1975. *In the Magic Land of Peyote*. Translated by John Upton. New York: Warner Books.

Benítez, Guillermo, *et al.* 2018. "The genus Datura L. (Solanaceae) in Mexico and Spain Ethnobotanical perspective at the interface of medical and illicit uses," in *Journal of Ethnopharmacology,* Volume 219, 12 June: pp. 133-151

Benzi, Marino. 1972. *Les Derniers Adorateurs du Peyotl*. Paris: Editions Gallinard.

Bernardello, Luis M. and Armando T. Hunziker, 1987. "A Synoptic Revision of *Solandra* (Solanaceae)," in *Nordic Journal of Botany* 7 (6) pp. 639-652.

Blackburn, Thomas C. 1975. *December's Child: A Book of Chumash Oral Narratives*. Berkeley, CA: University of California Press.

Brenner, Anita, 2002. *Idols Behind Altars: Modern Mexican Art and its Cultural Roots*. Mineola, N.Y.: Dover Publications (original 1929).

Brundage, Burr C. 1983 (paperback ed., original 1979). *The Fifth Sun: Aztec Gods, Aztec World*. Austin, TX: University of Texas Press.

Castaneda, Carlos. (1969). *The Teachings of Don Juan: a Yaqui Way of Knowledge* (2nd edition.). New York, N.Y.: Ballantine Books. (original edition 1968).

——————— (1972). *A separate reality: further conversations with Don Juan*. New York: Pocket Books. (Original edition 1971).

——————— (1973). *Journey to Ixtlan: The lessons of Don Juan*. New York: Touchstone Books. (Original edition 1972).

Collings, Peter R. 2000. *The Huichol of México: The Shaman*. Puerto Vallarta, MX. Casa Isabel.

Coyle, Philip E. 2001. *Náyari History, Politics, and Violence*. Tucson: University of Arizona Press.

——————— 2020. Email to Jay Fikes dated July 5.

Deloria, Vine. 2006. *The World We Used to Live In*. Golden, CO: Fulcrum Publishing.

DeMille, Richard. 1978. *Castaneda's Journey: The Power and the Allegory*. (Second ed.). Santa Barbara, CA: Capra Press.

——————— (ed.). 1980. *The Don Juan Papers: Further Castaneda Controversies*. Santa Barbara, CA: Ross-Erikson Publishers.

Densmore, Frances. 1992. *Teton Sioux Music and Culture*. Lincoln: University of Nebraska Press (Bison Books 1st edition 1992, original 1918).

Eliade, Mircea. 1964. *Shamanism: Archaic Techniques of Ecstasy*. Translated by Willard Trask. Bollingen Series No. 76. New York: Pantheon Books.

Ellison, Katherine. 1992. "The gods must be around here someplace," *San Jose Mercury News* (May 3, 1992): pp. 8-9, 12-13,15, 29.

Evans, W.C., Ghani, A. and Woolley, V.A. 1972. "Alkaloids of Solandra Species," in Phytochemistry Vol. 11 (1): pp. 470-472.

Fabila, Alfonso. 1959. *Los Huicholes de Jalisco*. México, D.F.: Instituto Nacional Indigenista.

Fikes, Jay C. 1978. "Native American Education: Cognitive Styles, Cultural Conflict, and Contract Schools," in *Michigan Discussions in Anthropology*, Vol.4, (Fall): pp. 31-51.

———— 1985. *Huichol Indian Identity and Adaptation*. Unpublished doctoral dissertation, Ann Arbor: University of Michigan.

———— 1993. *Carlos Castaneda, Academic Opportunism, and the Psychedelic Sixties*. Victoria, B.C. Canada: Millenia Press.

———— 1993b. "Anthropological Visualization of the Huichol in Ethnographic Film: A Discussion of the Problem of Contextualization," in *Anthropological Film and Video in the 1990s*. Edited by Jack R. Rollwagen. Brockport, N.Y.: The Institute, Inc.: pp. 221-240.

———— 1996. *Reuben Snake: Your Humble Serpent*. Edited by Jay C. Fikes. Santa Fe, N.M.: Clear Light Publishers.

———— 1996b. "Carlos Castaneda and Don Juan," in The Encyclopedia of the Paranormal, Edited by Gordon Stein. Amherst, NY: Prometheus Books: pp. 135-143.

———— 1997. *Huichol Indian Ceremonial Cycle*. Documentary film available at www.jayfikes.com

———— 1999. "Examining Ethics, Benefits and Perils of Tours to México," in *International Heritage, Multicultural Attractions and Tourism, Conference Proceedings (Vol. 1)* Istanbul, Turkey: Bosphorus University: pp. 407-421.

———— 2002. "Jay Fikes Speaks (Interviewed by Tom Lyttle)," in *The Entheogen Review*, Vol. XI, No. 3, Autumn: pp. 81-93.

———— 2003. *The Man Who Ate Honey*. Taos, N.M.: Ambrosia Books.

———— 2008. "Castaneda, Carlos," in *International Encyclopedia of the Social Sciences,* 2nd edition., ed. William A. Darity, Jr., Vol.

1: Detroit: Macmillan Reference USA: pp. 456-57.

———— 2011. *Unknown Huichol: Shamans and Immortals, Allies Against Chaos*. New York: Alta Mira Press.

———— 2011b. "Scrutinizing Self-Proclaimed Shamans and Appropriation of Huichol Peyote Pilgrimages: Making Apprentice-Shamans Chic," in *The American Mosaic: The American Indian Experience*. Santa Barbara, CA: ABC-CLIO. Accessed 13 Jan., 2012.

Fikes, Jay C. and Phil C. Weigand. 1998. *La Mitologia de los Huicholes*,(Spanish translation of Robert Zingg's *Huichol Mythology*) Zamora, Michoacan, México: Colegio de Michoacan.

———— 2004. "Sensacionalismo y etnografía: el caso de los Huicholes de Jalisco," in *Relaciones*, Vol. 25 (Spring): pp. 50-68.

Furst, Peter T., and Barbara G. Myerhoff. 1966. "Myth as History: The Jimson Weed Cycle of the Huichols of Mexico," in *Antropológica* 17: pp. 3-39.

Furst, Peter. 1969. *To Find our Life: The Peyote Hunt of the Huichols of Mexico*. Los Angeles, CA: Film distributed by the Latin American Center of U.C.L.A.

———— 1972. "To Find our Life: Peyote Among the Huichol Indians of Mexico," in *Flesh of the Gods: The Ritual Uses of Hallucinogens*, pp. 136-184. New York: Praeger.

Guttman, Hannah. 2016. "An Outlook on the Future of Peyote: A Religious and Environmental Issue" downloaded from Academia.edu website on 9-29-2019.

Hers, Marie-Areti. 1982. "Santuarios huicholes en la Sierra de Tenzompa, Jalisco," in *Anales del Instituto de Investigaciones Estéticas*, 50, Universidad Nacional Autónoma de México: pp. 35-41.

Hers, Marie-Areti. 1989. *Los toltecas en tierras chichimecas*. México D.F.: Universidad Nacional Autónoma de México.

Heuer, Bronwen. 2006. Emails to Jay Fikes: 1-04-06, 1-15-06, 1-23-06, phone conversation 1-15-06.

Hutton, Ronald. 2001. *Shamans: Siberian Spirituality and the Western Imagination*. London: Hambledon and London.

Knab, Timothy J. 1977. "Notes Concerning the Use of Solandra among the Huichol," in *Economic Botany,* 31(1): pp. 80-86.

Kvinta, Paul. 1999. "Culture Clash." *Outside Magazine,* June.

LaBarre, Weston. 1989. *The Peyote Cult.* Norman: University of Oklahoma Press.

Lewis, Ioan M. 1989, 2nd edition. *Ecstatic Religion: A Study of Shamanism and Spirit Possession.* London and New York: Routledge.

Liffman, Paul M. 2002. *Huichol Territoriality: Land Claims and Cultural Representation in Western Mexico.* Unpublished dissertation from University of Chicago. ProQuest: Ann Arbor: Michigan.

——————— 2011. *Huichol Territory and the Mexican Nation.* Tucson: University of Arizona Press.

——————— 2020. Emails to Jay Fikes dated September 6, 24, 26, & 27.

Lumholtz, Carl. 1900. *Symbolism of the Huichol Indians.* New York: American Museum of Natural History, Memoirs 1(2).

——————— 1902. *Unknown México, Vols. 1 and 2.* Reprint, Glorieta, New México: Rio Grande Press, 1973.

Mason, J. Alden, 2018. "Tepecano Prayers," in *International Journal of American Linguistics*, Vol. 1: pp. 91-153.

——————— 1981. "The Ceremonialism of the Tepecano Indians of Azqueltan, Jalisco," in *Themes of Indigenous Acculturation in Northwest Mexico.* Edited by Thomas B. Hinton and Phil C. Weigand. Tucson: University of Arizona Press: pp. 62-76.

McCarty, Kieran and Dan S. Matson. 1975. "Franciscan Report on the Indians of Nayarit, 1673," in *Ethnohistory* 22 (3): pp. 193-222.

Myerhoff, Barbara G. *The Deer-Maize-Peyote Complex among the Huichol Indians of Mexico.* Unpublished doctoral dissertation, UCLA, 1968.

——————— 1974. *Peyote Hunt: The Sacred Journey of the Huichol Indians.* Ithaca, New York: Cornell University Press, 1974.

Nathan, Debbie. 1998. "A fatal—and foolish?—trip to Ixtlan," in *San Antonio Current* (Dec. 31, 1998-Jan. 6, 1999): p. 8.

Negrín, Juan. 1975. *The Huichol Creation of the World.* Sacramento: E.B. Crocker Art Gallery.

——————— 1977. *El Arte Contemporaneo de los Huicholes.* Guadalajara: Universidad de Guadalajara.

——————— 2001. *"An Appreciation of Huichol Culture."* in *Entheos: Journal of Psychedelic Spirituality. 1(2)*: pp. 27-37.

Neurath, Johannes. 2005. *Arte Huichol*. México, D.F.: Artes de México, Número 75.

Ortega, José. 1754. *Maravillosa Reduccion y Conquista de la Provincia de San Joseph del Gran Nayar*. Reprint, México, D.F.: Editorial Layac, 1944.

Polanyi, Karl. 1957. *The Great Transformation*. Reprint, Boston: Beacon Press, 2001.

Rappaport, Roy A. 1979. *Ecology, Meaning, and Religion*. Richmond, CA: North Atlantic Books.

Rivard, Robert. 2005. *Trail of Feathers*. New York: Public Affairs.

Rivard Emails to Jay Fikes dated 2-6-2006, 2-13-2006, 2-14-2006, 2-15-2006

Rojas, Beatriz. 1992. *Los Huicholes: Documentos Historicos*. México, D.F.: Instituto Nacional Indigenista.

——————— 1993. *Los Huicholes en la Historia*. México, D.F.: Centro de Estudios Mexicanos y Centroamericanos.

Spiro, Melford E. 1984. "Some reflections on cultural determinism and relativism with special reference to emotion and reason," in *Culture Theory*, eds. Richard A. Shweder and Robert A. LeVine, London: Cambridge University Press: pp. 323–46.

Téllez Lozano, Víctor M. 2011. *Xatsitsarie, territorio, gobierno local, y ritual en una comunidad huichola*. Zamora, Michoacán México: El Colegio de Michoacán.

Thompson, K. 1994. "Portrait of a sorcerer: an interview with Carlos Castaneda," in *New Age Journal*: pp. 66-71, 152-153.

True, Martha. 2005. Telephone conversation with Jay Fikes, December 7.

Underhill, Ruth M. 1946. *Papago Indian Religion*. Reprint, New York: AMS Press, 1969.

Wallace, Paul A.W. 1994. *The Iroquois Book of Life: White Roots of Peace*. Santa Fe, N.M.: Clear Light Publishers.

Walter, Mariko N. and Fridman, Eva J. Neumann. 2004. *Shamanism, An Encyclopedia of World Beliefs, Practices, and Culture*, Vols. 1-2. Santa Barbara, CA: ABC-CLIO.

Wasson, R. Gordon. 1980. *The Wondrous Mushroom.* New York: McGraw-Hill.

Weigand, Phil C. 1969. "The Role of an Indianized Mestizo in the 1950 Huichol Revolt," in *Special* No. 1 (*Inter-Americana* No. 1). Carbondale: Latin American Institute, Southern Illinois University.

———— 1972. "Cooperative Labor Groups in Subsistence Activities Among the Huichol Indians," in *Mesoamerican Studies,* No. 7. Carbondale: Southern Illinois University Museum.

———— 1975. "Possible References to La Quemada in Huichol Mythology," in *Ethnohistory* 22 (1): pp 15-20.

———— 1978. "Contemporary Social and Economic Structure," in *Art of the Huichol Indians.* Eds. K. Berrin and T.K. Seligman. New York: Harry N. Abrams, Inc.: pp. 101-115.

———— 1981. "Differential Acculturation Among the Huichol Indians," in *Themes of Indigenous Acculturation in Northwest México.* Eds. Thomas B. Hinton and Phil C. Weigand. Tucson: University of Arizona Press: pp. 9-21.

———— 2000. "Huichol Society Before the Arrival of the Spanish," in *Journal of the Southwest.* Eds. Phil Coyle and Paul Liffman. Tucson: University of Arizona Press, Vol. 42, No. 1, Spring: pp. 13-36.

———— 2002. Ed. *Estudio Histórico y Cultural sobre los Huicholes.* Colotlán, Jalisco, Mexico: Universidad de Guadalajara (Campus Universitario del Norte).

Yasumoto, Masaya. 1996. "The Psychotropic Kieri in Huichol Culture," in *People of the Peyote,* Edited by Stacy B. Schaefer and Peter T. Furst. Albuquerque: University of New México Press: pp. 235-263.

Zarembo, Alan. 1999. "Death in the Mountains," in *Newsweek* (March 22): pp. 10-15.

Zingg, Robert M. *The Huichols: Primitive Artists.* New York: G.E. Stechert, 1938.

———— 2004. *Huichol Mythology.* Eds. Jay C. Fikes, Phil C. Weigand and Acelía Garcia de Weigand. Tucson: University of Arizona Press.

INDEX

deer
  Huichol shaman rapport with ancestral
      spirits associated with, 4
  as required offering in Huichol rituals, 45
deer hunting
  ban on bathing during, 44
  bond between Kieri and, 21, 78, 96–100, 104
  by Jesús González, 11, 37, 38, 43–46, 71–72
  Vicente González shooting "accident" and,
      96–100, 104, 106–107
  and Kieri veneration at Tenzompa Catholic church,
      5–6, 93–104, 106–107, 212n3
  maize and, 43–46
  Mexican government's harassment of traditional
      Huichols and, 159, 160
  offerings to Grandfather Fire and, 45–46, 70, 208–209n3
  popularization of Huichol life and, 161
  ritual items from "peyote pilgrimages" and, 45, 211–212n1
  rituals of, 43–46, 70, 89, 208–209n3
  salt fast during, 44
  sexual abstinence during, 21, 44, 67
  as source of animal protein, 110
  Ututawi Kieri and, 103–104, 171, 175, 212n3
  White Antlers Kieri and, 170f, 171, 232, 233f
  winiyeri (traps for strangling deer) in, 43–44
Deer Person
  Tamatsi Paritsika (shamans' helping spirit, linked to Kieri,
      Deer Person, wind) and, 17–21, 28–29, 106
Deer Shaman. *see* Tamatsi (Our Elder Brother, incarnate in Kieri)
Deganawida, superhuman status of, 68
Deloria, Vine, 87, 166–167, 181
DeMille, Richard, 152–153
Densmore, Frances, 181
Diaz, Margarito, 144–145

E

Elder Brother. *see* Tamatsi (Our Elder Brother, incarnate in Kieri)
Eliade, Mircea, 10–11
  Archaic Techniques of Ecstasy, 1
Ellison, Katherine, 149–150, 193

V

Villa, Pancho, 214–215n4

Voss, Gilbert, 83

votive arrows, 16, 18*f*, 23, 29–31, 43, 44, 46, 57, 76, 262

votive candles, 17, 52, 76, 99, 183, 208, 262

votive gourd bowls, 10, 11, 28, 30, 31, 41–43, 46, 57, 69, 76, 79–80, 99, 184, 205–206n1, 209–210n5

W

waiyeyeri (path Wixarika ancestors made, righteous trail), 45, 82

Wallace, Paul A. W., 68

Walter, Mariko N., 10–11

Wasson, R. Gordon, 166, 176–177

Watakame (first Huichol ancestor to acquire maize and plant it), 74–76

water

    Jesús González pilgrimages to the Pacific Ocean, 3, 10–11, 23–25, 27–30, 47, 71–73, 167–168

    k+puri (eternal Water Spirit), 61, 66, 76, 206–207n2

    from sacred sites, 46

    see also Hay+rime (budding, germinating or everlasting water used in various rituals); Rain Mothers

Watet+apa (primordial underworld), 53, 55, 82, 204–205n1

Weigand, Acelia Garcia de, 217n3

Weigand, Phil C., 79, 90, 91, 110, 124, 130, 140, 143, 151, 152, 161, 165, 173, 197, 199, 217n3, 219–220n1

White Antlers Kieri, 170*f*, 171, 262, 263*f*

wikuxa (bundle of threads, years of life, controlled by Tatei Werika Wimari), 25, 61, 66.

    see also Tatei Werika Wimari

Wind God

    association with Kieri, 212–213n4

winiyeri (traps for strangling deer), 43–44

Winkelman, Michael, 152

Winter, Joe, 220–221n4

Wirikuta, peyote pilgrimages simulated during First Fruits ritual, 79–84

Wir+k+ Tewiyari (Tatei Werika Wimari's partner, Tamatsi's benefactor). *see* Buzzard Person

Wixarika (Chapalagana Huichol)

    "baptism" rituals of, 94–95, 102

Z

Fig. 7. Fernando Serratos, kawiteru at Santa Catarina.

Our White Antlered Elder-Brother is Feasted and Consecrated

Our Elder-Brother White-Antlers, Tamatsí 'Awatusa, was a plant that could turn into a person; like other shrubs called the 'tree of the wind', or kieri, (a solaneous brevicalyx species, it is endowed with psychotropic powers). The pollen from its flowers made the hummingbirds faint and the bees would lose their sense of orientation. Thus, Our Elder-Brother manifested his power to Our Ancestors, who endowed him with a sacred spirit.

Our Ancestors gathered in Teakata, the ceremonial center of Our Grandfather Fire, Tatewarí. They prepared a celebration to grant 'Awatusa (White Antler) status as a deity, now that he had earned their acceptance to occupy the spot he had chosen. In recognition of his attributes, he received the 'ɨrɨ (a painted-votive arrow), the symbol and instrument of his power. The Arrow, decorated with a bow, small footwear and a mat on which his spirit can rest, is placed at the base of his plant form. Thereafter, pilgrims who devoutly seek wisdom will bring such arrows, known as Tamatsí 'Awatusa 'ɨrɨya, to White Antler so they can receive some of its power.

A bull is sacrificed to him so that its blood may nurture his spirit, which is now becoming one with his plant. The spirit and soul of the bull will go to rest with the Kieri, as it requests before it expires. Incense is burned in a three-legged clay vessel to honor the bull. Our Great Grandmother Oracle of Insight, Takutsi Nakawé, and Our Grandfather Fire dedicate votive candles to the spirit of Kieri. Tsítsika Temai (Young Bee Person) conveys his complements from all the other Ancestors and asks for luck in finding blossoms.

Like other Ancestors, Kieri 'Awatusa is served by his official animal companions and messengers. Xaye, the rattlesnake, conveys his gratitude to the Ancestors for receiving charge of guarding the Kieri. 'Awatsay, the crested woodpecker, will alert the Kieri spirit to the presence of those who approach. Kieri nectar is expelled from its beak. Tɨki, the pollen of Kieri, surrounds its flower.

The Moon and the Sun each offer him their personal mirror of insight, nierika, so he can be in contact with their spirits. Takutsi Metseri, Our Great Grandmother Moon, is communing with 'Awatusa particularly, for they are spiritually akin in their androgynous nature, each taking on the appearance of a man to women and of a woman to men. The Moon smiles broadly, greeting her companion. She has painted her face to give the appearance of a pregnant woman whose skin changes hues. Thus Kieri 'Awatusa gained his place among the Ancestor-Spirits.

Painting by Tutukila Carrillo 1974
Explanation and interpretation by Juan Negrín
based on a taped explanation with the artist
Dimensions: 32" x 48 1/8"

Fig. 8. Our White-Antlered Elder-Brother is Feasted and Consecrated

Fig. 9. Jesús González with Jay Fikes in Santa Rosa, CA in 2003.
Photo courtesy of Elisa Regalado.

"Today we are living together.
I will eventually go to the spirit world. The day they lay me in the
grave ... only my words will linger in the wind.
What I reveal now comes from my heart.
Henceforth you all will decide what to do about it."
- Jesús González

www.ingramcontent.com/pod-product-compliance
Lightning Source LLC
Chambersburg PA
CBHW041213030426
42336CB00023B/3331